Ionic 2 Cookbook

Second Edition

Over 30 life-changing recipes to help you create cutting edge, hybrid apps with Ionic 2

Hoc Phan

BIRMINGHAM - MUMBAI

Ionic 2 Cookbook

Second Edition

First published: October 2015

Second edition: November 2016

Production reference: 1251116

Published by Packt Publishing Ltd.
Livery Place
35 Livery Street
Birmingham B3 2PB, UK.

ISBN 978-1-78646-596-2

www.packtpub.com

Credits

Author
Hoc Phan

Reviewers
Massimiliano Giroldi
Indermohan Singh

Commissioning Editor
Amarabha Banerjee

Acquisition Editor
Reshma Raman

Content Development Editor
Narendrakumar Tripathi

Technical Editor
Huzefa Unwala

Copy Editor
Shaila Kusanale

Project Coordinator
Devanshi Doshi

Proofreader
Safis Editing

Indexer
Rekha Nair

Graphics
Jason Monteiro

Production Coordinator
Shraddha Falebhai

Cover Work
Shraddha Falebhai

About the Author

Hoc Phan is a technologist with a wide range of experiences in frontend development, cloud computing, and big data. He started programming at the age of 12, with Pascal and Assembly, on the Intel 80286 computer. He learned to start practicing right away, even before figuring out the important concepts. Hoc worked on many JavaScript projects in the past by teaching himself the framework using various online sources. He was one of the first few developers who tested Ionic for its feasibility as a JavaScript replacement of the native language of a device. He wrote the *Ionic Cookbook* (for more information, visit `https://www.amazon.com/Ionic-Cookbook-Hoc-Phan/dp/1785287974`), which was very well received.

He has worked for both start-ups and large companies. By frequently speaking at local meetups as well as cloud computing/big data industry events and conferences, he learns from other experts. He holds an MBA degree from the University of Washington's Michael G. Foster School of Business.

I would like to thank my wife, Nga Nguyen, for putting up with my late night writing sessions and taking care of our son ("little Brian"). Even though this is my third book on the same topic, the road to success is as difficult as the first two. Without the encouragement and understanding from my family, the completion of this book would not have been possible.

I would also like to thank all the Ionic team members and the community on Ionic Forum. They have been extremely helpful in addressing all of my questions when I ran into issues, especially with the changes between Ionic 1 and Ionic 2. There is definitely a small learning curve for all of us to solve the most interesting problem in the industry.

About the Reviewers

Massimiliano Giroldi is passionate about creative coding, martial arts, human rights, parachuting, photography, and more; he is not strictly a "tech guy."

He started to feel the relevance of the learner's point of view when he tried to model *love* on a C=64. Long after translating (technical and not technical) documentation, apps, and, primarily, taking his only Java certification reinforced this concept.

He uses :q to shut down the terminal when working on personal projects and can be reached on Twitter at `@max_devjs`.

I wish to thank the author, Hoc Phan, for proposing the review of this book—without him, I would not write these words. I'd also like to thank the Ionic team and community. Also, the entire Packt team, especially Devanshi Doshi (Project Coordinator-Content) and Reshma Raman (Senior Acquisition Editor). I'd also like to thank the readers of this book.

Everyone I met in my life—I have learned a lot from all of you.

Last but not least, my family, including the pugs, of course.

Indermohan Singh is a software developer from India running a mobile app development studio in the city of Ludhiana. He is the founder of the Indian Classical Music Learning app, *Ragakosh*. He blogs at `http://inders.in` and hosts the AngularJS Ludhiana meetup. He is also the author of another Ionic 2 book, named *Ionic 2 Blueprint*, for Packt. He loves teaching at `https://codementor.io/imsingh`. He also loves to give presentations on various JavaScript topics. When he is not in front of his laptop, you can find him singing with his tanpura.

He also worked as a technical reviewer of *Learning Ionic* by Arvind Ravulavaru.

I am thankful to my family—my father, mother, and brother—for supporting me during reviewing. Finally, I want to thank God for giving me the strength and education to be able to review this wonderful book.

---

www.PacktPub.com

eBooks, discount offers, and more

Did you know that Packt offers eBook versions of every book published, with PDF and ePub files available? You can upgrade to the eBook version at www.PacktPub.com and as a print book customer, you are entitled to a discount on the eBook copy. Get in touch with us at customercare@packtpub.com for more details.

At www.PacktPub.com, you can also read a collection of free technical articles, sign up for a range of free newsletters and receive exclusive discounts and offers on Packt books and eBooks.

https://www.packtpub.com/mapt

Get the most in-demand software skills with Mapt. Mapt gives you full access to all Packt books and video courses, as well as industry-leading tools to help you plan your personal development and advance your career.

Why Subscribe?

- Fully searchable across every book published by Packt
- Copy and paste, print, and bookmark content
- On demand and accessible via a web browser

Table of Contents

Preface

The world of mobile development is fragmented, with many platforms, frameworks, and technologies. Ionic is intended to fill that gap, with its open source HTML5 mobile app framework that lets developers build native-feeling apps using web technologies such as HTML, CSS, and AngularJS. Ionic makes it easy for frontend developers to become app developers. The framework provides superior performance with deep Cordova integration and a comprehensive set of tools for prototyping, backend support, and deployment.

This book will take you through the process of developing a cross-platform mobile app using just HTML5 and Javascript based on Ionic 2, which is the latest version of Ionic using the Angular 2 framework. You will start by getting familiar with the CLI and learning how to build and run an app. You will touch on common features of real-world mobile applications, such as authenticating a user, getting data, and saving data using either Firebase or local storage. Next, the book will explain how Ionic integrates with Cordova to support native device features using ngCordova and take advantage of the existing modules around its ecosystem. You will also explore advanced topics of extending Ionic to create new components. Finally, the book will show you how to customize the Ionic theme and build an app for all platforms.

What this book covers

Chapter 1, Creating Our First App with Ionic 2, introduces the Ionic 2 framework with instructions on how to set up the development environment and quickly create and run your first app.

Chapter 2, Adding Ionic 2 Components, walks you through some examples of how to manage pages, states, and the overall navigation within the app.

Chapter 3, Extending Ionic 2 with Angular 2 Building Blocks, takes a deep dive into the AngularJS components, directives, and the customization of pipes. You will learn how to leverage the Ionic 2 module architecture to create shared services.

Chapter 4, Validating Forms and Making HTTP Requests, explains how to create a complex form with input validation, retrieve data via REST API calls, and integrate with Stripe for online payment.

Chapter 5, Adding Animation, provides instructions on how to embed a video as background, create a physics-based CSS animation, and bind gestures to the animation state.

Chapter 6, User Authentication and Push Notification Using Ionic Cloud, takes a deep dive into registering and authenticating users using Ionic Cloud and sending and receiving push notifications.

Chapter 7, Supporting Device Functionalities Using Ionic Native, explains how to use Ionic Native to access native device functionalities, such as camera, social sharing, InAppBrowser, and map.

Chapter 8, Theming the App, provides instructions on how to customize the app for different platforms using Sass variables.

Chapter 9, Publishing the App for Different Platforms, looks into the process of performing the final steps of getting the app published.

What you need for this book

- A Mac computer with Mac OS X El Capitan and root privileges
- iPhone 5 or later version
- Any Android device with Android 5.x or later version (optional)
- Any Windows Phone device (optional)

Who this book is for

Ionic 2 Cookbook is intended for frontend developers who want to take advantage of their existing skills to develop cross-platform mobile apps. This book will help you become an intermediate or advanced Ionic Framework developer by covering topics about AngularJS, Cordova, and Sass in depth. Since Ionic is open source, there is a large community supporting this framework for you to continue the learning journey.

Sections

In this book, you will find several headings that appear frequently (Getting ready, How to do it, How it works, There's more, and See also).

To give clear instructions on how to complete a recipe, we use these sections as follows:

Getting ready

This section tells you what to expect in the recipe, and describes how to set up any software or any preliminary settings required for the recipe.

How to do it...

This section contains the steps required to follow the recipe.

How it works...

This section usually consists of a detailed explanation of what happened in the previous section.

There's more...

This section consists of additional information about the recipe in order to make the reader more knowledgeable about the recipe.

See also

This section provides helpful links to other useful information for the recipe.

Conventions

In this book, you will find a number of text styles that distinguish between different kinds of information. Here are some examples of these styles and an explanation of their meaning.

Code words in text, database table names, folder names, filenames, file extensions, pathnames, dummy URLs, user input, and Twitter handles are shown as follows: "There is no need to modify the `/platforms` or `/plugins` folder manually unless troubleshooting needs to be done."

A block of code is set as follows:

```
<ion-tabs>
  <ion-tab [root]="tab1Root" tabTitle="One"
  tabIcon="water"></ion-tab>
  <ion-tab [root]="tab2Root" tabTitle="Two"
  tabIcon="leaf"></ion-tab>
  <ion-tab [root]="tab3Root" tabTitle="Three"
  tabIcon="flame"></ion-tab>
```

```
</ion-tabs>
```

Any command-line input or output is written as follows:

```
$ sudo npm install -g cordova ionic ios-sim
```

New terms and **important words** are shown in bold. Words that you see on the screen, for example, in menus or dialog boxes, appear in the text like this: "In this section, you will learn how to create an attribute directive that can prevent certain characters from being input in the **Username** as well as showing another DOM node (where it says **You are typing username**) by toggling its visibility."

Warnings or important notes appear in a box like this.

Tips and tricks appear like this.

Reader feedback

Feedback from our readers is always welcome. Let us know what you think about this book—what you liked or disliked. Reader feedback is important for us as it helps us develop titles that you will really get the most out of.

To send us general feedback, simply e-mail `feedback@packtpub.com`, and mention the book's title in the subject of your message.

If there is a topic that you have expertise in and you are interested in either writing or contributing to a book, see our author guide at `www.packtpub.com/authors`.

Customer support

Now that you are the proud owner of a Packt book, we have a number of things to help you to get the most from your purchase.

Downloading the example code

You can download the example code files for this book from your account at `http://www.packtpub.com`. If you purchased this book elsewhere, you can visit `http://www.packtpub.com/support` and register to have the files e-mailed directly to you.

You can download the code files by following these steps:

1. Log in or register to our website using your e-mail address and password.
2. Hover the mouse pointer on the **SUPPORT** tab at the top.
3. Click on **Code Downloads & Errata**.
4. Enter the name of the book in the **Search** box.
5. Select the book for which you're looking to download the code files.
6. Choose from the drop-down menu where you purchased this book from.
7. Click on **Code Download**.

You can also download the code files by clicking on the **Code Files** button on the book's webpage at the Packt Publishing website. This page can be accessed by entering the book's name in the **Search** box. Please note that you need to be logged in to your Packt account.

Once the file is downloaded, please make sure that you unzip or extract the folder using the latest version of:

- WinRAR / 7-Zip for Windows
- Zipeg / iZip / UnRarX for Mac
- 7-Zip / PeaZip for Linux

The code bundle for the book is also hosted on GitHub at `https://github.com/PacktPublishing/Ionic-2-Cookbook`. We also have other code bundles from our rich catalog of books and videos available at `https://github.com/PacktPublishing/`. Check them out!

Downloading the color images of this book

We also provide you with a PDF file that has color images of the screenshots/diagrams used in this book. The color images will help you better understand the changes in the output. You can download this file from `https://www.packtpub.com/sites/default/files/downloads/Ionic2Cookbook_ColorImages.pdf`.

Errata

Although we have taken every care to ensure the accuracy of our content, mistakes do happen. If you find a mistake in one of our books—maybe a mistake in the text or the code—we would be grateful if you could report this to us. By doing so, you can save other readers from frustration and help us improve subsequent versions of this book. If you find any errata, please report them by visiting `http://www.packtpub.com/submit-errata`, selecting your book, clicking on the **Errata Submission Form** link, and entering the details of your errata. Once your errata are verified, your submission will be accepted and the errata will be uploaded to our website or added to any list of the existing errata under the Errata section of that title.

To view the previously submitted errata, go to `https://www.packtpub.com/books/content/support` and enter the name of the book in the search field. The required information will appear under the **Errata** section.

Piracy

Piracy of copyrighted material on the Internet is an ongoing problem across all media. At Packt, we take the protection of our copyright and licenses very seriously. If you come across any illegal copies of our works in any form on the Internet, please provide us with the location address or website name immediately so that we can pursue a remedy.

Please contact us at `copyright@packtpub.com` with a link to the suspected pirated material.

We appreciate your help in protecting our authors and our ability to bring you valuable content.

Questions

If you have a problem with any aspect of this book, you can contact us at `questions@packtpub.com`, and we will do our best to address the problem.

1

Creating Our First App with Ionic 2

In this chapter, we will cover the following topics:

- Setting up a development environment
- Creating a HelloWorld app via the CLI
- Creating a HelloWorld app via Ionic Creator
- Viewing the app using your web browser
- Viewing the app using the Ionic CLI
- Viewing the app using Xcode for iOS
- Viewing the app using Genymotion for Android
- Viewing the app using Ionic View

Introduction

There are many options for developing mobile applications today. Native applications require a unique implementation for each platform, such as iOS, Android, and Windows phone. It's required for some cases such as high-performance CPU and GPU processing with lots of memory consumption. Any application that does not need over-the-top graphics and intensive CPU processing could benefit greatly from a cost-effective, write once and run anywhere HTML5 mobile implementation.

For those who choose the HTML5 route, there are many great choices in this active market. Some options may be very easy to start, but they could be very hard to scale or could face performance problems. Commercial options are generally expensive for small developers to discover product and market fit. The best practice is to think of the users first. There are instances where a simple responsive design website is a better choice; for example, when a business mainly has fixed content with minimal updating required or the content is better off on the web for SEO purposes.

The Ionic Framework has several advantages over its competitors, as shown:

- It's written on top of AngularJS. Ionic 1.x was based on AngularJS 1.x, while Ionic 2.0 is on top of AngularJS 2.0.
- UI performance is strong because of its usage of the `requestAnimationFrame()` technique.
- It offers a beautiful and comprehensive set of default styles, similar to a mobile-focused twitter Bootstrap.
- **Sass** is available for quick, easy, and effective theme customization.

There have been many significant changes between the launch of AngularJS 1.x and 2.0. All of these changes are applicable to Ionic 2 as well. Consider the following examples:

- AngularJS 2.0 utilizes **TypeScript**, which is a superset of the **ECMAScript 6** (**ES6**) standard, to build your code into JavaScript. This allows the developers to leverage TypeScript features, such as type checking, during the complication step.
- There will be no more Controllers and Directives in AngularJS. Earlier, a controller was assigned to a DOM node while a directive converted a template into a component-like architecture. However, it is very hard to scale and debug large AngularJS 1.x applications due to the misuse of Controllers and/or issues with conflicting directives. Moving to AngularJS 2.0, there is only a single concept of Component, which eventually has a selector corresponding to an HTML template and a class containing functions.
- The `$scope` object will no longer exist in AngularJS 2.0 because all properties are now defined inside a component. This is actually good news because debugging errors in `$scope` (especially with nested scenarios) is very difficult in AngularJS 1.x.
- Finally, AngularJS 2.0 promises to have better performance and supports both ES5 and ES6 standards. You could write AngularJS 2.0 in TypeScript, Dart or just pure JavaScript.

In this chapter, you will go through several HelloWorld examples to Bootstrap your Ionic app. This process will give you a quick skeleton to start building more comprehensive apps. The majority of apps have similar user experience flows, such as tabs and side menus.

Setting up a development environment

Before you create your first app, your environment must have the required components ready. These components ensure a smooth process of development, build and test. The default Ionic project folder is based on Cordova's. Therefore, you need the Ionic CLI to automatically add the correct platform (that is, iOS, Android, or Windows phone) and build the project. This will ensure all Cordova plugins are included properly. The tool has many options to run your app in the browser or simulator with live reload.

Getting ready

You need to install Ionic and its dependencies to get started. Ionic itself is just a collection of CSS styles, AngularJS components, and standard Cordova plugins. It's also a command-line tool to help manage all technologies, such as Cordova and Bower. The installation process will give you a command line to generate the initial code and build the app.

Ionic uses npm as the installer, which is included when installing Node.js. Please install the latest version of Node.js from `https://nodejs.org/en/download/`.

You will need to install Cordova, `ios-sim` (iOS Simulator) and Ionic:

```
$ npm install -g cordova ionic ios-sim
```

You can install all three components with this single command line instead of issuing three command lines separately. The `-g` parameter is to install the package globally (not just in the current directory).

For Linux and Mac, you may need to use the `sudo` command to allow system access, as shown:

```
$ sudo npm install -g cordova ionic ios-sim
```

The following are a few common options for an **Integrated Development Environment** (**IDE**):

- Xcode for iOS
- Android Studio for Android
- Microsoft Visual Studio Code (VS Code)
- Sublime Text (`http://www.sublimetext.com/`) for web development

All of these have a free license. You could code directly in Xcode or Android Studio but those are somewhat heavy-duty for web apps, especially when you have a lot of windows open and just need something simple to code. Sublime Text is free for non-commercial developers but you have to purchase a license if you are a commercial developer. Most frontend developers would prefer to use Sublime Text for coding HTML and JavaScript because it's very lightweight and comes with a well-supported developer community. Sublime Text has been around for a long time and is very user-friendly. However, there are many features in Ionic 2 that make Visual Studio Code very compelling. For example, it has the look and feel of a full IDE without being bulky. You could debug JavaScript directly inside VS Code as well as getting autocomplete (for example, IntelliSense). The following instructions cover both Sublime Text and VS Code, although the rest of this book will use VS Code.

How to do it...

VS Code works on Mac, Windows, and Linux. Here are the instructions:

1. Visit `https://code.visualstudio.com`.
2. Download and install for your specific OS.
3. Unzip the downloaded file.
4. Drag the `.app` file into the `Applications` folder and drag it to Mac's Dock.
5. Open Microsoft Visual Studio code.
6. Press *Ctrl* + *Shift* + *p* to open command palette.
7. Type `shell command` in command palette.
8. Click on the `Shell Command: Install 'code' command in PATH` command to install the script to add Visual Studio Code in your terminal `$PATH`.
9. Restart Visual Studio Code to take effect.
10. Later on, you can just do `code.` (including the dot) directly from the Ionic project folder and VS Code will automatically open that folder as a project:

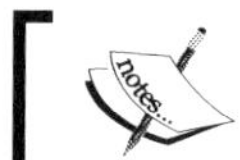

Note that the following screenshots are done via Mac.

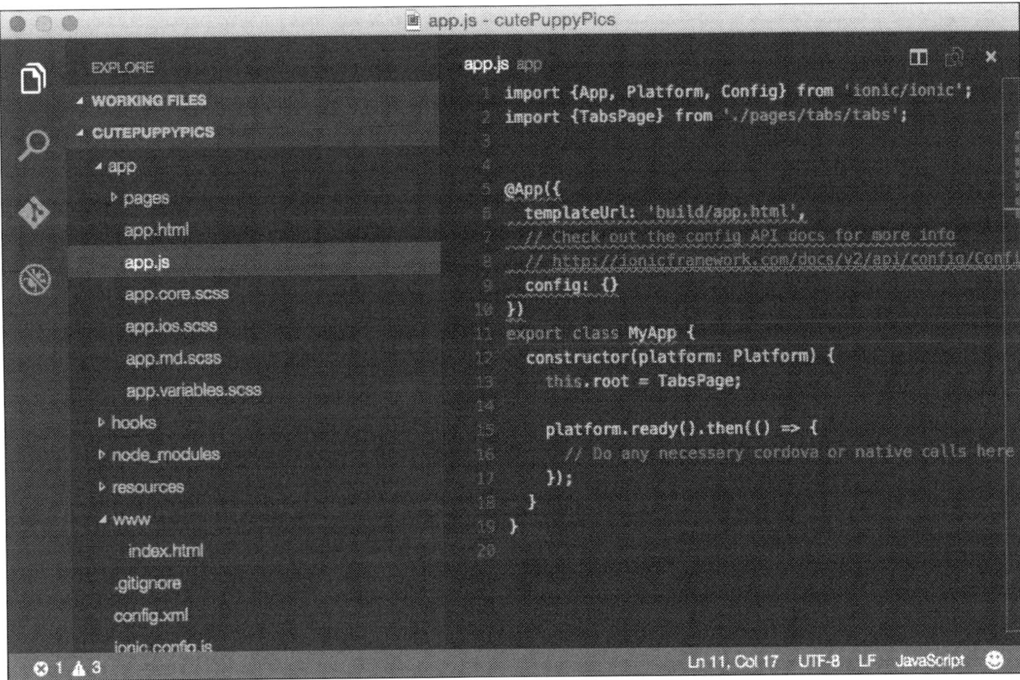

11. If you decide to use Sublime Text, you will need Package Control (`https://packagecontrol.io/installation`), which is similar to a **Plugin Manager**. Since Ionic uses Sass, it's optional to install the Sass Syntax Highlighting package.
12. Navigate to **Sublime Text** | **Preferences** | **Package Control**:

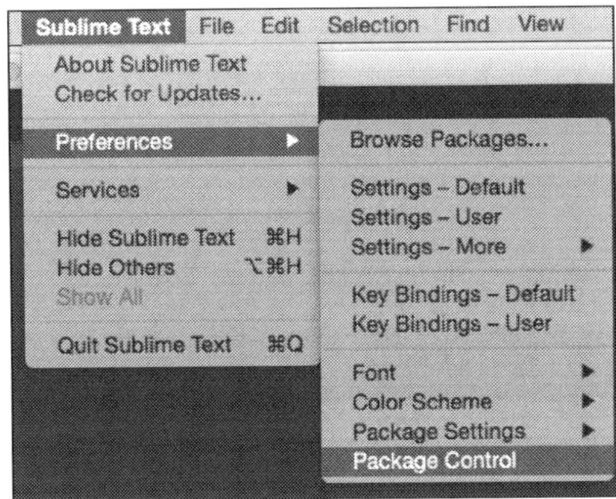

13. Go to **Package Control: Install Package**. You could also just type the commands partially (that is, `inst`) and it will automatically select the right option:

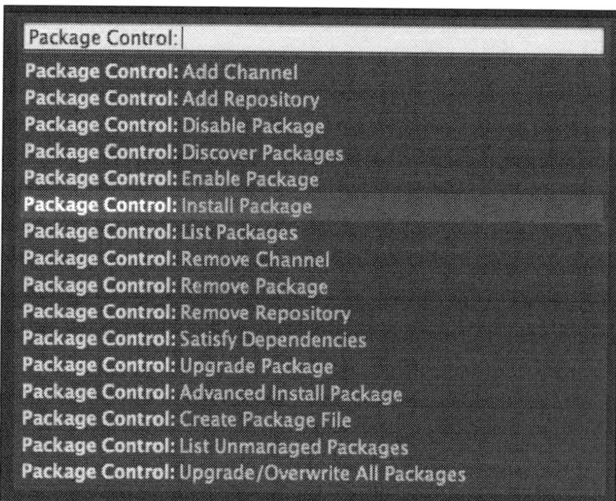

14. Type `Sass` and the search results will show one option for **TextMate & Sublime Text**. Select that item to install:

Sass
Sass support for TextMate & Sublime Text (2 & 3)
v2015.01.06.16.00.00; github.com/nathos/sass-textmate-bundle

There's More...

There are tons of Sublime Text packages that you may want to use, such as HTML, JSHint, JSLint, Tag, and ColorPicker You can visit `https://sublime.wbond.net/browse/popular` for additional needs.

Creating a HelloWorld app via the CLI

It's quickest to start your app using the existing templates. Ionic gives you the following three standard out-of-the-box templates via the command line:

- **Blank**: This is a simple page with minimal JavaScript code.
- **Tabs**: These are multiple pages with routes. A route URL goes to a tab.
- **Side menu**: This is a template with a left/right menu with center content area.

How to do it...

1. To set up the app with a blank template from Ionic, use this command:

```
$ ionic start HelloWorld_Blank blank --v2
```

If you don't have an account in `ionic.io`, the command line will ask for it. You could either press *y* or *n* to continue. It's not mandatory to have an account at this step.

2. If you replace blank with tabs, it will create a tab template, as shown:

```
$ ionic start HelloWorld_Tabs tabs
```

3. Similarly, the following command will create an app with a side menu:

```
$ ionic start HelloWorld_Sidemenu sidemenu --v2
```

The side menu template is the most common template as it provides a very nice routing example with different pages in the `/app/pages` folder.

Additional guidance for the Ionic CLI is available on the GitHub page, `https://github.com/driftyco/ionic-cli`.

How it works...

This chapter will show you how to quickly start your code base and visualize the result. More details about AngularJS 2.0 and its template syntax will be discussed across various chapters of this book. However, the core concepts are as follows:

- **Component**: AngularJS 2.0 is very modular because you could write your code in a file and use an export class to turn it into a component. If you are familiar with AngularJS 1.x, this is similar to a Controller and how it binds with a DOM node. A component will have its own private and public properties and methods (that is, functions). To tell whether a class is an AngularJS component or not, you have to use the `@Component` decorator. This is another new concept in TypeScript since you could enforce characteristics (metadata) on any class so that they behave in a certain way.
- **Template**: A template is an HTML string or a separate `.html` file that tells AngularJS how to render a component. This concept is very similar to any other frontend and backend framework. However, AngularJS 2.0 has its own syntax to allow simple logic on the DOM, such as repeat rendering (`*ngFor`), event binding (click), or custom tags (`<my-tag>`).
- **Directive**: This allows you to manipulate the DOM, since the directive is bound to a DOM object. So, `*ngFor` and `*ngIf` would be examples of directives because they alter the behavior of that DOM.

- **Service**: This refers to the abstraction to manage models or collections of complex logic beside get/set required. There is no service decorator as with a component. So, any class could be a service.
- **Pipe**: This is mainly used to process an expression in the template and return some data (that is, rounding numbers and adding currency) using the `{{ expression | filter }}` format. For example, `{{amount | currency}}` will return `$100` if the `amount` variable is `100`.

Ionic automatically creates a project folder structure that would look as follows:

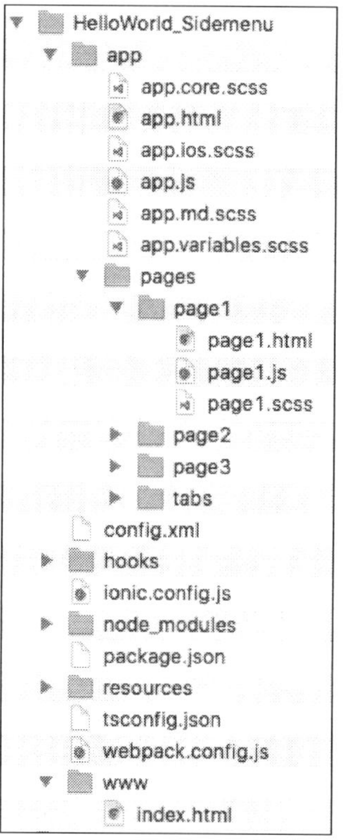

You will spend most of your time in the `/app` folder, because that's where your application components will be placed. This is very different from Ionic 1.x because the /www folder here is actually compiled by TypeScript. If you build the app for iOS, the Ionic build command line will also create another copy at `/platforms/ios/`www, which is specifically for Cordova to point to. Another interesting change in AngularJS 2.0 is that all custom JS and CSS files are placed in the same subfolder or in `/app/pages`. Since AngularJS 2.0 is component based, each component will come with HTML, CSS, and JS. If you add in more JavaScript modules, you can put them in the `/app` folder, or a better practice is to use `npm install` so that it's automatically added in the `/node_modules` folder. Ionic 2 completely got rid of Grunt and Bower. Everything is simplified into just `package.json`, where your third-party dependencies will be listed.

There is no need to modify the `/platforms` or `/plugins` folder manually unless troubleshooting needs to be done. Otherwise, the Ionic or Cordova CLI will automate the content inside these folders.

By default, from the Ionic template, the AngularJS app name is called `MyApp`. You will see something like this in `app.js`, which is the Bootstrap file for the entire app:

```
@App({
  templateUrl: 'build/app.html',
  config: {}
})
export class MyApp {
  constructor(platform: Platform) {
    this.root = TabsPage;

    platform.ready().then(() => {
    });
  }
}
```

This is acting as the `root` of your app and all content will be injected inside `<ion-app></ion-app>` of `index.html`.

Note that if you double-click on the `index.html` file to open it in the browser, it will show a blank page. This doesn't mean that the app isn't working. The reason for this is that the Angular component of Ionic dynamically loads all the `.js` files and this behavior requires server access via the `http://` protocol. If you open a file locally, the browser automatically treats it as a file protocol (`file://`), and therefore Angular will not have the ability to load additional `.js` modules to run the app properly. There are several methods of running the app, which will be discussed later.

Creating a HelloWorld app via Ionic Creator

Another way to start your app codebase is to use **Ionic Creator**. This is a great interface builder to accelerate your app development with the drag and drop style. You can quickly take the existing components and position them to visualize how it should look in the app via a web-based interface. Most common components, such as buttons, images, and checkboxes, are available.

Ionic Creator allows the user to export everything as a project with all `.html`, `.css`, and `.js` files. You should be able edit content in the `/app` folder to build on top of the interface.

Getting ready

Ionic Creator requires registration for a free account at `https://creator.ionic.io/` to get started.

How to do it...

1. Create a new project called **myApp**:

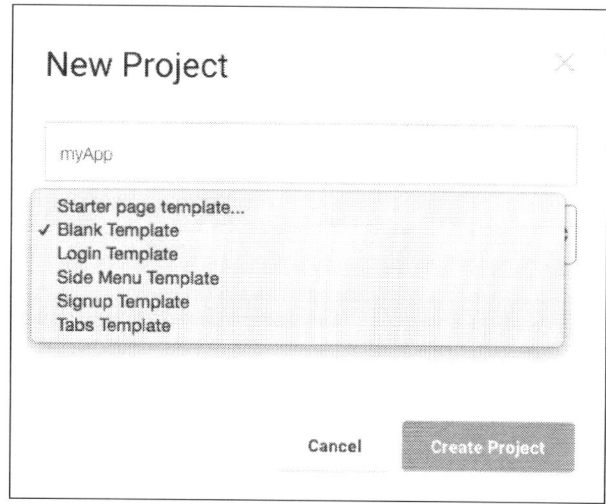

2. Validate to ensure that you see the following screen:

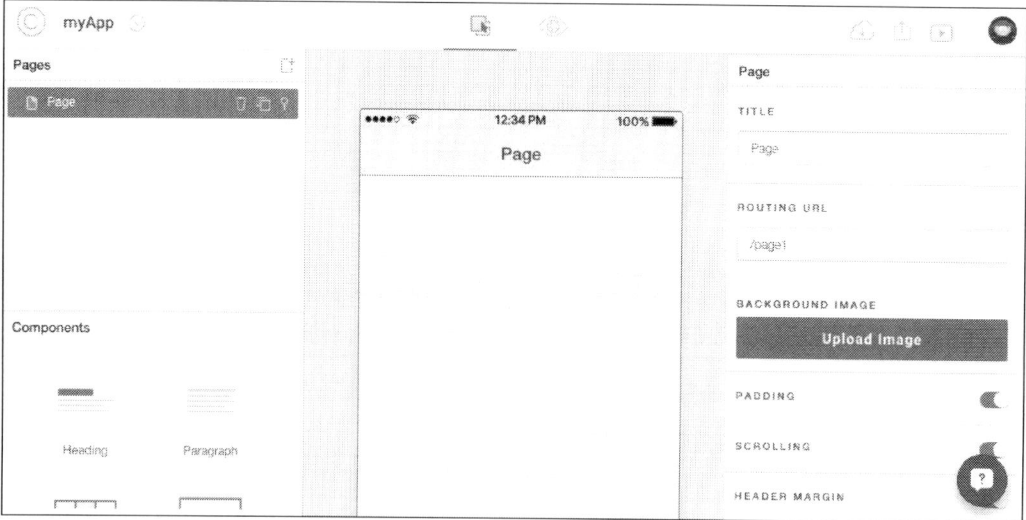

The center area is your app interface. The left side gives you a list of **Pages**. Each page is a single route. You also have access to a number of UI components that you would normally have to code by hand in an html file. The panel on the right shows the properties of any selected component.

You're free to do whatever you need to do here by dropping components to the center screen. If you need to create a new page, you have to click on the plus sign in the **Pages** panel. Each page is represented as a link, which is basically a route in Angular UI Router's definition. To navigate to another page (for example, after clicking a button), you can just change the link property and point to that page.

There is an edit button on top where you can toggle back and forth between the edit mode and preview mode. It's very useful to see how your app will look and behave.

3. Once completed, click the export button on the top in the navigation bar. You have the following four options:
    - Use the Ionic CLI tool to get the code
    - Download the project as a ZIP file
    - Export it to native code (similar to PhoneGap Build), as shown:

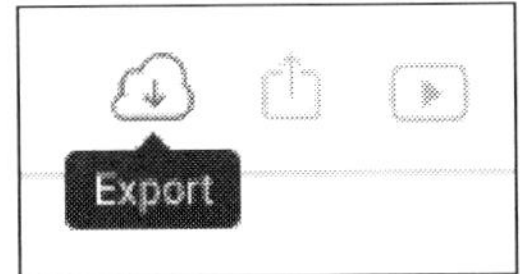

- Export it to the preview mode using the Creator app, as follows:

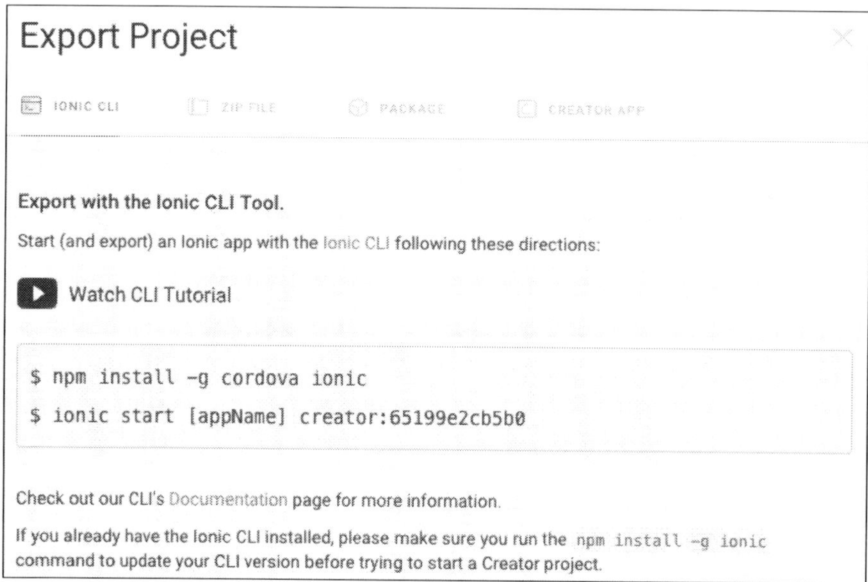

The best way to learn Ionic Creator is to play with it. You can add a new page and pick out any of the existing templates. The following example shows a **Login** page template:

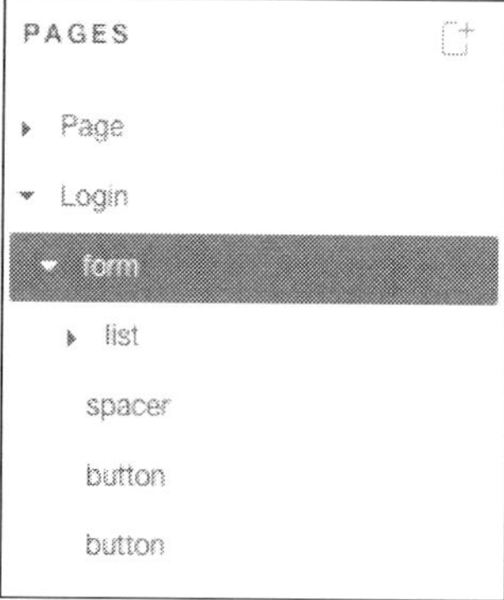

Here is how it should look out of the box (after export or download):

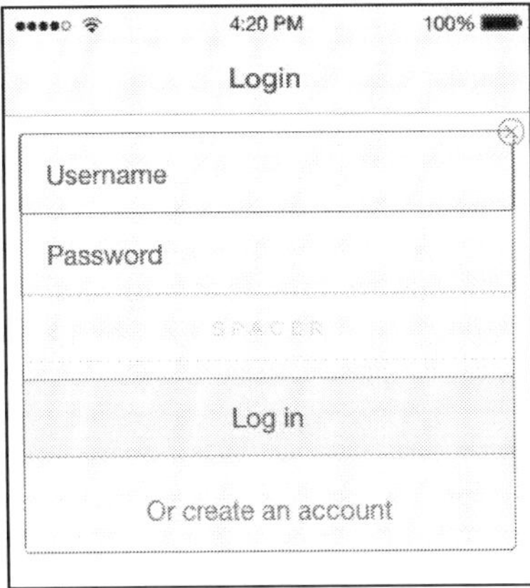

There's More...

To switch to the preview mode, where you can see the UI in a device simulator, click on the switch button in the top right to enable Test, as illustrated:

In this mode, you should be able to interact with the components in the web browser as if they're actually deployed on the device.

If you break something, it's very simple to start a new project. It's a great tool to use for prototyping and to get the initial template or project scaffolding. You should continue coding in your regular IDE for the rest of the app. Ionic Creator doesn't do everything for you, yet. For example, if you want to access specific Cordova plugin features, you have to write that code separately.

Also, if you want to tweak the interface outside of what is allowed within Ionic Creator, it will also require specific modifications to the `.html` and `.css` files.

Viewing the app using your web browser

In order to run the web app, you need to turn your `/www` folder into a web server. Again, there are many methods to do this and people tend to stick with one or two ways to keep things simple. A few other options are unreliable, such as Sublime Text's live watch package or static page generator (for example, the Jekyll and Middleman apps). They are slow to detect changes and may freeze your IDE. So those won't be mentioned here.

Getting ready

The recommended method is to use the `ionic serve` command line. It basically launches an HTTP server so that you can open your app in a desktop browser.

How to do it...

1. First, you need to be in the `project` folder. Let's assume that it is the Side Menu HelloWorld:

   `$ cd HelloWorld_Sidemenu`

2. From there, just issue the simple command line, as shown:

   `$ ionic serve`

That's it! There is no need to go into the `/www` folder or figure out which port to use. The command line will provide the following options while the web server is running:

```
Δ Compiling and bundling with Webpack...
√ Using your webpack.config.js file

Δ Compiling Sass to CSS
√ Matching patterns: app/app.+(ios|md).scss

Δ Copying fonts
√ Matching patterns: node_modules/ionic-framework/fonts/**/*.ttf

Δ Copying HTML
√ Matching patterns: app/**/*.html

√ Sass compilation complete
√ Fonts copied to www/build/fonts
√ HTML copied to www/build

Hash: 1b03f7bea7292b8fd911
Version: webpack 1.12.10
Time: 6455ms
         Asset     Size  Chunks             Chunk Names
app.bundle.js  2.58 MB       0  [emitted]  main
    [0] multi main 76 bytes {0} [built]
     + 356 hidden modules

√ Webpack complete

Δ Starting dev server.

√ Running live reload server: http://localhost:35729
√ Running dev server:  http://localhost:8100
√ Watching: 0=www/build/**/*.html, 1=www/build/**/*.js, 2=www/build/**/*.css
Ionic server commands, enter:
  restart or r to restart the client app from the root
  goto or g and a url to have the app navigate to the given url
  consolelogs or c to enable/disable console log output
  serverlogs or s to enable/disable server log output
  quit or q to shutdown the server and exit
```

The most common option to use here is `r` to restart or `q` to quit when you are done.

There are additional steps to view the app with the correct device resolution:

1. Install Google Chrome if it's not already on your computer.
2. Open the link (for example, `http://localhost:8100/`) from ionic serve in Google Chrome.
3. Turn on Developer Tools. For example, in Mac's Google Chrome, navigate to **View** | **Developer** | **Developer Tools**.

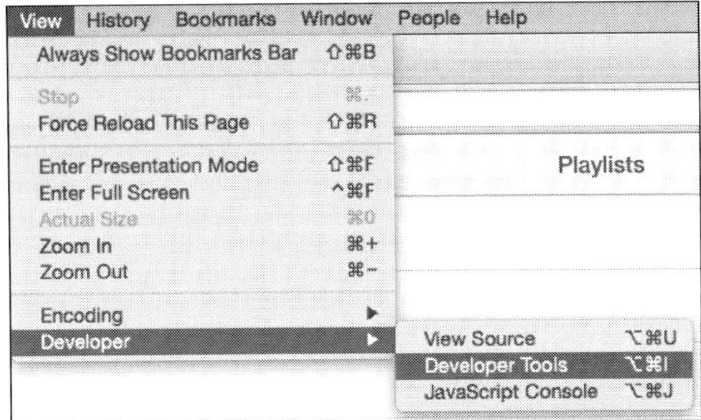

4. Click on the small mobile icon in the Chrome Developer Tools area, as illustrated:

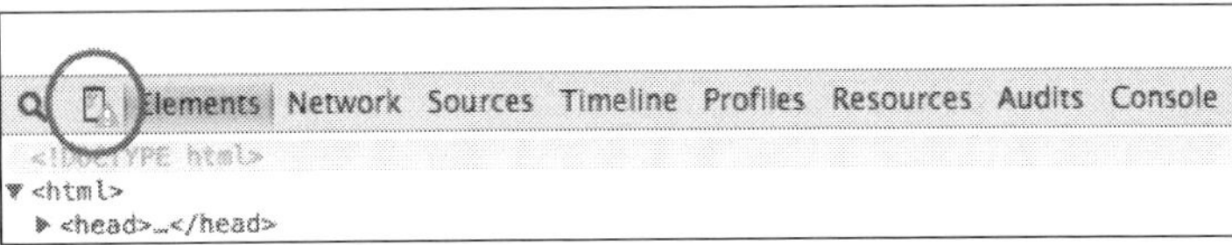

5. There will be a long list of devices to pick from, as shown:

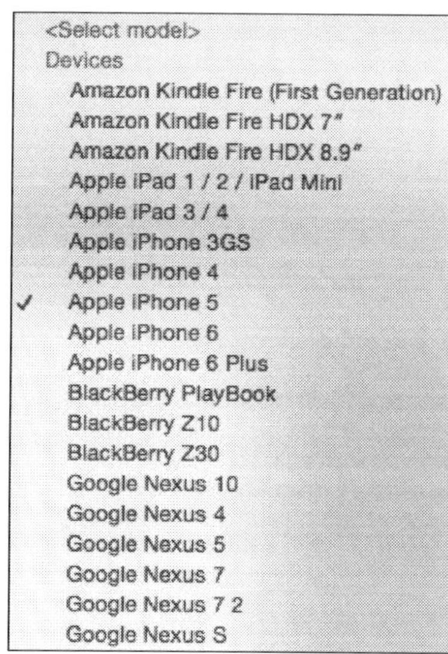

6. After selecting a device, you need to refresh the page to ensure that the UI is updated. Chrome should give you the exact view resolution of the device.

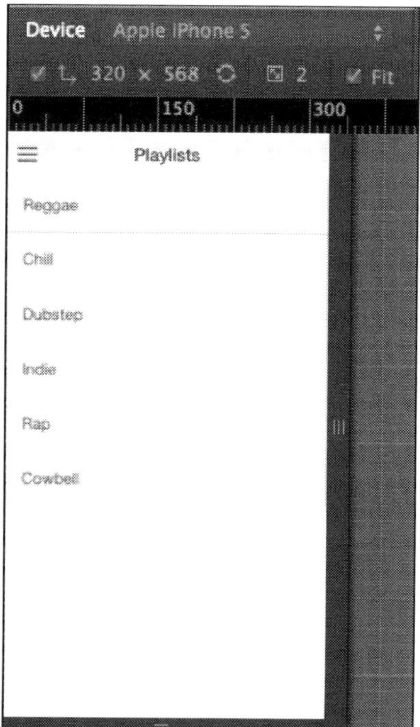

Most developers would prefer to use this method to code as you can debug the app using Chrome Developer Tools. It works exactly like any other web application. You can create breakpoints or output variables to the console.

How it works...

Note that ionic serve is actually watching everything under the `/app` folder and transpiling the TypeScript code into JavaScript under `/www` on the fly. This makes sense because there is no need for the system to scan through every single file when the probability for it to change is very small.

While the web server is running, you can go back to the IDE and continue coding. For example, let's open `page1.html` or any other template file and change the first line to this:

```
<ion-view view-title="Updated Playlists">
```

Go back to the web browser where Ionic opened the new page; the app interface will change the title bar right away without requiring you to refresh the browser. This is a very nice feature when there is a lot of back and forth between code change and checking on how it works or looks in the app instantly.

Viewing the app using the Ionic CLI

So far, you have been testing the web app portion of Ionic. Most of the time, you will need to actually run the app on a physical device or at least an emulator to see how the app behaves and whether all native features work.

Getting Ready

You will need to have the emulator installed. iOS emulator comes when you do `npm install -g ios-sim` and the Android emulator comes with Android Studio. To test the app on a physical device, you must connect the device to your computer via a USB connection.

How to do it...

1. Add the specific platform (such as iOS) and build the app using the following command line:

```
$ ionic platform add ios
$ ionic build ios
```

Note that you need to do the `platform add` before building the app. However, if you use the standard template from the Ionic CLI, it should already have the iOS platform included. To build and run for Android, you can replace iOS with Android.

2. To emulate the app using the iOS emulator, use the following command line:

```
$ ionic emulate ios
```

3. To run the app on the actual physical iPhone device, use the command line as shown:

```
$ ionic run ios --device
```

Viewing the app using Xcode for iOS

You could run the app using Xcode (in Mac) as well.

How to do it...

1. Go to the `/platforms/ios` folder.
2. Look for the folder with `.xcodeproj` and open it in Xcode.
3. Click on the iOS Device icon and select your choice of iOS simulator:

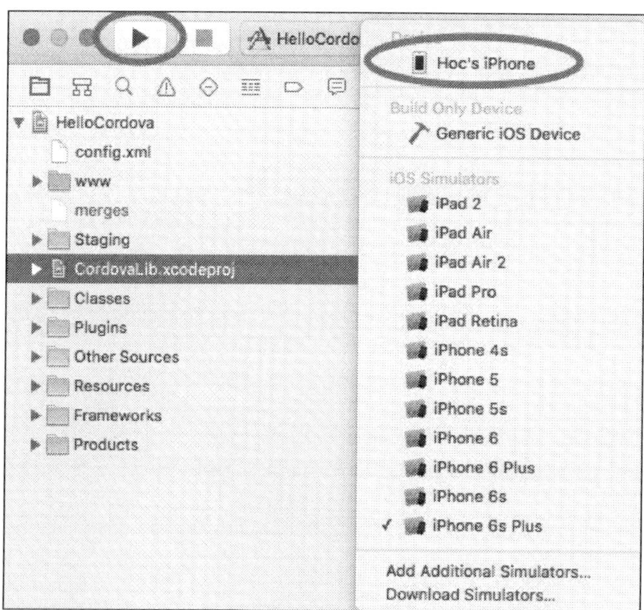

4. Click on the run button and you should be able to see the app running in the simulator.

There's more...

You can connect a physical device via a USB port and it will show up in the iOS Device list for you to pick. Then, you can deploy the app directly on your device. Note that iOS developer membership is required for this. This method is more complex than just viewing the app via a web browser.

However, it's a must when you want to test out your code related to device features, such as camera or maps. If you change code in the `/app` folder and want to again run it in Xcode, you have to do `ionic build ios` first, because the running code is in the `Staging` folder of your Xcode project, as illustrated:

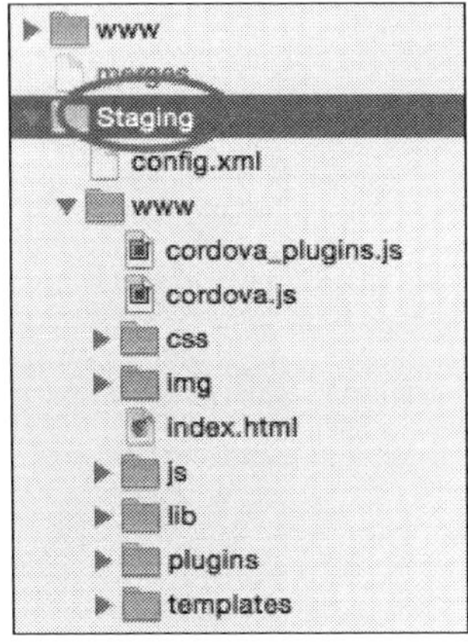

For debugging, the Xcode Console can output JavaScript logs as well. However, you could use the more advanced features of Safari's **Web Inspector** (which is similar to Google Chrome's Developer Tools) to debug your app. Note that only Safari can debug a web app running on a connected physical iOS device because Chrome does not support this on a Mac. It's easy to enable this capability, and it can be done with the following steps:

1. Allow remote debugging for iOS device by navigating to `Settings` | **Safari** | **Advanced** and enabling **Web Inspector**:

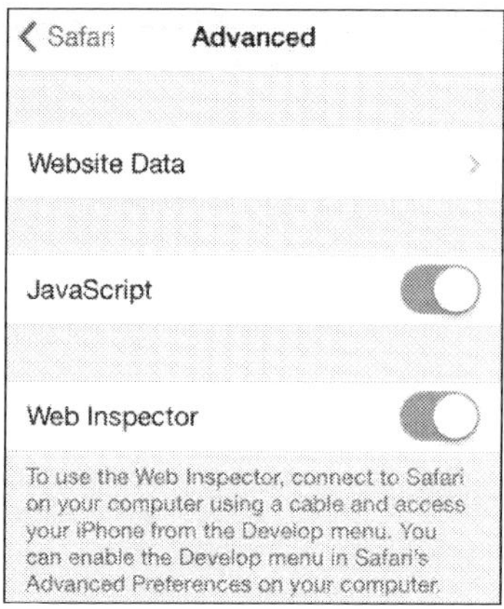

2. Connect the physical iOS device to your Mac via USB and run the app.
3. Open the Safari browser.
4. Select **Develop** | **your device's name (or iOS Simulator)** | **index.html**, as shown:

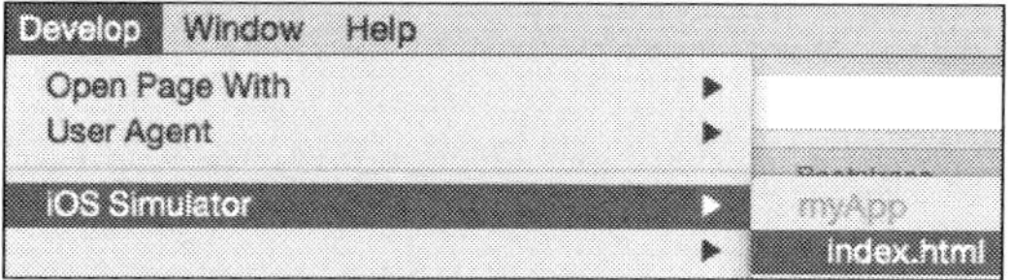

If you don't see the **Develop** menu in Safari, you need to navigate to **Preferences** > **Advanced** and check on **Show Develop menu in menu bar**

Safari will open a new console just for that specific device just as it's running within the computer's Safari.

Viewing the app using Genymotion for Android

While it's possible to install the Google Android simulator, many developers have an inconsistent experience on a Mac. There are many commercial and free alternatives that offer more convenience and a wide range of device support. **Genymotion** provides some unique advantages, such as allowing users to switch the Android model and version, supporting networking from within the app, and allowing SD card simulation.

In this section, you will learn how to set up Android developer environment (on a Mac in this case) first. Then, you will install and configure Genymotion for mobile app development.

How to do it...

1. The first step is to set up the Android environment properly for development. Download and install Android Studio from `https://developer.android.com/studio/index.html`.

You might be asked to install other libraries if your machine doesn't have the correct dependencies. If that is the case, you should run `sudo apt-get install lib32z1 lib32ncurses5 lib32bz2-1.0 lib32stdc++6` from the command line to install.

2. Run Android Studio.

3. You need to install all the required packages, such as Android SDK. Just click **Next** twice at the setup wizard screen and click on the **Finish** button to start the packages' installation.

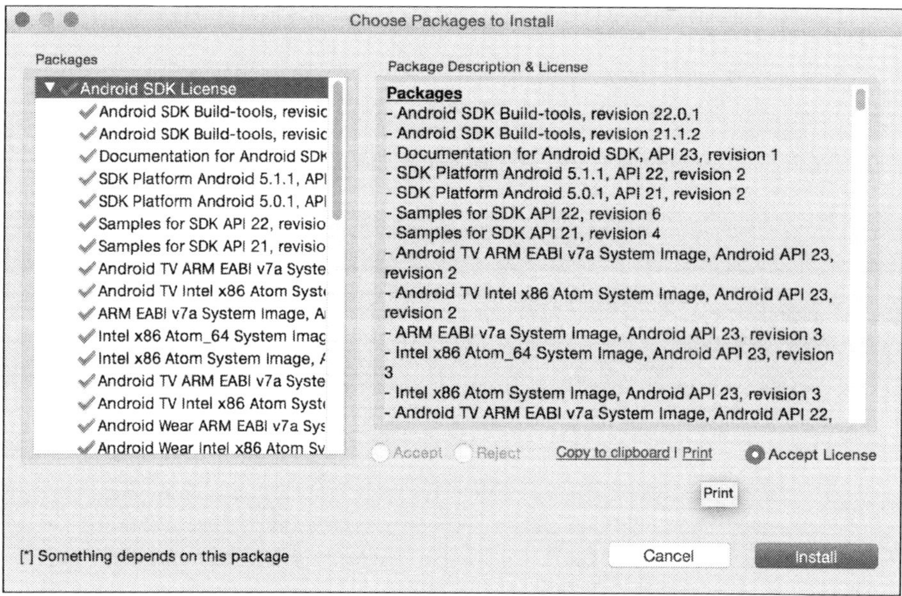

4. After the installation is completed, you need to install additional packages and other SDK versions. On the **Quick Start** screen, select **Configure**, as illustrated:

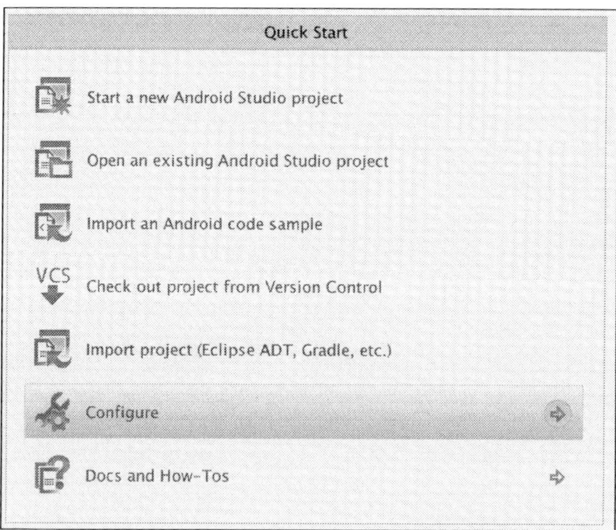

5. After this, select **SDK Manager**, as shown:

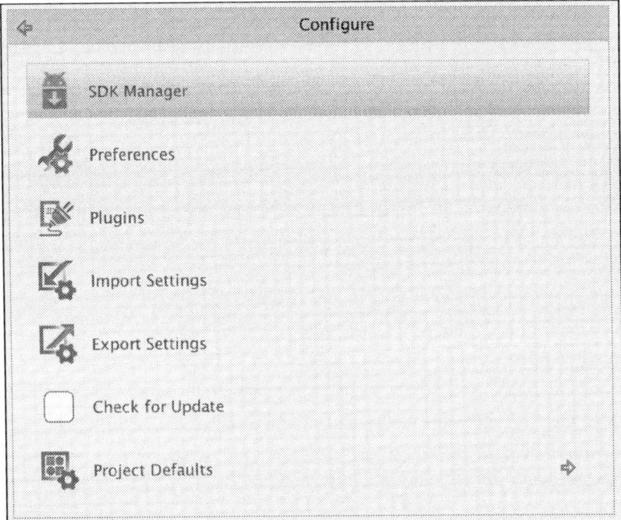

6. It's good practice to install the previous version, such as **Android 5.0.1** and **5.1.1**. You may also want to install all `Tools` and `Extras` for later use:

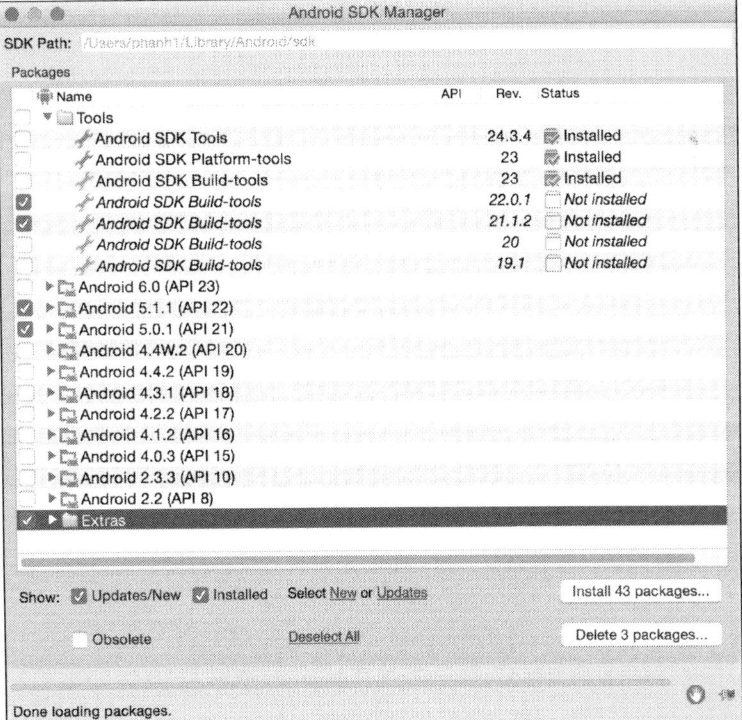

7. Click on the **Install packages...** button.
8. Check the box on **Accept License** and select **Install**.
9. The SDK Manager will give you an SDK Path on the top. Make a copy of this path because you need to modify the environment path.
10. Go to the terminal and type the following command:

```
$ touch ~/.bash_profile; open ~/.bash_profile.
```

11. This will open a text editor to edit your `bash profile` file. Insert the following line where `/YOUR_PATH_TO/android-sdk` should be the SDK Path that you copied earlier:

```
export ANDROID_HOME=/YOUR_PATH_TO/android-sdk
export PATH=$ANDROID_HOME/platform-tools:$PATH
export PATH=$ANDROID_HOME/tools:$PATH
```

12. Save and close that text editor.
13. Go back to terminal and type.

```
$ source ~/.bash_profile
$ echo $ANDROID_HOME
```

14. You should see the output as your SDK Path. This verifies that you have correctly configured the Android developer environment.
15. The next step is to install and configure Genymotion. Download and install Genymotion and Genymotion Shell from `genymotion.com`.
16. Run Genymotion.
17. Click on the **Add** button to start adding a new Android device, as illustrated:

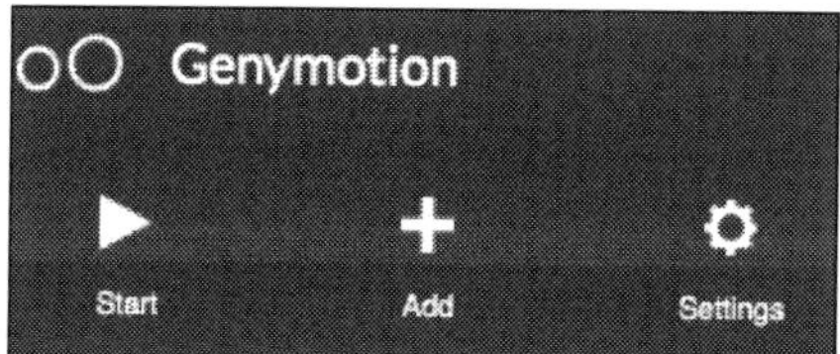

18. Select a device that you want to simulate. In this case, let select **Samsung Galaxy S5**, as follows:

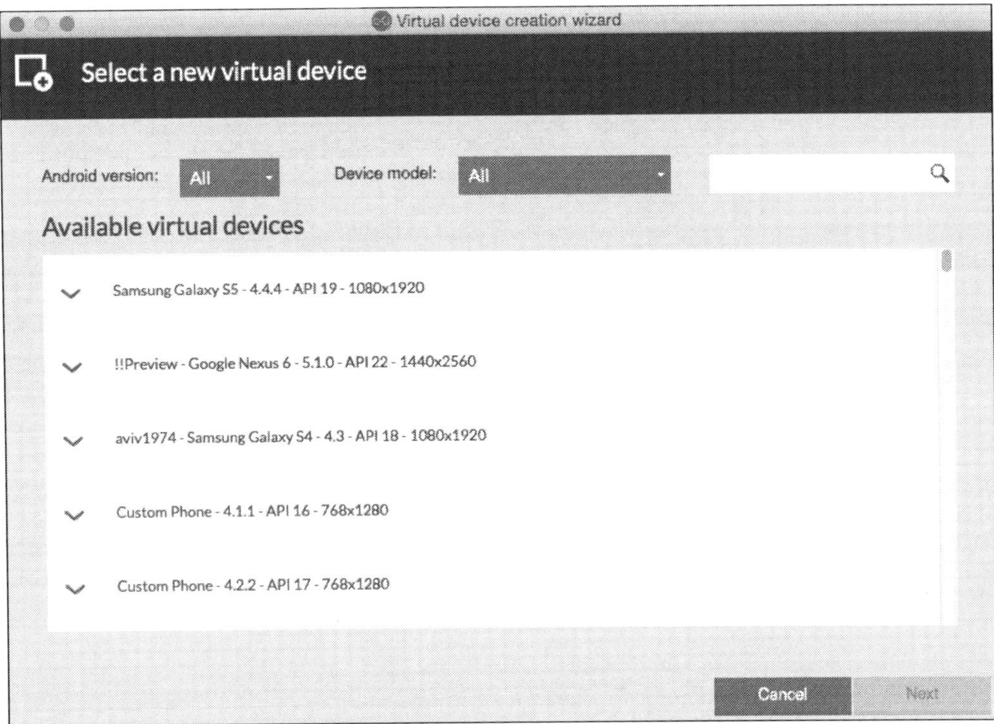

19. You will see the device being added to your virtual devices. Click on that device.

20. Then click on **Start**:

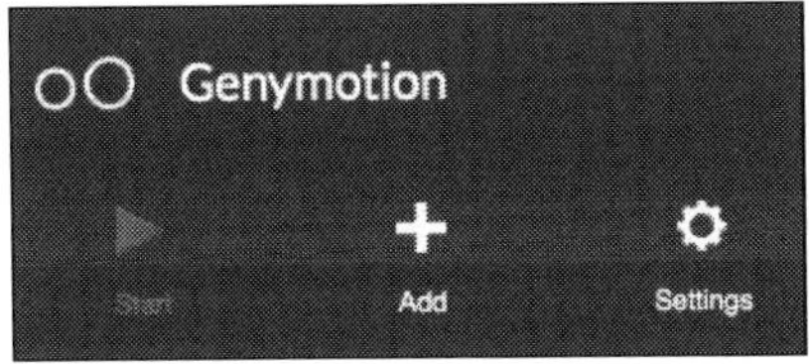

21. The simulator will take a few seconds to start and will show another window. This is just a blank simulator without your app running inside yet:

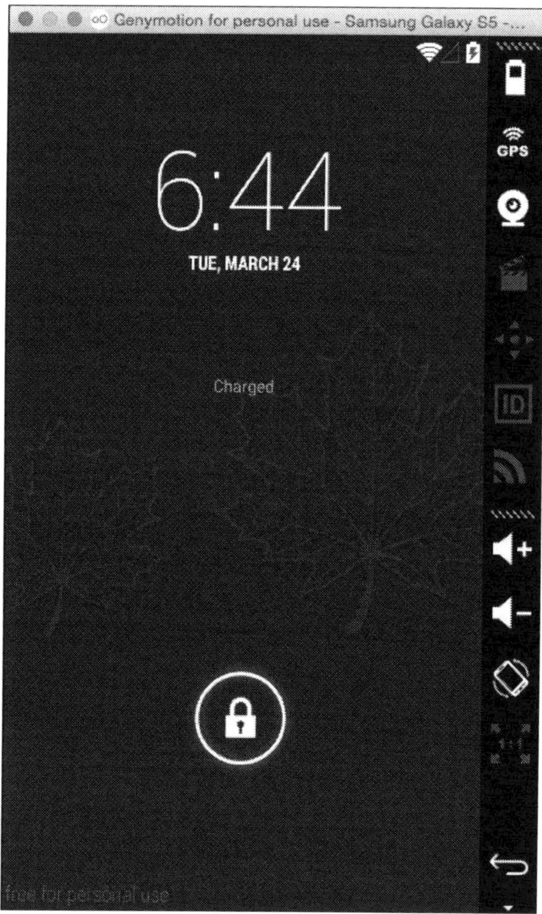

22. Run Genymotion Shell.
23. From Genymotion Shell, you need to get a device list and keep the IP address of the device attached, which is Samsung Galaxy S5. Type `devices list`:

```
Genymotion Shell > devices list
Available devices:

 Id | Select |     Status     |   Type   |   IP Address    |      Name
----+--------+----------------+----------+-----------------+---------------
  0 |    *   |             On |  virtual |  192.168.56.101 | Samsung Galaxy S5 -
4.4.4 - API 19 - 1080x1920
```

24. Type `adb connect 192.168.56.101` (or whatever the IP address was that you saw earlier from the `devices list` command line).
25. Type `adb devices` to confirm that it is connected.
26. Type `ionic platform add android` to add Android as a platform for your app.
27. Finally, type `ionic run android`.
28. You should be able to see the Genymotion window showing your app.

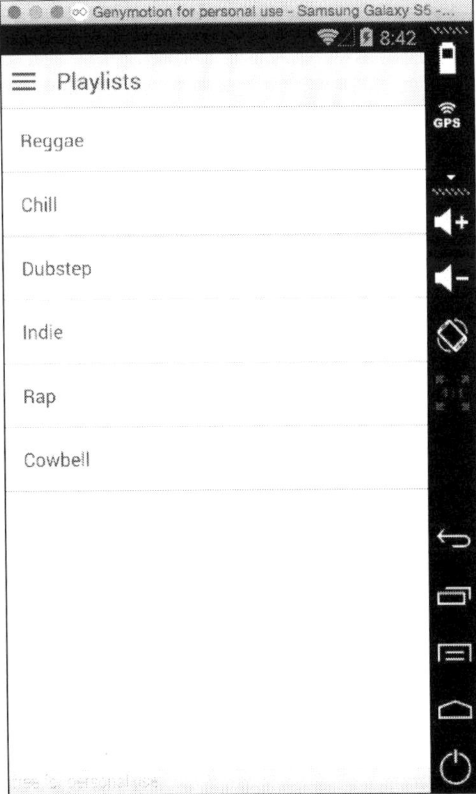

Although there are many steps to get this working, it's a lot less likely that you have to go through the same process over. Once your environment is set up, all you need to do is to leave Genymotion running, while writing code. If there is a need to test the app in different Android devices, it's easy to add another virtual device in Genymotion and connect to it.

Viewing the app using Ionic View

Ionic View is an app viewer that you can download from the App Store or Google Play. When you are in the development process and the app is not completed, you don't want to submit it to either Apple or Google right away but limit access to your testers. Ionic View can help load your own app inside Ionic View and make it behave like a real app with some access to native device features. Additionally, Ionic View lets you use your app on an iOS device without any certificate requirement.

Since Ionic View uses Cordova **InAppBrowser** plugin to launch your app, all the device features have to be hacked to make it work. Currently, Ionic View only supports SQLite, battery, camera, device motion, device orientation, dialog/notification, geolocation, globalization, network information, vibration, keyboard, status bar, barcode scanner, and zip. It's a good idea to check the updated support list prior to using Ionic View to ensure that your app works properly.

How to do it...

There are two ways to use Ionic View. You can either upload your own app or load someone else's app ID. If you test your own app, follow these steps:

1. Download Ionic View from either App Store or Google Play.
2. Make sure to register an account on `ionic.io`.
3. Go to your app's `project` folder.
4. Search for ionic upload.
5. Enter your credentials.
6. The CLI will upload the entire app and give you the app ID, which is `152909f7` in this case. You may want to keep this app ID to share with other testers later.

```
Uploading app...
Successfully uploaded (152909f7)

Share your beautiful app with someone:

$ ionic share EMAIL
```

7. Open the Ionic View app on the mobile device and log in if you haven't done so already.
8. Now you should be able to see the app name on your **MY APPS** page. Go ahead and select the app name (**myApp** in this case), as illustrated:

9. Select **VIEW APP** to run the app, as shown:

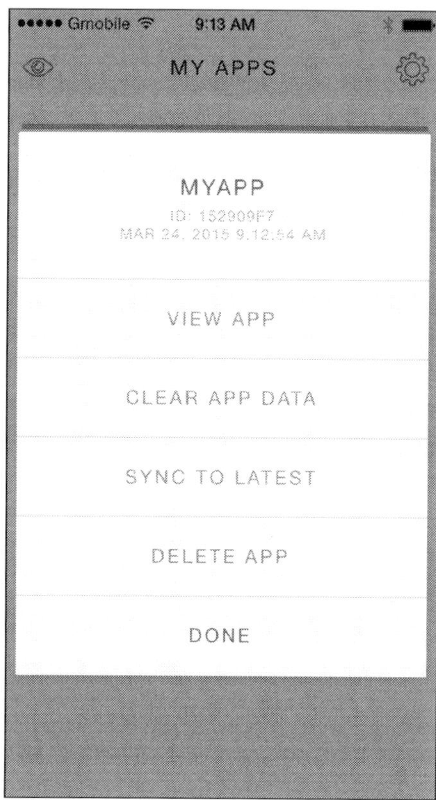

10. You will see that the app interface appears with initial instructions on how to exit the app. Since your app will cover the full screen of Ionic View, you need to swipe down using three fingers, as illustrated, to exit back to Ionic View:

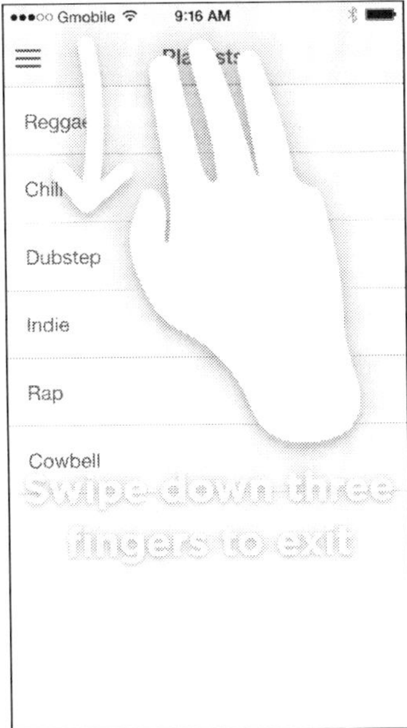

If there is no code update, the process is the same except that you need to select **SYNC TO LATEST** from the menu.

There's more...

To summarize, there are several benefits of using Ionic View, some of which are as follows:

- It's convenient because there is only one command line to push the app
- Anyone can access your app by entering the app ID
- There is no need to even have iOS developer membership to start developing with Ionic. Apple has its own `TestFlight` app, in which the use case is very similar
- You can stay agile in the developer process by having testers test the app as you develop it
- Ionic View has a wide range of device feature support and continues to grow

2

Adding Ionic 2 Components

In this chapter, we will cover the following tasks related to using Ionic 2 components:

- Adding multiple pages using tabs
- Adding left and right menu navigation
- Navigating multiple pages with state parameters

Introduction

It's possible to write a simple app with a handful of pages. Ionic provides a lot of out-of-the-box components that allow simple plug-n-play operations. When the app grows, managing different views and their custom data at a specific time or triggered event could be very complex. Ionic 2 comes with some changes in handling state and navigation. In Ionic 1, you could use UI-Router for advanced routing management mechanism. In Ionic 2, `NavController` will enable the push/pop implementation of the navigation.

Since Ionic 2 introduces many new components, you have to understand how these components impact your app state hierarchy and when each state is triggered.

Adding multiple pages using tabs

This section will explain how to work with the Ionic tab interface and expand it for other cases. The example used is very basic with three tabs and some sample Ionic components in each tab. This is a very common structure that you will find in many apps. You will learn how Ionic 2 structures the tab interface and how it translates to individual folders and files.

In this example, you will build three tabs, as follows:

- Showing a simple text-only page to explain where to fit the components
- Showing a sign up form
- Showing a horizontal slider box

Although the app is very straightforward, it will teach you a lot of key concepts in Angular 2 and Ionic 2. Some of them are the component decorators, theme and the TypeScript compiler process.

Here is a screenshot of the app where the middle tab is selected:

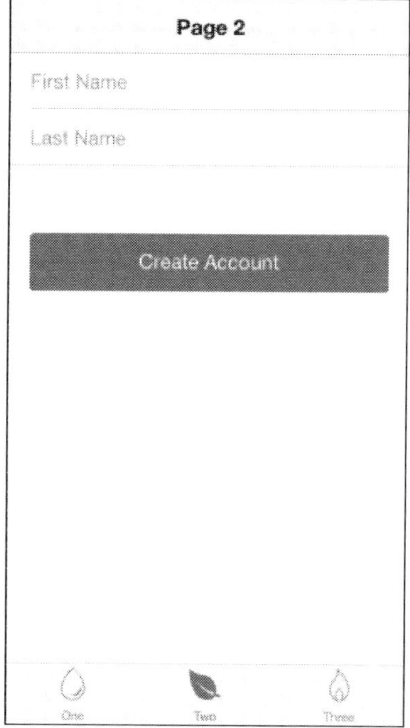

Getting ready

Since this is your first app being built from scratch, you need to ensure that you have followed through *Chapter 1, Creating Our First App with Ionic 2*, to set up the environment and Ionic CLI. If you already had Ionic 1, it must be updated. For this, you can use the same command line as to install, which is as follows:

```
$ sudo npm install -g cordova ionic ios-sim
```

How to do it...

The following are the instructions:

1. Create a new `PagesAndTabs` app using the `tabs` template and go into the `PagesAndTabs` folder to start Visual Studio Code, as shown:

   ```
   $ ionic start PagesAndTabs tabs --v2
   $ cd PagesAndTabs
   $ code .
   ```

2. The blank template only gives you a basic page. Open the `Finder` app in Mac or Windows Explorer in Windows to see the following folder structure:

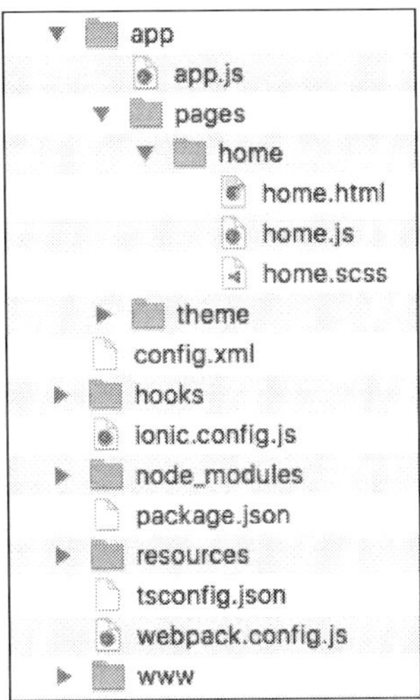

> You will only modify what is inside the `/src` folder and not `/www`, as in Ionic 1. Everything in the `/src` folder will be built, and the `/www` folder will be created automatically. We will also reserve the folder names and filenames as much as possible, since the main goal here is to understand how the tab template works and the areas you can modify.

3. Open and edit the `/src/pages/tabs/tabs.html` template file with the following code:

```
<ion-tabs>
  <ion-tab [root]="tab1Root" tabTitle="One"
  tabIcon="water"></ion-tab>
  <ion-tab [root]="tab2Root" tabTitle="Two"
  tabIcon="leaf"></ion-tab>
  <ion-tab [root]="tab3Root" tabTitle="Three"
  tabIcon="flame"></ion-tab>
</ion-tabs>
```

> The new template only updates the title and icons. This is because this example wants to reserve the naming of tab `root` variables. You could add more tabs using <ion-tab>, as needed.

4. To add a page, you need to ensure that `tab1Root` points to an existing folder and template. Since you will reuse the existing tab structure, you can just modify the `/src/pages/home/home.html` template, as shown, as this is your first page:

```
<ion-header>
  <ion-navbar>
    <ion-title>One</ion-title>
  </ion-navbar>
</ion-header>

<ion-content padding>
  <h2>Welcome to Ionic 2 Tabs!</h2>
  <p>
    This starter project comes with simple tabs-based
    layout for apps
    that are going to primarily use a Tabbed UI.
  </p>
</ion-content>
```

5. Also, in the same `/home`, folder, edit `home.ts` that corresponds to the same template, and enter the code here:

```
import { Component } from '@angular/core';

import { NavController } from 'ionic-angular';

@Component({
  selector: 'page-home',
  templateUrl: 'home.html'
})
export class HomePage {

  constructor(public navCtrl: NavController) {

  }

  ionViewWillEnter() {
    console.log('Enter Page 1');
  }

}
```

6. For the second page, `tab2Root`, you will follow a similar process by editing the `/src/pages/about/about.html` template, as shown:

```
<ion-header>
  <ion-navbar>
    <ion-title>
      Two
    </ion-title>
  </ion-navbar>
</ion-header>

<ion-content>
  <ion-list>
    <ion-item>
      <ion-input type="text" placeholder="First
      Name"></ion-input>
    </ion-item>

    <ion-item>
      <ion-input type="text" placeholder="Last Name"></ion-
      input>
```

```
      </ion-item>
    </ion-list>
    <div padding>
      <button ion-button primary block>Create
      Account</button>
    </div>
  </ion-content>
```

7. Edit `about.ts`, in the same folder from the preceding step:

```
import { Component } from '@angular/core';
import { NavController } from 'ionic-angular';

@Component({
  selector: 'page-about',
  templateUrl: 'about.html'
})
export class AboutPage {

  constructor(public navCtrl: NavController) {

  }

  ionViewWillEnter() {
    console.log('Enter Page 2');
  }
}
```

8. Finally, for the `tab3Root` page, you can change the template so that it will show a slider in `/src/pages/contact/contact.html`, as follows:

```
<ion-header>
  <ion-navbar>
    <ion-title>
      Three
    </ion-title>
  </ion-navbar>
</ion-header>

<ion-content>
  <ion-slides #mySlider index=0 (ionDidChange)="onSlideChanged($ev
    ent)">

    <ion-slide style="background-color: green">
      <h2>Slide 1</h2>
```

```
    </ion-slide>

    <ion-slide style="background-color: blue">
      <h2>Slide 2</h2>
    </ion-slide>

    <ion-slide style="background-color: red">
      <h2>Slide 3</h2>
    </ion-slide>

  </ion-slides>
</ion-content>
```

9. In the /contact folder, you need to edit contact.ts with the following code:

```
import { Component, ViewChild } from '@angular/core';
import { Slides, NavController } from 'ionic-angular';

@Component({
  selector: 'page-contact',
  templateUrl: 'contact.html'
})
export class ContactPage {
  @ViewChild('mySlider') slider: Slides;

  constructor(public navCtrl: NavController) {

  }

  ionViewWillEnter() {
    console.log('Enter Page 3');
  }

  onSlideChanged(e) {
    let currentIndex = this.slider.getActiveIndex();
    console.log("You are on Slide ", (currentIndex + 1));
  }

}
```

10. Go to your terminal and type the following command line to run the app:

```
$ ionic serve
```

How it works...

There is actually a lot of new information and a lot of concepts in this simple app. At a higher level, this is how the app is structured:

- When you run the app, Cordova loads the `/www/index.html` file first to open. All of your code and templates are combined into one file, `/www/build/main.js`.
- The `/app` folder is where most of your logic belongs. It starts with `app.component.ts` as the Bootstrap file.
- Each subfolder under the `/pages` folder will represent a page, which is a new concept in Ionic 2. A page consists of an HTML template, TypeScript code, and an `.scss` file to customize that specific template only.
- The `/theme` folder will contain variables and customizations at the global level to override the default theme from Ionic 2.

Now, let's start with everything inside the `/app` folder.

The `app.component.ts` file only imports all the required pages and components to start the app. This example needs the following four imports by default:

```
import { Component } from '@angular/core';
import { Platform } from 'ionic-angular';
import { StatusBar } from 'ionic-native';
import { TabsPage } from '../pages/tabs/tabs';
```

You must always import `Component`, `Platform`, and `StatusBar` from Ionic, because that will give you the `@Component` decorator to Bootstrap your app. A decorator is placed in front of its class to provide metadata for the class. The following example tells that the `MyApp` class has the characteristics of a component with a `template` property:

```
@Component({
  template: `<ion-nav [root]="rootPage"></ion-nav>`
})
export class MyApp {
  rootPage = TabsPage;

  constructor(platform: Platform) {
    platform.ready().then(() => {
      StatusBar.styleDefault();
    });
  }
}
```

Since this is a simple example, you don't need to declare a lot except the template information. Similar to Ionic 1, you can use either `template` or `templateUrl` to point to a local file.

Class is another new concept in ES6. However, developers have been declaring class in various programming languages, such as Java and C#. In ES6, you can use class to be able to efficiently reuse code with better abstraction. A class could exist within that file context only. Consider the following example:

```
class Example {}
```

However, if you want to use that class somewhere else, you have to export:

```
export class Example {}
```

In a class, you can have the following:

- Variable, such as `this.a` or `this.b`
- Method, such as `doSomething()`
- Constructor that automatically executes (or initializes) when an object is created using the class

More information about classes can be found at `https://developer.mozilla.org/en-US/docs/Web/JavaScript/Reference/Classes`.

Another nice thing about ES6 here is the arrow function, as shown:

```
platform.ready().then(() => {

});
```

The preceding is the same as:

```
platform.ready().then(function() {

});
```

An example (by passing a parameter) is as follows:

```
var a1 = a.map( s => s.length );
```

The same code can be rewritten as shown:

```
var a1 = a.map(function(s){ return s.length });
```

More information about arrow function can be found at `https://developer.mozilla.org/en-US/docs/Web/JavaScript/Reference/Functions/Arrow_functions`.

One important thing in `app.component.ts` is that you must declare a `root` page. You can see that from the template via `[root]="rootPage"`,and then again in the constructor via `this.rootPage = TabsPage`. The square brackets, `[]`, around `root` mean that it's a property of that DOM node. This is a new concept from Angular 2 as it's trying to get rid of using a DOM property, such as `ngmodel` (which tends to result in lower performance). The assignment here is to tell Ionic 2 that you will use `TabsPage`, which was imported earlier, and assign that as a `root` page. Then, the `ion-nav` directive will look at its own `root` property to start rendering the page. There seem to be a lot of abstractions and boilerplate compared to Ionic 1. However, this practice is recommended to ensure better separation and scaling.

Once you understand how `app.component.ts` works, it's easier to grasp the concepts from the other pages. Let's take a look at the `/pages/tabs/tabs.ts` file because that is where you define the `TabsPage` class. From this file, you need to import three other pages, which are the following:

```
import { Component } from '@angular/core';
import { HomePage } from '../home/home';
import { AboutPage } from '../about/about';
import { ContactPage } from '../contact/contact';
```

The template for this page is in `tabs.html`. However, you could also put the template in a string inside the `.ts` file, as follows:

```
@Component({
  template:
  ` <ion-tabs>
      <ion-tab [root]="tab1Root" tabTitle="One"
      tabIcon="water"></ion-tab>
      <ion-tab [root]="tab2Root" tabTitle="Two"
      tabIcon="leaf"></ion-tab>
      <ion-tab [root]="tab3Root" tabTitle="Three"
      tabIcon="flame"></ion-tab>
    </ion-tabs>`
})
```

ES6 also introduces a new feature, called a multiline template string. You probably realize that the preceding template string does not have any `join()` or string combine (`+`) operator. The reason is that you can use back-tick (`` ` ` ``) to allow a multiline template.

So, instead of doing this:

```
console.log("string text line 1\n"+
"string text line 2");
```

You can now do this:

```
console.log(`string text line 1
string text line 2`);
```

Below the page decorator, you need to export `TabsPage` (so that you can use in `app.component.ts`) and tell the constructor to use `tab1Root`, `tab2Root`, and `tab3Root` as root, as shown, for other pages in tab navigation:

```
export class TabsPage {
  tab1Root: any = HomePage;
  tab2Root: any = AboutPage;
  tab3Root: any = ContactPage;

  constructor() {
  }
}
```

Ionic 2 tab declaration is very similar to Ionic 1, shown as follows:

```
<ion-tabs>
    <ion-tab><ion-tab>
</ion-tabs>
```

You just have to make sure that the `root` property is pointing to another page.

`tab1Root` is actually very simple to understand because it's a text page where you add your own content and design within the `<ion-content>` element, as shown:

```
<ion-content padding>
  <h2>Welcome to Ionic 2 Tabs!</h2>
  <p>
    This starter project comes with simple tabs-based layout for
    apps that are going to primarily use a Tabbed UI.
  </p>
</ion-content>
```

If you want to change the title, you can simply change the following line:

```
<ion-title>One</ion-title>
```

`tab2Root` and `tab3Root` are very similar in terms of how they are structured. Ionic 2 gives you the convenience of binding to an event right in the `page` class, as shown:

```
import { Component } from '@angular/core';
import { NavController } from 'ionic-angular';

@Component({
  selector: 'page-about',
```

```
  templateUrl: 'about.html'
})
export class AboutPage {

  constructor(public navCtrl: NavController) {

  }

  ionViewWillEnter() {
    console.log('Enter Page 2');
  }
}
```

In the preceding example from `about.ts`, if the user enters `tab2Root`, it will call the `ionViewWillEnter ()` function automatically. This is a significant improvement because, in Ionic 1, you had to use `$ionicView.enter` on the `$scope` variable. Again, the concept of `$scope` no longer exists in Angular 2.

For a scalable app, it's better to separate templates into different files and avoid co-mingling templates inside the JavaScript code. The `templateUrl` must always point to the relative location of the `.html` file.

In `./src/pages/contact/contact.html`, you can use slider box and bind to slide the change event, as shown:

```
<ion-header>
  <ion-navbar>
    <ion-title>
      Three
    </ion-title>
  </ion-navbar>
</ion-header>

<ion-content>
  <ion-slides #mySlider index=0
  (ionDidChange)="onSlideChanged($event)">

    <ion-slide style="background-color: green">
      <h2>Slide 1</h2>
    </ion-slide>

    <ion-slide style="background-color: blue">
      <h2>Slide 2</h2>
```

```
    </ion-slide>

    <ion-slide style="background-color: red">
      <h2>Slide 3</h2>
    </ion-slide>

  </ion-slides>
</ion-content>
```

To get an event in Angular 2 (or Ionic 2), you have to use the parentheses, ( ), because the concept of `ng-click` or similar is no longer available. In this case, if the slide is changed based on `ionDidChange`, the `ion-slides` directive will trigger the `onSlideChanged()` function in the `ContactPage` class.

You cannot really run the TypeScript directly without having TypeScript to transpile the code into JavaScript. This process happens automatically behind the scenes when you run ionic serve. Also, when you change some code in the project, Ionic will detect the changes and rebuild the files before updating the browser. There is no need to hit the Refresh button every time.

See also

- Mozilla developer network has a very extensive documentation on ECMAScript 6 that you can find at the following link at `https://developer.mozilla.org/en-US/docs/Web/JavaScript/New_in_JavaScript/ECMAScript_6_support_in_Mozilla`.
- For Angular 2 specific information, you can read directly from the Angular 2 documentation at `https://angular.io/docs/ts/latest/index.html`.

Adding left and right menu navigation

Menu navigation is a very common component in many mobile apps. You can use menu to allow users to change to different pages in the app, including login and logout. The menu could be placed on the left or right of the app. Ionic 2 also lets you detect events and customize the menu's look and feel further.

This is a screenshot of the app you will develop:

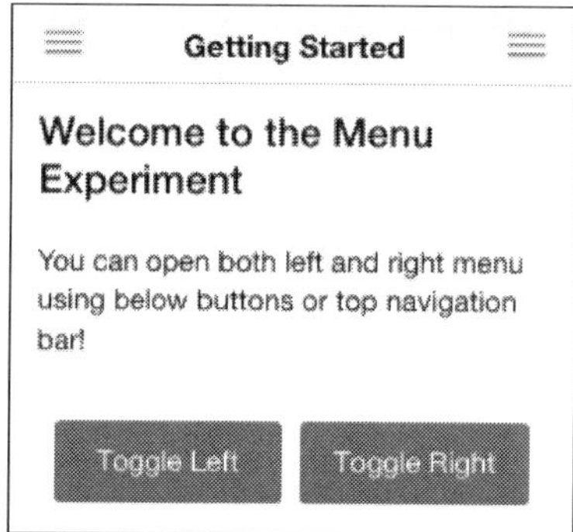

The app will have two pages and two menus. You can toggle either the left or right menu (but not both at the same time). In reality, it is much less likely that you will have both menus, but for the purposes of demonstration, this app will include both menus as the app will show the different properties of the menus that you can set. The left menu will change the page and the right menu will allow you to capture the exact item that is clicked on.

Getting ready

This app can run on your web browser, so there is no need to have a physical device available. Again, you only need to have Ionic 2 available on your computer.

How to do it...

Here are the instructions:

1. Create a new `LeftRightMenu` app using the `sidemenu` template, as shown, and go to the `LeftRightMenu` folder:

   ```
   $ ionic start LeftRightMenu sidemenu --v2
   $ cd LeftRightMenu
   ```

2. Verify your app folder structure to ensure that it's similar to the following:

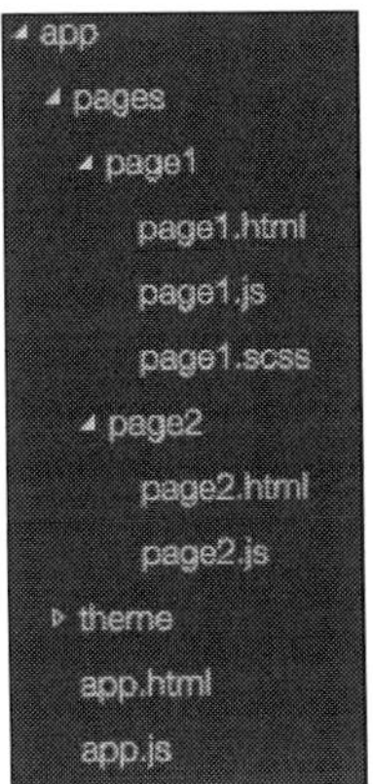

3. Edit `./src/app/app.component.ts` and replace with the following code:

```
import { Component, ViewChild } from '@angular/core';
import { Nav, Platform } from 'ionic-angular';
import { StatusBar, Splashscreen } from 'ionic-native';

import { Page1 } from '../pages/page1/page1';
import { Page2 } from '../pages/page2/page2';


@Component({
  templateUrl: 'app.html'
})
export class MyApp {
  @ViewChild(Nav) nav: Nav;
  text: string = '';
  rootPage: any = Page1;
  pages: Array<{title: string, component: any}>;

  constructor(public platform: Platform) {
    this.initializeApp();

    // used for an example of ngFor and navigation
    this.pages = [
      { title: 'Page One', component: Page1 },
      { title: 'Page Two', component: Page2 }
    ];

  }

  initializeApp() {
```

```
    this.platform.ready().then(() => {
      // Okay, so the platform is ready and our plugins are
      available.
      // Here you can do any higher level native things you
      might need.
      StatusBar.styleDefault();
      Splashscreen.hide();
    });
  }

  openPage(page) {
    // Reset the content nav to have just this page
    // we wouldn't want the back button to show in this
    scenario
    this.nav.setRoot(page.component);
  }

  rightMenuClick(text) {
    this.text = text;
  }
}
```

4. Create ./src/app/app.html with the following code:

```
<ion-menu id="leftMenu" [content]="content" side="left"
type="overlay">
  <ion-header>
    <ion-toolbar>
      <ion-title>Menu</ion-title>
    </ion-toolbar>
  </ion-header>

  <ion-content>
    <ion-list>
      <button menuClose ion-item *ngFor="let p of pages"
      (click)="openPage(p)">
        {{p.title}}
      </button>
    </ion-list>
  </ion-content>

</ion-menu>

<ion-menu id="rightMenu" [content]="content" side="right"
type="reveal">
  <ion-header>
```

```
    <ion-toolbar>
      <ion-title>Items</ion-title>
    </ion-toolbar>
  </ion-header>

  <ion-content>
    <ion-list>
      <button ion-item (click)="rightMenuClick('Item
      One')">
        Item One
      </button>
      <button ion-item (click)="rightMenuClick('Item
      Two')">
        Item Two
      </button>
    </ion-list>

    <ion-card *ngIf="text">
      <ion-card-content>
        You just clicked {{ text }}
      </ion-card-content>
    </ion-card>
  </ion-content>

</ion-menu>

<!-- Disable swipe-to-go-back because it's poor UX to combine STGB
with side menus -->
<ion-nav [root]="rootPage" #content swipeBackEnabled="false"></
ion-nav>
```

There are two menus as siblings in this template. They are also at the same level as `ion-nav` and not as parent or child. This structure is important for menu navigation to work.

5. Now, let's create two pages, for which you only have to modify the standard pages from the "sidemenu" template. Open and edit the `./src/app/pages/page1/page1.html` template:

```
<ion-header>
  <ion-navbar>
    <ion-title>Getting Started</ion-title>

    <ion-buttons start>
```

```
        <button ion-button menuToggle="leftMenu">
          <ion-icon name="menu"></ion-icon>
        </button>
      </ion-buttons>

      <ion-buttons end>
        <button ion-button menuToggle="rightMenu">
          <ion-icon name="menu"></ion-icon>
        </button>
      </ion-buttons>
    </ion-navbar>
  </ion-header>

  <ion-content padding class="getting-started">
    <h3>Welcome to the Menu Experiment</h3>
    <p>
       You can open both left and right menu using below
       buttons or top navigation bar!
    </p>
    <ion-row>
      <ion-col width-50>
        <button ion-button primary block
        menuToggle="leftMenu">Toggle Left</button>
      </ion-col>
      <ion-col width-50>
        <button ion-button primary block
        menuToggle="rightMenu">Toggle Right</button>
      </ion-col>
    </ion-row>

  </ion-content>
```

6. In the same folder, open and edit the `css` classes via `page1.scss`, as shown:

```
.getting-started {

  p {
    margin: 20px 0;
    line-height: 22px;
    font-size: 16px;
  }

}

.bar-button-menutoggle {
```

```
  display: inline-flex;
}
```

Note that since you're using the sidemenu template, it already comes with a second page (for example, page2). There is no need to modify that page in this specific example.

7. Open and edit the template for the second page at `./src/pages/page2/page2.html`, as shown:

```
<ion-header>
  <ion-navbar>
    <ion-title>Page Two</ion-title>

    <ion-buttons start>
      <button ion-button menuToggle="leftMenu">
        <ion-icon name="menu"></ion-icon>
      </button>
    </ion-buttons>

    <ion-buttons end>
      <button ion-button menuToggle="rightMenu">
        <ion-icon name="menu"></ion-icon>
      </button>
    </ion-buttons>
  </ion-navbar>
</ion-header>

<ion-content>
  <ion-list>
    <button ion-item *ngFor="let item of items"
    (click)="itemTapped($event, item)">
      <ion-icon [name]="item.icon" item-left></ion-icon>
      {{item.title}}
      <div class="item-note" item-right>
        {{item.note}}
      </div>
    </button>
  </ion-list>
  <div *ngIf="selectedItem" padding>
    You navigated here from <b>{{selectedItem.title}}</b>
  </div>
</ion-content>
```

8. Finally, since you added a `scss` file in the `page1` folder, you need to ensure that it's imported in `/src/app/app`, which you can do as shown: Scss

   ```
   @import "../pages/page1/page1";
   ```

9. Go to your terminal and run the app:

   ```
   $ ionic serve
   ```

How it works...

Since this app is just an introduction to menu navigation, it will not manage page routing and state parameters. At a higher level, this is how the app flows:

- `app.js` loads up both the menu templates in `app.html`
- The left menu will trigger the `openPage()` function to open PageTwo
- The right menu will trigger the `rightMenuClick()` function to change the `this.text` property and display on the screen

In the `app.html` template, the left menu has the following properties:

```
side="left" type="overlay"
```

However, the right menu has the following assigned instead:

```
side="right" type="reveal"
```

The `side` property will determine where, on the screen, the menu should show. There are two types of menus. The `overlay` option will leave the center page as it is, without moving. The `reveal` option would push the entire screen to show the menu. It depends on your app design to pick different types.

Each `ion-menu` directive must have `[content]="content"` declared because it will use the content area to bind swipe left or right. In this case, it is basically a local variable in `ion-nav`, as follows:

```
<ion-nav id="nav" [root]="rootPage" #content
swipeBackEnabled="false"></ion-nav>
```

The use of the `ion-toolbar` inside `ion-menu` is optional if you want to have the title for your menu. The key to having a menu item displayed, is to use `ion-list` and `ion-item`. You can loop through an array to display the menu items dynamically, as illustrated:

```
<ion-list>
  <button menuClose ion-item *ngFor="let p of pages"
  (click)="openPage(p)">
    {{p.title}}
  </button>
</ion-list>
```

`*ngFor` is a replacement for `ng-repeat` in Ionic 1. You need to use `#p` because it's the same as declaring a local variable named `p`. This is best practice for variable isolation. Otherwise, the concept is very similar to Ionic 1 as you can grab `p.title` for each item in the `pages` array.

On the right menu, instead of going to a different page via `nav.setRoot()`, you just set some text and dynamically display the text inside the menu, as shown:

```
<ion-card *ngIf="text">
  <ion-card-content>
    You just clicked {{ text }}
  </ion-card-content>
</ion-card>
```

So, if the text variable doesn't exist (which means that the user has not clicked on anything yet), the `ion-card` will not show anything via `*ngIf`.

For each page, you have to declare the same `ion-navbar`. Otherwise, you will lose the top navigation and buttons to the menus:

```
<ion-header>
  <ion-navbar>
    <ion-title>Getting Started</ion-title>

    <ion-buttons start>
      <button ion-button menuToggle="leftMenu">
        <ion-icon name="menu"></ion-icon>
      </button>
    </ion-buttons>

    <ion-buttons end>
      <button ion-button menuToggle="rightMenu">
        <ion-icon name="menu"></ion-icon>
      </button>
    </ion-buttons>
  </ion-navbar>
</ion-header>
```

Note that `leftMenu` and `rightMenu` must be the same `id` you used earlier, in the `app.html` template.

On the first page, there are two buttons to trigger the menus from within the content page as well, as shown:

```
<ion-row>
  <ion-col width-50>
    <button primary block menuToggle="leftMenu">Toggle
    Left</button>
  </ion-col>
  <ion-col width-50>
    <button primary block menuToggle="rightMenu">Toggle
    Right</button>
  </ion-col>
</ion-row>
```

These two buttons also call `menuToggle` to trigger the menu. The buttons are placed within the Ionic grid system. Since Ionic uses flexbox, it is very simple to use as you just need to create `ion-col` and `ion-row`. The `width` property, with a number, will determine the width percentage.

See also

- For further usage of the Ionic menu, you can check out the following link: `http://ionicframework.com/docs/v2/components/#menus`
- The API document for the Ionic menu is also available at `http://ionicframework.com/docs/v2/api/components/menu/Menu/`

Navigating multiple pages with state parameters

App navigation is an important topic because it's the core of a user's experience. You want to manage the user's expectation on what would happen after they submit a form or after they go to a new tab. In addition, you may want to ensure that the user data is available on the correct page or in the correct state. This could also get more complicated when the requirement of a back navigation is involved.

This section will teach you how to work with `NavController` and `NavParams`, which are the two important base classes to manage all navigation for the app. This is a screenshot of the app you will develop:

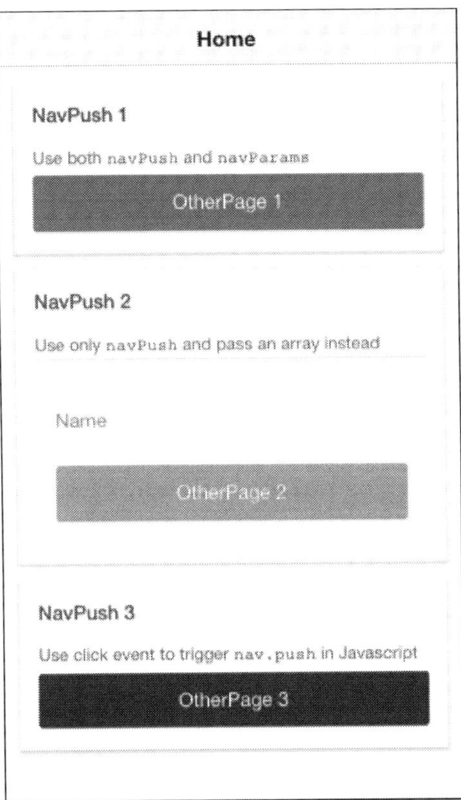

This app has three different examples of how to navigate to a different page and how to pass the parameters. When you click on any button, it will show the second page, which is as follows:

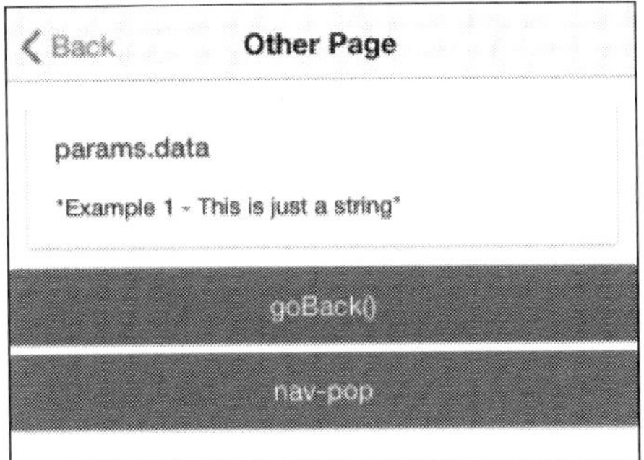

The second page, basically, captures the parameters and displays them on the screen. It also gives you three different options to navigate back to the previous page.

In this app, you will learn the following:

- How to use `NavController` and `NavParams`
- How to use `[navPush]` and `[navParams]` directly in the template
- How to add two-way data binding in an input box
- How to use **pipe** to convert a JSON object to a string and render it on the screen

Getting ready

You only need to have the Ionic 2 CLI available to run this app.

How to do it...

Here are the instructions:

1. Create a new `Navigation` app using the blank template, as shown, and go into the `Navigation` folder:

   ```
   $ ionic start Navigation blank --v2
   $ cd Navigation
   ```

2. Edit `./src/app/app.module.ts` with the following code:

   ```
   import { NgModule } from '@angular/core';
   import { IonicApp, IonicModule } from 'ionic-angular';
   import { MyApp } from './app.component';
   import { HomePage } from '../pages/home/home';
   import { OtherPage } from '../pages/otherPage/otherPage';

   @NgModule({
     declarations: [
       MyApp,
       HomePage,
       OtherPage
     ],
     imports: [
       IonicModule.forRoot(MyApp)
     ],
     bootstrap: [IonicApp],
     entryComponents: [
       MyApp,
   ```

```
    HomePage,
    OtherPage
  ],
  providers: []
})
export class AppModule {}
```

The main reason you have to modify this file is to declare `OtherPage` as a dynamically loaded module via `NgModule`. You will have to declare `OtherPage` again in the `home.ts` file.

3. Edit `./src/app/pages/home/home.html` with the following code:

```
<ion-header>
  <ion-navbar>
    <ion-title>
      Home
    </ion-title>
  </ion-navbar>
</ion-header>

<ion-content padding>
  <ion-card>
    <ion-card-header>
      NavPush 1
    </ion-card-header>
    <ion-card-content>
      <p>Use both <code>navPush</code> and <code>navParams</
      code></p>
      <button ion-button block [navPush]="otherPage"
      [navParams]="myString">OtherPage 1</button>
    </ion-card-content>
  </ion-card>

  <ion-card>
    <ion-card-header>
      NavPush 2
    </ion-card-header>
    <ion-card-content>
      <p>Use only <code>navPush</code> and pass an array
      instead</p>
      <ion-list>
        <ion-item>
          <ion-label floating>Name</ion-label>
```

```
          <ion-input type="text"
          [(ngModel)]="myJSON.text"></ion-input>
        </ion-item>
      </ion-list>
      <div>
        <button ion-button block color="secondary"
        [navPush]="otherPage" [navParams]="myJSON">
        OtherPage 2</button>
      </div>
    </ion-card-content>
  </ion-card>

  <ion-card>
    <ion-card-header>
      NavPush 3
    </ion-card-header>
    <ion-card-content>
      <p>Use click event to trigger <code>nav.push</code>
      in Javascript </p>
      <button ion-button block color="dark"
      (click)="gotoOtherPage()">OtherPage 3</button>
    </ion-card-content>
  </ion-card>
</ion-content>
```

4. Edit ./src/app/pages/home/home.ts with the following code:

```
import { Component } from '@angular/core';
import { NavController } from 'ionic-angular';
import { OtherPage } from '../otherPage/otherPage';

@Component({
  selector: 'page-home',
  templateUrl: 'home.html'
})
export class HomePage {
  public myString: string = 'Example 1 - This is just a
  string';
  public myJSON: any = {text: ''};
  otherPage: any = OtherPage;

  constructor(public navCtrl: NavController) {
  }

  gotoOtherPage() {
```

```
        this.navCtrl.push(OtherPage, {text: 'Example 3 - This
        is an object'});
    }
}
```

5. Create the `./src/app/pages/otherPage` folder.
6. Create the `otherPage.html` file in the previously created `otherPage` folder:

```
<ion-header>
  <ion-navbar>
    <ion-title>
      Other Page
    </ion-title>
  </ion-navbar>
</ion-header>

<ion-content>
  <ion-card *ngIf="params.data">
    <ion-card-header>
      params.data
    </ion-card-header>
    <ion-card-content>
      {{ params.data | json }}
    </ion-card-content>
  </ion-card>

  <button ion-button block (click)="goBack()">
    goBack()
  </button>
  <button ion-button block navPop>
    nav-pop
  </button>
</ion-content>
```

7. In the same folder, add `otherPage.ts` as well, with the following code:

```
import { Component } from '@angular/core';
import { NavController, NavParams } from 'ionic-angular';

@Component({
  selector: 'other-page',
  templateUrl: 'OtherPage.html'
})
export class OtherPage {
  constructor(public navCtrl: NavController, public params:
  NavParams) {
```

```
    }

    goBack() {
      this.navCtrl.pop();
    }

    onPageWillEnter() {
      console.log('Enter OtherPage');
    }
  }
```

8. Go to your terminal and run the app:

   ```
   $ ionic serve
   ```

How it works...

At a high level, this is how the app is structured:

- The app will Bootstrap via `app.ts` and load `home.html` as the `root` page
- Everything in the `/home` folder is your first page
- Everything in the `/otherPage` folder is your second page
- These two pages are communicated using `NavParams` (or `navParams` from the template)

Let's take a look at `home.ts`. You must import both `NavController` and `NavParams`:

```
import {Page, NavController, NavParams} from 'ionic/ionic';
```

For your constructor, you need to do a few things, which are as follows:

```
public myString: string = 'Example 1 - This is just a string';
public myJSON: any = {text: ''};
otherPage: any = OtherPage;

constructor(public navCtrl: NavController) {
}
```

The `this.navCtrl` variable will reference the imported `NavController`. You are supposed to bring it in like this in order to use the navigation feature internally. The `myString` and `myJSON` are just variables that you will pass in the parameter to the second page. You also have to bring in the class for `OtherPage` and make it accessible to `navPush`, later, in your template.

The gotoOtherPage() method, as shown, does one simple thing—it will push the page to the current navigation:

```
gotoOtherPage() {
  this.navCtrl.push(OtherPage, {text: 'Example 3 - This is an
  object'});
}
```

By doing so, your app will switch to OtherPage page right away and this will also include the parameters.

The home.html template for the first page is to demonstrate the following three scenarios:

- You can use [navPush] and [navParams] directly inside the template. You just need to pass the internal object of the class handling this page. So, in this case, you have to pass otherPage, and not OtherPage (notice the uppercase O):

  ```
  <button block [navPush]="otherPage"
  [navParams]="myString">OtherPage 1</button>
  ```

- You can also pass a JSON object as a param into [navPush]:

  ```
  <button ion-button block color="secondary"
  [navPush]="otherPage" [navParams]="myJSON">OtherPage
  2</button>
  ```

- The third scenario is to navigate to a new page manually, as shown, using a method implemented inside the page class:

  ```
  <button block dark (click)="gotoOtherPage()">OtherPage 3</button>
  ```

Unlike Angular 1 or Ionic 1, you cannot use ng-model to do two-way binding anymore. The new syntax will be [(ngModel)] for any input element instead.

In your second page, you just need to make the NavController and NavParams available in the class from the constructor.

Let's take a look at your otherPage.js file:

```
constructor(public navCtrl: NavController, public params: NavParams) {
}
```

The template for the second page (that is, otherPage.html) is very simple. First, the navigation bar on the top is to enable the default back button:

```
<ion-header>
  <ion-navbar>
    <ion-title>
```

```
        Other Page
      </ion-title>
    </ion-navbar>
  </ion-header>
```

The back button is an automatic mechanism in Ionic 2 so that you don't have to worry about when it would show.

The following code will display the variable content if the state parameter exists:

```
<ion-card *ngIf="params.data">
  <ion-card-header>
    params.data
  </ion-card-header>
  <ion-card-content>
    {{ params.data | json }}
  </ion-card-content>
</ion-card>
```

The `ion-card` leverages `*ngIf` to decide whether this DOM should be rendered or not. Since `params.data` could be a JSON object, you need to convert it to a string to display it on the screen. Angular 1 has a filter but Angular 2 renamed this feature as pipe. However, the basic concept is the same. The `{{ params.data | json }}` code basically tells Angular 2 to apply the `json` function to `params.data`, and render the output.

You could go back to the previous page using the `nav.pop()` function, as shown:

```
<button block (click)="goBack()">
  goBack()
</button>
```

Alternatively, you could go back using a directive `navPop` and put that inside your button, as shown:

```
<button block navPop>
  nav-pop
</button>
```

So, those are the possibilities within the Ionic 2 navigation features.

See also

For more information refer to the official Ionic 2 documentation for `NavController` and `NavParams`, at the following links:

- `http://ionicframework.com/docs/v2/api/components/nav/NavController/`
- `http://ionicframework.com/docs/v2/api/components/nav/NavParams/`

To read more about how Angular Pipe works, you can review the following page for the previous example on JSON pipe at:

- `https://angular.io/docs/js/latest/api/common/JsonPipe-class.html`

3
Extending Ionic 2 with Angular 2 Building Blocks

In this chapter, we will cover the following tasks related to creating custom components, directives, and filters with Angular 2:

- Creating a custom pizza ordering component
- Creating a custom username input directive
- Creating a custom pipe
- Creating a shared service to provide data to multiple pages

Introduction

Most of Ionic's out-of-the-box features are actually prebuilt components. In this section, you will learn how to create your own custom component using the `html` template, which contains Ionic components as well.

Components actually define Angular 2. A component is no more than just a class with self-describing features. For example, `<ul>` is a component that you are already familiar with. Previously, you used various Ionic components, such as `<ion-list>` and `<ion-item>`. A component is a decorator (that is, `@Component`) to add metadata to a class to describe the following:

- **selector**: This is the name that is to be used in the DOM (for example, `<my-component>`)

- **template or templateUrl**: This refers to the way the component is rendered
- **directives**: This refers to a list of directive dependencies you plan to use inside the component
- **providers**: This is a list of providers (that is, services) you plan to use inside the component

Of course, there are many other options, but the preceding four options are the most common ones.

Creating a custom pizza ordering component

In this section, you will build an app to demonstrate a custom component with its private variables and template. Observe the following screenshot of the pizza ordering component:

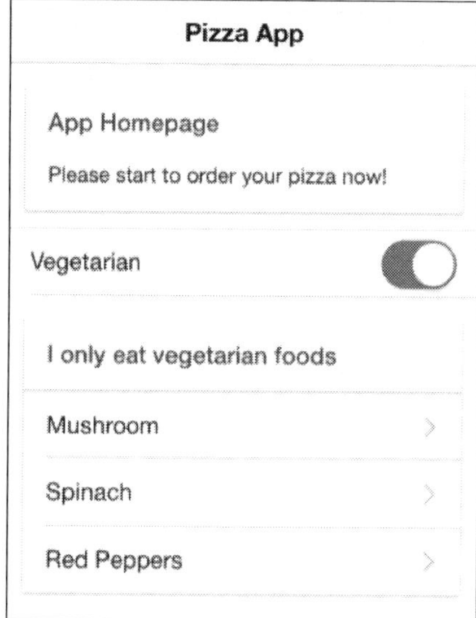

The user will not notice which area is a part of the page as opposed to a self-contained component. Your custom component here is the only area where the list is *listening* to the **Vegetarian** checkbox:

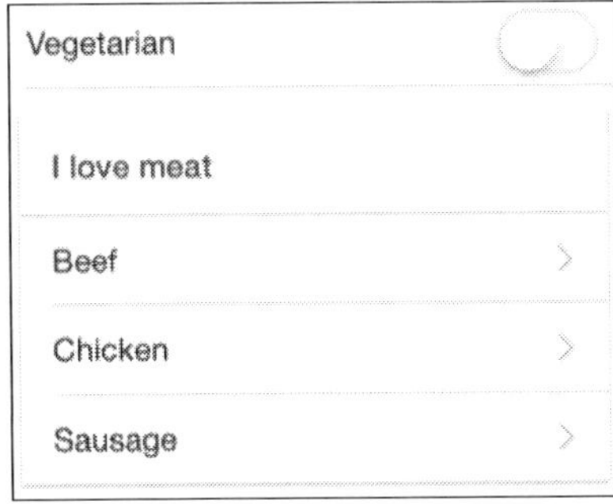

Getting ready

This app example could work either in a browser or in a physical device.

How to do it...

Perform the following instructions:

1. Create a new MyComponent app using the blank template as shown, and go into the MyComponent folder:

   ```
   $ ionic start MyComponent blank --v2
   $ cd MyComponent
   ```

2. Open the ./app/pages/home/home.html file and replace the content with the following code:

   ```
   <ion-header>
     <ion-navbar>
       <ion-title>
         Pizza App
       </ion-title>
     </ion-navbar>
   </ion-header>

   <ion-content padding>
     <ion-card>
       <ion-card-header>
         App Homepage
       </ion-card-header>
       <ion-card-content>
         Please start to order your pizza now!
   ```

```
    </ion-card-content>
  </ion-card>

  <my-component></my-component>
</ion-content>
```

This is your root page containing `<my-component>`, which will be defined later.

3. Open `./app/pages/home/home.ts` for editing globally with the following code:

```
import { Component } from '@angular/core';
import { NavController } from 'ionic-angular';
import { MyComponent } from '../../components/foo';

@Component({
  selector: 'page-home',
  templateUrl: 'home.html'
})
export class HomePage {

  constructor(public navCtrl: NavController) {

  }

}
```

You simply have to declare `MyComponent` as a dependency. A component is basically just a directive with a template, assuming you are familiar with the directive concept of Angular 1.

4. Now, let's create the component by first creating a directive, as illustrated in the following code:

```
$ mkdir ./src/components
```

5. Create a `foo.ts` file in the `components` directory that you just created, as shown in the following code:

```
import { Component } from '@angular/core';

@Component({
  selector: 'my-component',
  templateUrl: 'foo.html'
})
export class MyComponent {
  public data: any = {myToggle: true};

  constructor() {
```

```
  }

  isClicked(val) {
    console.log('Vegetarian: ' + val);
  }

}
```

6. Create `foo.html` in the `./src/components` folder, as follows:

```
<ion-list>
  <ion-item>
    <ion-label>Vegetarian</ion-label>
    <ion-toggle (click)="isClicked(data.myToggle)"
    [(ngModel)]="data.myToggle"></ion-toggle>
  </ion-item>

  <ion-card *ngIf="data.myToggle">
    <ion-card-header>
      I only eat vegetarian foods
    </ion-card-header>

    <ion-list>
      <button ion-item>
        Mushroom
      </button>
      <button ion-item>
        Spinach
      </button>
      <button ion-item>
        Red Peppers
      </button>
    </ion-list>
  </ion-card>

  <ion-card *ngIf="!data.myToggle">
    <ion-card-header>
      I love meat
    </ion-card-header>

    <ion-list>
      <button ion-item>
        Beef
      </button>
```

```
        <button ion-item>
          Chicken
        </button>
        <button ion-item>
          Sausage
        </button>
      </ion-list>
    </ion-card>

</ion-list>
```

7. Modify `./src/app/app.module.ts`, as illustrated, so that you can declare `MyComponent`. Observe the following code:

```
import { NgModule } from '@angular/core';
import { IonicApp, IonicModule } from 'ionic-angular';
import { MyApp } from './app.component';
import { HomePage } from '../pages/home/home';
import { MyComponent } from '../components/foo';

@NgModule({
  declarations: [
    MyApp,
    HomePage,
    MyComponent
  ],
  imports: [
    IonicModule.forRoot(MyApp)
  ],
  bootstrap: [IonicApp],
  entryComponents: [
    MyApp,
    HomePage,
    MyComponent
  ],
  providers: []
})
export class AppModule {}
```

8. Go to your terminal and run the app using the following command:

```
$ ionic serve
```

How it works...

You may wonder why it's necessary to create a component just to toggle a list (of pizza topping options). The answer is that this is just a demonstration of how you can compartmentalize your app using a component. The key things that you have done are as follows:

- You created a custom component, called `<my-component>`, which can be used anywhere, including outside your app.
- The data within your component is completely private. This means that nobody else can access it without calling a method within your component's class.
- You can add or change behaviors within your component without impacting other areas outside the component.

To create a component, you need to ensure that you import the `decorator`, as shown, from Angular 2 itself (and not from Ionic 2):

```
import { Component } from '@angular/core';

@Component({
  selector: 'my-component',
  templateUrl: 'foo.html'
})
```

In your component template, everything is local to what is inside the component class. So, you can bind the click event using `click`, as shown in the following code:

```
<ion-item>
  <ion-label>Vegetarian</ion-label>
  <ion-toggle (click)="isClicked(data.myToggle)"
  [(ngModel)]="data.myToggle"></ion-toggle>
</ion-item>
```

Just like Angular 1, you need to use `[(ngModel)]` to declare that you want `data.myToggle` to be your model. The `[(..)]` part is to tell Angular 2 that this is a two-way binding.

There are two lists of pizza toppings. The first one is as follows:

```
<ion-card *ngIf="data.myToggle">
  <ion-card-header>
    I only eat vegetarian foods
  </ion-card-header>

  <ion-list>
    <button ion-item>
      Mushroom
```

```
        </button>
        <button ion-item>
          Spinach
        </button>
        <button ion-item>
          Red Peppers
        </button>
      </ion-list>
    </ion-card>
```

The second list of pizza toppings is as shown:

```
    <ion-card *ngIf="!data.myToggle">
      <ion-card-header>
        I love meat
      </ion-card-header>

      <ion-list>
        <button ion-item>
          Beef
        </button>
        <button ion-item>
          Chicken
        </button>
        <button ion-item>
          Sausage
        </button>
      </ion-list>
    </ion-card>
```

To toggle the visibility of each list based on the `data.myToggle` model, you can use `*ngIf`, which is very similar to `ng-if` from Angular 1.

See also

- For more information about components in the Angular 2 documentation, you can visit `https://angular.io/docs/ts/latest/guide/architecture.html#!#component`.

Creating a custom username input directive

Since you have gone through the process of creating a component in the preceding section, you may wonder what the difference is between a component and a directive. If you have some experience with Angular 1, you may notice that it had no definition of a component. Starting in Angular 2, there are the following three kinds of directive:

Kind	Description
Components	They have a template and a class associated with the component (that is, `ion-input`)
Structural directives	They change the DOM structure within the scope of where it is (that is, `*ngIf` or `*ngFor`)
Attribute directives	They change the appearance of the current DOM by intercepting its display or events

You may have a mix of both structural and attribute characteristics in the same directive. In this section, you will learn how to create an attribute directive that can prevent certain characters from being input in the **Username** as well as showing another DOM node (where it says **You are typing username**) by toggling its visibility. Observe the following screenshot of the app:

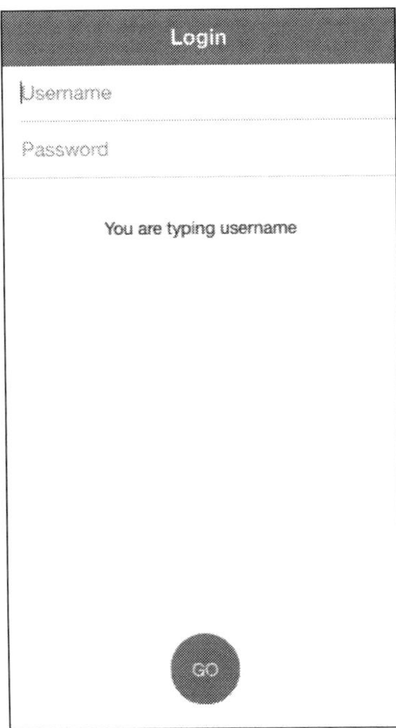

The **GO** button is there just for cosmetic purposes, and you will not need to write any code for it.

Getting ready

This app example could work either in a browser or on a physical device.

How to do it...

Observe the following instructions:

1. Create a new `MyIonicInputDirective` app using the `blank` template, as shown, and go into the `MyIonicInputDirective` folder:

   ```
   $ ionic start MyIonicInputDirective blank --v2
   $ cd MyIonicInputDirective
   ```

2. Open the `./src/app/pages/home/home.html` file and replace the content with the following code:

   ```
   <ion-header>
     <ion-navbar color="danger">
       <ion-title>
         Login
       </ion-title>
     </ion-navbar>
   </ion-header>

   <ion-content padding>
     <ion-list>

       <ion-item >
         <ion-input type="text" placeholder="Username"
         [(ngModel)]="username"
         [myIonicInput]="myStyles"></ion-input>
       </ion-item>

       <ion-item>
         <ion-input type="password"
         placeholder="Password"></ion-input>
       </ion-item>

     </ion-list>
     <p *ngIf="myStyles.showUsername" class="hint">
       You are typing username
     </p>

     <ion-fab bottom center>
   ```

```
    <button ion-fab>GO</button>
  </ion-fab>
</ion-content>
```

As mentioned earlier, the **GO** button is just an example of the new floating button feature from Ionic 2. All you need to do is include `bottom` and `center` in order to position it. These are actually good examples of attribute directives.

3. Open `home.ts`, in the same folder as in the preceding step, to edit and insert the following code:

```
import { Component } from '@angular/core';
import { NavController } from 'ionic-angular';

@Component({
  selector: 'page-home',
  templateUrl: 'home.html'
})
export class HomePage {
  private myStyles: Object = {showUsername: false};

  constructor(public navCtrl: NavController) {
  }

}
```

4. Create the `./src/directives` folder, as shown in the following command:

```
$ mkdir ./src/directives
```

5. Create the `my-ionic-input.ts` file in the `directives` folder and copy the following code:

```
import {Directive, ElementRef, Input} from '@angular/core';

@Directive({
  selector: '[myIonicInput]',
  host: {
    '(mouseenter)': 'onMouseEnter()',
    '(mouseleave)': 'onMouseLeave()'
    // '(keypress)': 'onKeyPress'
  }
})
export class MyIonicInputDirective {
  @Input('myIonicInput') myStyles: any;

  constructor(private el: ElementRef) {
```

```
      el.nativeElement.onkeypress = function(e) {
        console.log(e);

        if ('~!@#$%^&*()-
        ='.includes(String.fromCharCode(e.keyCode))) {
          e.preventDefault();
          return;
        }
      }
    }
    onMouseEnter() {
      this.myStyles.showUsername = true;
    }

    onMouseLeave(e) {
      this.myStyles.showUsername = false;
    }

    // onKeyPress will not work with ion-input directly
    because the actual input element is a child of ion-input
    // onKeyPress() {
    //   console.log("onKeyPress");
    // }
  }
```

6. Open and edit `./src/app/app.module.ts` to declare your new directive, as follows:

```
import { NgModule } from '@angular/core';
import { IonicApp, IonicModule } from 'ionic-angular';
import { MyApp } from './app.component';
import { HomePage } from '../pages/home/home';
import { MyIonicInputDirective } from '../directives/my-
ionic-input';

@NgModule({
  declarations: [
    MyApp,
    HomePage,
    MyIonicInputDirective
  ],
  imports: [
    IonicModule.forRoot(MyApp)
  ],
```

```
  bootstrap: [IonicApp],
  entryComponents: [
    MyApp,
    HomePage
  ],
  providers: []
})
export class AppModule {}
```

7. Go to your terminal and run the app, as shown:

```
$ ionic serve
```

How it works...

The home page template (`home.html`) is very typical with `ion-list` and `ion-item`, which contain your input elements. However, there are two important things to take note of. First, there is an attribute, called `myIonicInput`, in the `ion-input` component. Observe the following code:

```
<ion-item >
  <ion-input type="text" placeholder="Username"
  [(ngModel)]="username" [myIonicInput]="myStyles"></ion-input>
</ion-item>
```

Second, the `myStyles` object is now used to toggle the visibility of the `<p>` element, as shown:

```
<p *ngIf="myStyles.showUsername" class="hint">
  You are typing username
</p>
```

This `myStyles` object is actually a `private` variable in your `HomePage` class in the `home.ts` file, as follows:

```
export class HomePage {
  private myStyles: Object = {showUsername: false};
}
```

With TypeScript, you could assign a type (that is, object) to a variable with a default value. You may also note that `MyIonicInputDirective` should be declared for a dependency to be injected into the template directives.

To create a basic directive, you must import at least `Directive` and `ElementRef` in order to manipulate the DOM. However, since this `Directive` has input (that is, `myStyles`), you should also import `Input` in your `my-ionic-input.ts`, as illustrated in the following code:

```
import {Directive, ElementRef, Input} from '@angular/core';
```

You have `selector` and `host` metadata in your directive, as shown:

```
@Directive({
  selector: '[myIonicInput]',
  host: {
    '(mouseenter)': 'onMouseEnter()',
    '(mouseleave)': 'onMouseLeave()'
    // '(keypress)': 'onKeyPress'
  }
})
```

The `myIonicInput` selector will be queried from the DOM and will trigger *actions* on that DOM node. For event detection on the DOM, you have to map the event name to the class method. For example, the `mouseenter` event will trigger a call to the `onMouseEnter()` method in the directive's class, which is `MyIonicInputDirective`.

Now, let's look more closely in the directive's class:

```
export class MyIonicInputDirective {
  @Input('myIonicInput') myStyles: any;

  constructor(private el: ElementRef) {
    el.nativeElement.onkeypress = function(e) {
      console.log(e);

      if ('~!@#$%^&*()-
      ='.includes(String.fromCharCode(e.keyCode))) {
        e.preventDefault();
        return;
      }
    }
  }
  onMouseEnter() {
    this.myStyles.showUsername = true;
  }

  onMouseLeave(e) {
```

```
        this.myStyles.showUsername = false;
      }

      // onKeyPress will not work with ion-input directly because the
      actual input element is a child of ion-input
      // onKeyPress() {
      //   console.log("onKeyPress");
      // }
    }
```

The @Input decorator is used to declare that you will bring in a variable from the template. This is the reason why you must have the square brackets in [myIonicInput]="myStyles". Otherwise, myStyles would just be a string instead of an expression referring to the myStyles object from the HomePage class. Another interesting thing to note here is the code inside the constructor. The ElementRef is pointing to the same DOM where you placed your attribute directive. You want to modify the behavior of the keyboard using el.nativeElement.onkeypress so that special characters won't be allowed. If the user enters a special character, it will trigger e.preventDefault() and nothing will happen. The keyboard event is basically discarded. You may wonder why we cannot just use the keypress event and map it to onKeyPress, which was intentionally commented out. The reason is that you are placing the myIonicInput directive on top of ion-input. But the actual <input> DOM is just a child of ion-input. Therefore, if you listen to the keypress event on the parent ion-input, you won't be able to bind it.

The onMouseEnter and onMouseLeave methods are very self explanatory because they just toggle the myStyles.showUsername variable. Again, this myStyles object is just a reference back to the myStyles of HomePage. So, if you change the variable here, it will change at the home page's level as well.

See also

- For more information about Angular 2 directives, you can refer to the official documentation at https://angular.io/docs/ts/latest/guide/attribute-directives.html
- Since this is the first section where TypeScript appears, it might be helpful to go through the handbook at http://www.typescriptlang.org/docs/tutorial.html, for more details

Creating a custom pipe

Pipes are also a feature of Angular 2 and are not specific to Ionic. If you are familiar with Angular 1, a *pipe* is exactly the same thing as a *filter*. The main reason you might want to use pipes is to display data in a different format in the view. You don't want to change the actual value in the component. This makes things very convenient because you don't have to decide on the specific format within the code, while leaving flexibility in the view layer. Here is a list of some useful built-in pipes (from `https://angular.io/docs/ts/latest/api/#!?apiFilter=pipe`):

- AsyncPipe
- DatePipe
- NumberPipe
- SlicePipe
- DecimalPipe
- JsonPipe
- PercentPipe
- UpperCasePipe
- LowerCasePipe
- CurrencyPipe
- ReplacePipe

In this section, you will learn how to create a custom pipe using the `@Pipe` decorator. The following is a screenshot of the app:

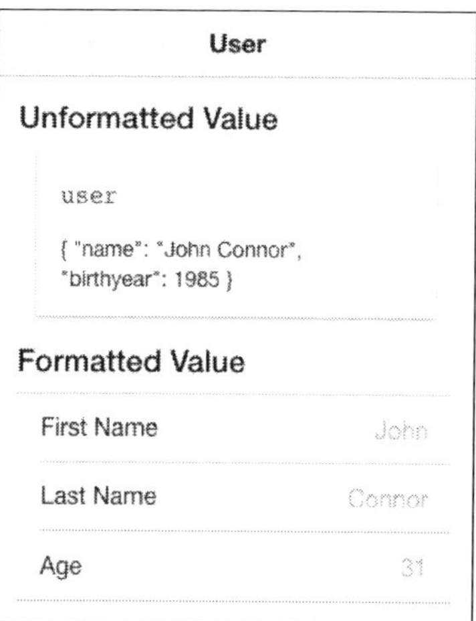

While the app interface is very simple, this example is to show you how to create a pipe to extract object data.

Getting ready

There is no need to test in a physical device because the Angular 2 pipe will work just fine in the web browser.

How to do it...

Observe the following instructions:

1. Create a new `CustomPipe` app using the `blank` template, as shown, and go to the `CustomPipe` folder:

   ```
   $ ionic start CustomPipe blank --v2
   $ cd CustomPipe
   ```

2. Open the `./src/pages/home/home.html` file and modify the content with the following code:

   ```
   <ion-header>
     <ion-navbar>
       <ion-title>
         User
       </ion-title>
     </ion-navbar>
   </ion-header>

   <ion-content padding>

     <h4>Unformatted Value</h4>
     <ion-card>

       <ion-card-header>
         <code>user</code>
       </ion-card-header>

       <ion-card-content>
         {{ user | json }}
       </ion-card-content>

     </ion-card>

     <h4>Formatted Value</h4>
     <ion-list>

       <ion-item>
   ```

```
      <ion-label fixed>First Name</ion-label>
      <ion-note item-right>{{ user | userExtract :
      "firstname" }}</ion-note>
    </ion-item>

    <ion-item>
      <ion-label fixed>Last Name</ion-label>
      <ion-note item-right>{{ user | userExtract :
      "lastname" }}</ion-note>
    </ion-item>

    <ion-item>
      <ion-label fixed>Age</ion-label>
      <ion-note item-right>{{ user | userExtract : "age"
      }}</ion-note>
    </ion-item>

  </ion-list>
</ion-content>
```

You can quickly see that the template uses the `userExtract` pipe to render the correct information.

3. Then, replace the content of `./src/pages/home/home.ts` with the following code:

```
import { Component } from '@angular/core';
import { NavController } from 'ionic-angular';

@Component({
  selector: 'page-home',
  templateUrl: 'home.html'
})
export class HomePage {
  private user: any;

  constructor(public navCtrl: NavController) {
    this.user = {
      name: 'John Connor',
      birthyear: 1985
    }
  }

}
```

You don't have the `custom-pipe.ts` file yet, so, you need to create it next.

4. Create the `./src/utils` folder by using the following command:

   ```
   $ mkdir ./utils/utils
   ```

   You can call this folder anything. However, since, sometimes, pipes are considered *utility* functions, let's call it `utils`.

5. Create the `custom-pipe.ts` file in the `utils` folder and copy the following code:

   ```
   import { Pipe, PipeTransform } from '@angular/core';

   @Pipe({name: 'userExtract'})
   export class UserExtractPipe implements PipeTransform {
     transform(value: any, arg) : any {
       let newVal: any;
       if (arg == "firstname") {

         newVal = value.name ? value.name.split(' ')[0] : '';

       } else if (arg == "lastname") {

         newVal = value.name ? value.name.split(' ').splice(-
         1) : '';

       } else if (arg == "age") {
         var currentTime = new Date();

         newVal = value.birthyear ? currentTime.getFullYear()
         - value.birthyear : 0;
       }

       return newVal;
     }
   }
   ```

6. Add `UserExtractPipe` to `./src/app/app.module.ts` by replacing with the following code:

   ```
   import { NgModule } from '@angular/core';
   import { IonicApp, IonicModule } from 'ionic-angular';
   import { MyApp } from './app.component';
   import { HomePage } from '../pages/home/home';
   import { UserExtractPipe } from '../utils/custom-pipe'

   @NgModule({
     declarations: [
       MyApp,
   ```

```
      HomePage,
      UserExtractPipe
    ],
    imports: [
      IonicModule.forRoot(MyApp)
    ],
    bootstrap: [IonicApp],
    entryComponents: [
      MyApp,
      HomePage
    ],
    providers: []
  })
  export class AppModule {}
```

7. Go to your terminal and run the app, as follows:

```
$ ionic serve
```

How it works...

You can use an Angular 2 pipe in the view to simply convert or transform any value to a desired value. There is no limitation on how you want to structure the pipe. Angular 2 automatically detects the | sign in the template and turns the value in front of it to an input. To create a pipe, you must import the decorator and provide a name (see `custom-pipe.ts`), as shown:

```
import { Pipe, PipeTransform } from '@angular/core';

@Pipe({name: 'userExtract'})
```

The input from the template is the following `value` parameter:

```
transform(value: any, arg) : any {
```

The value returned by the `transform` method will be the output to the view, as shown in the following code:

```
return newVal;
```

In this example, you are taking a parameter for the pipe to process, as illustrated in the following code:

```
    if (arg == "firstname") {

      newVal = value.name ? value.name.split(' ')[0] : '';
```

```
} else if (arg == "lastname") {

  newVal = value.name ? value.name.split(' ').splice(-1) : '';

} else if (arg == "age") {
  var currentTime = new Date();

  newVal = value.birthyear ? currentTime.getFullYear() -
  value.birthyear : 0;
}
```

For example, this is what you had in the `home.html` template:

```
<ion-item>
  <ion-label fixed>First Name</ion-label>
  <ion-note item-right>{{ user | userExtract : "firstname"
  }}</ion-note>
</ion-item>
```

Each parameter is placed after a colon (`:`). Then, within your `@Pipe` class, you can refer to it using `arg`. The rest of the code is very simple as already shown in the preceding section. Observe the following

- If it's `firstname`, take the first word after splitting by space
- If it's `lastname`, take the last word
- If it's `age`, subtract the current year from birth year

Of course, you could have more complicated scenarios with pipes. However, the overall recommendation is to keep things simple at the view to ensure rendering performance. If you need to do heavy processing, it's best to handle it as a separate variable.

See also

- To understand more about Angular 2 pipes, you can check out the official documentation at `https://angular.io/docs/ts/latest/guide/pipes.html`

Creating a shared service to provide data to multiple pages

When you develop an app that involves a lot of pages and communication to the backend, you will need to have a way to communicate across the pages and components. For example, you may have a service to request user data from the backend and store it in a common local service. Then, you will need to provide a way for the user to update their user data and see the update in real time. When the user navigates to different pages, the same information will be pulled and rendered as well without making multiple trips to the backend. This is a very common scenario that requires the use of the `@Injectable` decorator in Angular 2.

Observe the following screenshot of the app you will build:

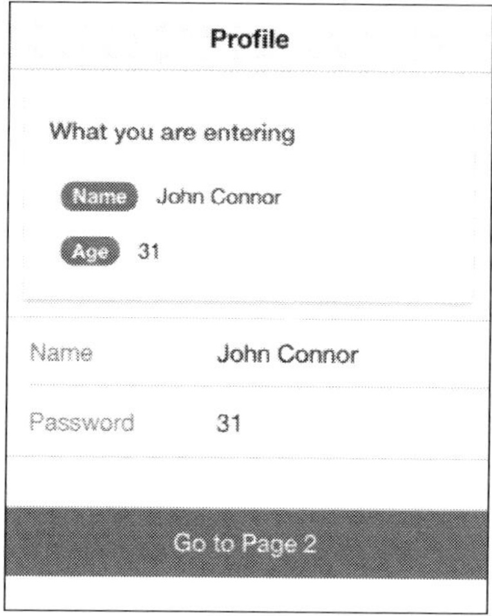

The user can fill out the form and see updates above it in real time. Then, they can move to the next page (**Go to Page 2**) and see the following screenshot:

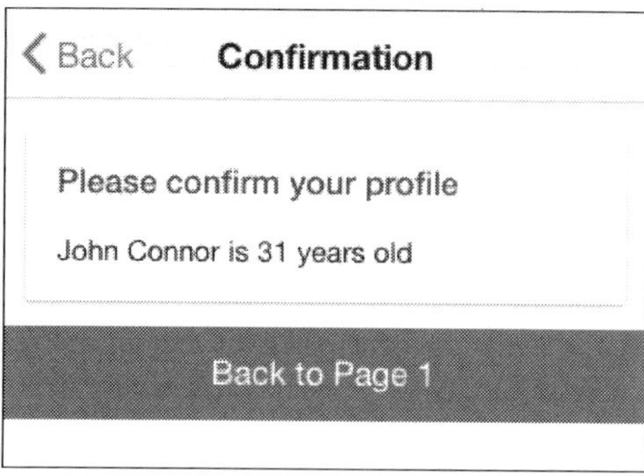

This page uses the same service as the preceding page and references the same date with the name and age. You will learn the following topics in this section:

- Creating a service using `@Injectable`
- Sharing a service across multiple pages
- Detecting changes using getters and setters inside the service

Getting ready

This app example could work either in a browser or on a physical device.

How to do it...

Observe the following instructions:

1. Create a new `SharedService` app using the `blank` template, as shown, and go to the `SharedService` folder:

   ```
   $ ionic start SharedService blank --v2
   $ cd SharedService
   ```

2. You will need to make several changes in the directory because you have two pages and a common service for both. Let's start by modifying the `./src/app/app.component.ts` file so that the `rootPage` is pointing to `Page1`:

   ```
   import { Component } from '@angular/core';
   import { Platform } from 'ionic-angular';
   import { StatusBar, Splashscreen } from 'ionic-native';
   import { Page1 } from '../pages/page1/page1';

   @Component({
     template: `<ion-nav [root]="rootPage"></ion-nav>`
   })
   export class MyApp {
     rootPage = Page1;

     constructor(platform: Platform) {
       platform.ready().then(() => {
         // Okay, so the platform is ready and our plugins are
         available.
         // Here you can do any higher level native things you
         might need.
         StatusBar.styleDefault();
         Splashscreen.hide();
       });
   ```

```
    }
}
```

3. Create `./src/pages/page1`, as shown in the following code:

   ```
   $ mkdir ./src/pages/page1
   ```

4. Create your first template, `page1.html`, in the `page1` folder with the following code:

   ```
   <ion-header>
     <ion-navbar>
       <ion-title>
         Profile
       </ion-title>
     </ion-navbar>
   </ion-header>

   <ion-content>
     <ion-card>
       <ion-card-header>
         What you are entering
       </ion-card-header>
       <ion-card-content>
         <ion-badge item-right>Name</ion-badge> {{ user.name
         }}
         <br><br>
         <ion-badge item-right>Age</ion-badge> {{ user.age }}
       </ion-card-content>
     </ion-card>
     <ion-list>

       <ion-item>
         <ion-label fixed>Name</ion-label>
         <ion-input type="text" [(ngModel)]="user.name"></ion-
         input>
       </ion-item>

       <ion-item>
         <ion-label fixed>Password</ion-label>
         <ion-input type="number"
         [(ngModel)]="user.age"></ion-input>
       </ion-item>

     </ion-list>

     <button ion-button full block (click)="goToPage2()">Go to
     Page 2</button>

   </ion-content>
   ```

5. Create `page1.ts` in the `page1` folder, as follows:

```
import { Component } from '@angular/core';
import { NavController } from 'ionic-angular';
import { UserService } from '../../services/user';
import { Page2 } from '../page2/page2';

@Component({
  selector: 'page-one',
  templateUrl: 'page1.html'
})
export class Page1 {
  private user: any;
  private nav: any;

  constructor(public navCtrl: NavController, user:
  UserService, nav: NavController) {
    console.log(user.name);
    this.user = user;
    this.nav = nav;
  }

  goToPage2(){
    this.nav.push(Page2);
  }
}
```

The file extension is `.ts`, and not `.js`, because you are going to use some TypeScript-specific features, such as getters and setters.

6. Similarly, create the `page2` folder using the following command:

```
$ mkdir ./src/pages/page1
```

7. Add the `page2.html` template in the `page2` folder as well, as follows:

```
<ion-header>
  <ion-navbar>
    <ion-title>
      Confirmation
    </ion-title>
  </ion-navbar>
</ion-header>

<ion-content class="home">
```

```
    <ion-card>
      <ion-card-header>
        Please confirm your profile
      </ion-card-header>
      <ion-card-content>
        {{ user.name }} is {{ user.age }} years old
      </ion-card-content>
    </ion-card>

    <button ion-button full block (click)="goToPage1()">Back
    to Page 1</button>
  </ion-content>
```

This is your second page with the same `name` and `age` information.

8. Create `page2.ts`, in the `page2` folder, with the following code:

```
import { Component } from '@angular/core';
import { NavController } from 'ionic-angular';
import { UserService } from '../../services/user';
import { Page1 } from '../page1/page1';

@Component({
  selector: 'page-two',
  templateUrl: 'page2.html'
})
export class Page2 {
  private user: any;
  private nav: any;

  constructor(public navCtrl: NavController, user:
  UserService, nav: NavController) {
    console.log(user.name);
    this.user = user;
    this.nav = nav;
  }

  goToPage1(){
    this.nav.push(Page1);
  }
}
```

9. Create the `services` folder with the following command:

```
$ mkdir ./src/services
```

10. Put `UserService` in the `user.ts` file in the `services` folder, as shown:

```
import {Injectable} from '@angular/core';

@Injectable()
export class UserService {
  private _name: string;
  private _age: number;

  constructor() {
    this._name = 'John Connor';
    this._age = 31;
  }

  get name() {
    return this._name;
  }

  set name(newVal) {
    console.log('Set name = ' + newVal);
    this._name = newVal;
  }

  get age() {
    return this._age;
  }

  set age(newVal) {
    console.log('Set age = ' + newVal);
    this._age = newVal;
  }
}
```

11. Open and edit `./src/app/app.module.ts` so that you can inject `UserService` as a global provider:

```
import { NgModule } from '@angular/core';
import { IonicApp, IonicModule } from 'ionic-angular';
import { MyApp } from './app.component';
import { Page1 } from '../pages/page1/page1';
import { Page2 } from '../pages/page2/page2';
import { UserService } from '../services/user';

@NgModule({
  declarations: [
    MyApp,
```

```
      Page1,
      Page2
    ],
    imports: [
      IonicModule.forRoot(MyApp)
    ],
    bootstrap: [IonicApp],
    entryComponents: [
      MyApp,
      Page1,
      Page2
    ],
    providers: [UserService]
  })
  export class AppModule {}
```

12. Verify your folder structure looks like the following screenshot:

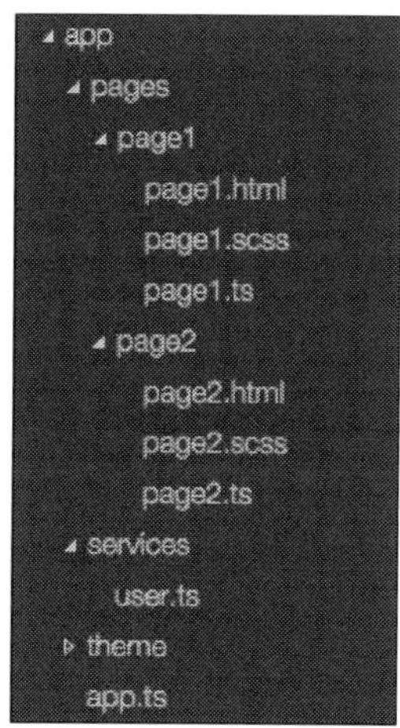

13. Go to your terminal and run the app as shown with the following command:

```
$ ionic serve
```

You can move from `page 1` to `page 2` and then back and the data persists across the pages.

How it works...

In general, if you want to use a common service across multiple pages, you must inject it at the highest level. In this example, you put `UserService` as a dependency at the start of `app.module.ts`, as follows:

```
providers: [UserService]
```

After that, other pages within the app can start using this common service without having to reinject it. The main reason is that, whenever you inject a service or class, it will instantiate a new object, which ends up erasing all the existing data in memory. If you want to keep the data persistent across the pages, it should be in the parent app to avoid reinjection.

To use the `UserService` in each page, you just need to import it, as illustrated in the following code:

```
import { UserService } from '../../services/user';
```

The way to "bring in" the service is to put the referencing in the constructor (page1.ts), as shown:

```
  constructor(user: UserService, nav: NavController) {
    console.log(user.name);
    this.user = user;
    this.nav = nav;
  }
```

This will pass down the `UserService` reference to a local private variable of the page (in this case, `this.user`).

From the template standpoint, there is no difference between using `{{ user.name }}` and `{{ user.age }}` to inject data.

Now, let's take a look at `UserService`:

```
import {Injectable} from '@angular/core';

@Injectable()
export class UserService {
  private _name: string;
  private _age: number;

  constructor() {
    this._name = 'John Connor';
    this._age = 31;
  }

  get name() {
    return this._name;
  }

  set name(newVal) {
    console.log('Set name = ' + newVal);
```

```
        this._name = newVal;
      }

      get age() {
        return this._age;
      }

      set age(newVal) {
        console.log('Set age = ' + newVal);
        this._age = newVal;
      }
    }
```

Actually, there are several things going on here. First, you need to import `Injectable` from `@angular/core`.

Don't forget the parentheses in `@Injectable()`.

Second, if you want to use getters and setters, you need to make separate variables, called `_name` and `_age`, to store the data. Then, you can use the get/set method to do additional processing when other pages access or set the variables in this common class. If you change the `name` or `age` from `Page 1`, you can see the following logs in the console:

```
Set name = John Conno
Set age = 3
>
```

This feature is very beneficial since you can use this as a replacement for `watch` or `observable`. If you recall from Angular 1, you have to use `$scope.$watch` for a similar approach.

See also

- For more information about Angular 2 services, visit the official documentation at `https://angular.io/docs/ts/latest/tutorial/toh-pt4.html`
- You can get great instructions on many techniques for component communication at `https://angular.io/docs/ts/latest/cookbook/component-communication.html`

4

Validating Forms and Making HTTP Requests

In this chapter, we will cover the following tasks related to creating form input validation, mocked API calls, and payment pages using Stripe:

- Creating a complex form with input validation
- Retrieving data via a mocked API using a static JSON file
- Integrating with Stripe for online payment

Introduction

All mobile apps require taking user input and sending it to a backend server. A simple example is filling out a form, such as a user registration or contact form. The information is validated against a set of rules before being sent to the backend. Also, there are many other scenarios where the information is captured based on user behavior from the app, such as where they touch or how much time they spend on a certain page. Regardless, you will run into many send and retrieve data scenarios.

This chapter will cover the following three basic examples:

- How to validate user inputs, such as text, number, and required versus not required, and communicate the data to another page
- How to render data without having an actual backend
- How to process payments using Stripe

All of these are actually available natively in Angular 2. However, since Angular 2 has a lot of changes compared to Angular 1 in terms of processing data and working with the backend server, it's worth covering these topics in detail.

Creating a complex form with input validation

In this section, you will build an app to demonstrate form validation using `ngForm` and `ngControl`. Here is a screenshot of the form:

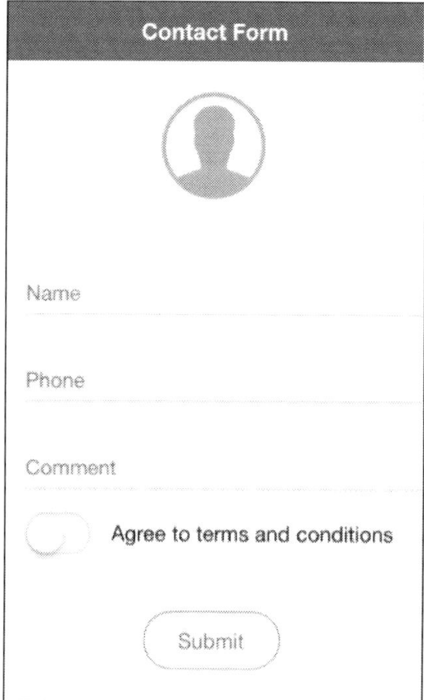

If the user tries to submit without providing valid information, the form will show the following error:

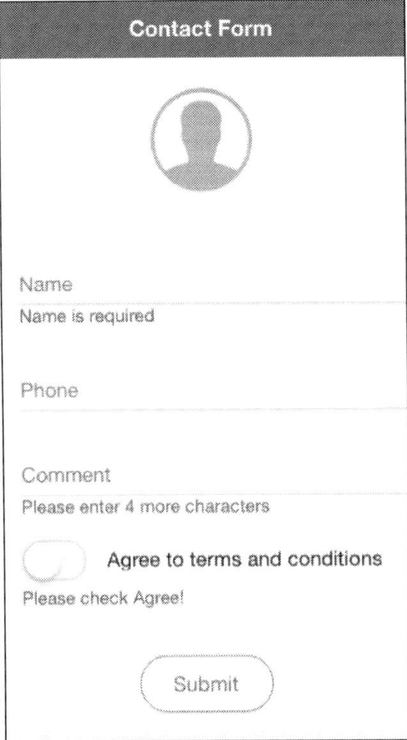

Basically, the **Name** field is required. The **Phone** field is the number type, but is optional. The **Comment** field is required and the user must enter at least four characters. Of course, this is just for demonstration of the input length. The user, finally, must agree to the terms and conditions via the toggle input.

After a successful validation, the user will be taken to the second screen with a summary of the previous screen, as illustrated in the following screenshot:

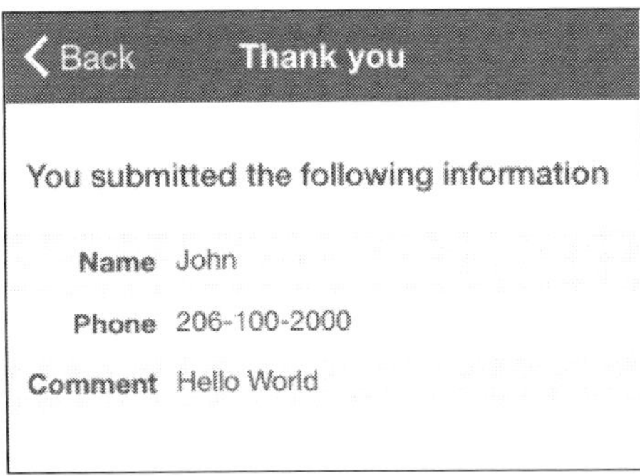

Getting ready

This app example could work either in a browser or on a physical device. However, you can optionally connect your physical device to verify the **Phone** field for number keypad.

How to do it...

Observe the following the instructions:

1. Create a new `MyFormValidation` app using the `blank` template, as shown, and go to the `MyFormValidation` folder:

   ```
   $ ionic start MyFormValidation blank --v2
   $ cd MyFormValidation
   ```

2. Open the `./src/app/app.module.ts` file and replace the content with the following code:

   ```
   import { NgModule } from '@angular/core';
   import { IonicApp, IonicModule } from 'ionic-angular';
   import { MyApp } from './app.component';
   import { HomePage } from '../pages/home/home';
   import { ThankyouPage } from '../pages/thankyou/thankyou';
   import { MyFormService } from '../services/myform';

   @NgModule({
     declarations: [
       MyApp,
       HomePage,
       ThankyouPage
     ],
     imports: [
       IonicModule.forRoot(MyApp)
     ],
     bootstrap: [IonicApp],
     entryComponents: [
       MyApp,
       HomePage,
       ThankyouPage
     ],
     providers: [MyFormService]
   })
   export class AppModule {}
   ```

   You may realize that there is a common service to be used across the app, called `MyFormService` here. This example also has a second page, called `ThankyouPage`.

3. Now, let's create the service by first creating a directory, as shown:

   ```
   $ mkdir ./src/services
   ```

4. Create the `myform.js` file in the component's directory that you just created, as follows:

   ```
   import {Injectable} from '@angular/core';

   @Injectable()
   export class MyFormService {
     public name: string = '';
     public phone: number;
     public comment: string = '';

     constructor() {
     }
   }
   ```

   This example will keep the service component simple for demonstration purposes.

5. Open and edit the `./src/pages/home/home.html` template, as shown:

   ```
   <ion-header>
     <ion-navbar color="primary">
       <ion-title>
         Contact Form
       </ion-title>
     </ion-navbar>
   </ion-header>

   <ion-content>
     <p class="center">
       <ion-icon class="large lighter" primary
       name="contact"></ion-icon>
     </p>
     <form #f="ngForm" novalidate (ngSubmit)="onSubmit(f)">
       <ion-list>

         <ion-item>
           <ion-label floating>Name</ion-label>
           <ion-input type="text" name="name" required
           [(ngModel)]="data.name"></ion-input>
         </ion-item>
         <div [hidden]="f.controls.name &&
         (f.controls.name.valid || (f.controls.name.pristine
         && !isSubmitted))" class="note danger">
   ```

```
      Name is required
    </div>

    <ion-item>
      <ion-label floating>Phone</ion-label>
      <ion-input type="tel" name="phone"
      [(ngModel)]="data.phone"></ion-input>
    </ion-item>

    <ion-item>
      <ion-label floating>Comment</ion-label>
      <ion-input type="text" required minlength=4
      name="comment" [(ngModel)]="data.comment"></ion-
      input>
    </ion-item>
    <div *ngIf="(isSubmitted && f.controls.comment &&
    f.controls.comment.pristine) || ((f.controls.comment)
    && (f.controls.comment.dirty &&
    f.controls.comment.errors))" class="note danger">
      Please enter {{ 4 -
      (f.controls.comment.errors.minlength ?
      f.controls.comment.errors.minlength.actualLength :
      0) }} more characters
    </div>

    <ion-item class="tos">
      <ion-toggle item-left [(ngModel)]="data.tos"
      name="tos" type="button"
      (click)="noSubmit($event)"></ion-toggle>
      <ion-label item-right>Agree to terms and
      conditions</ion-label>
    </ion-item>

    <div [hidden]="(!isSubmitted) || (f.controls.tos &&
    data.tos)" class="note danger">
      Please check Agree!
    </div>

  </ion-list>

  <div class="center">
    <button ion-button type="submit" round
    outline>Submit</button>
  </div>
</form>

</ion-content>
```

This is probably the most complicated part of the form validation process because there are many places where you have to embed validation logic for the input.

6. Open and replace the content of the `./src/pages/home/home.scss` file with the following code:

```
.center {
  text-align: center;
}

ion-icon.large {
  font-size: 7em;
}

ion-icon.lighter {
  opacity: 0.5;
}

ion-list > .item:first-child {
  border-top: 0;
}

ion-list > .item:last-child, ion-list > ion-item-
sliding:last-child .item {
  border-bottom: 0;
}

.tos {
  padding-top: 10px;

  ion-toggle {
    padding-left: 0px;
  }
  .item-inner {
    border-bottom: 0;
  }
}

.item ion-toggle {
  padding-left: 0;
}

.note.danger {
  padding-left: 16px;
  color: #d14;
}
```

7. Open `./src/pages/home/home.ts` for editing with the following code:

```
import { Component } from '@angular/core';
import { NavController } from 'ionic-angular';
import { ThankyouPage } from '../thankyou/thankyou';
import { MyFormService } from '../../services/myform';

@Component({
  selector: 'page-home',
  templateUrl: 'home.html'
})
export class HomePage {
  private data: any;
  private isSubmitted: Boolean = false;

  constructor(public nav: NavController, private formData:
  MyFormService) {
    this.nav = nav;
    this.formData = formData;
    this.data = {
      name: '',
      phone: '',
      comment: '',
      tos: false
    }
  }

  onSubmit(myForm) {
    this.isSubmitted = true;
    console.log('onSubmit');
    console.log(myForm);

    if ((myForm.valid) && (myForm.value.tos)) {
      this.formData.name = this.data.name;
      this.formData.phone = this.data.phone;
      this.formData.comment = this.data.comment;
      this.nav.push(ThankyouPage);
    }
  }

  noSubmit(e) {
    e.preventDefault();
  }
}
```

You may note that there isn't much validation code in the JavaScript part. This means that the template takes care of a lot of the validations. There is also an `import` command for a `thankyou` page, which you will have to create next.

8. Now, let's create the `thankyou` folder, as follows:

   ```
   $ mkdir ./src/pages/thankyou
   ```

9. Create a `thankyou.js` file in the component's directory that you just created, as shown:

   ```
   import { Component } from '@angular/core';
   import { MyFormService } from '../../services/myform'

   @Component({
     templateUrl: 'thankyou.html'
   })
   export class ThankyouPage {

     constructor(private formData: MyFormService) {
       this.formData = formData;
     }

   }
   ```

   This page just renders the data from the `MyFormService` service. So, you can keep it very simple.

10. Create `thankyou.html` in the `./src/pages/thankyou`, folder, as illustrated:

    ```
    <ion-header>
      <ion-navbar color="secondary">
        <ion-title>
          Thank You
        </ion-title>
      </ion-navbar>
    </ion-header>

    <ion-content>
      <h6 class="padding">
        You submitted the following information
      </h6>

      <div class="my-table">
        <ion-row>
          <ion-col width-25 class="my-label">Name</ion-col>
    ```

```
      <ion-col width-75>{{ formData.name }}</ion-col>
    </ion-row>
    <ion-row>
      <ion-col width-25 class="my-label">Phone</ion-col>
      <ion-col width-75>{{ formData.phone }}</ion-col>
    </ion-row>
    <ion-row>
      <ion-col width-25 class="my-label">Comment</ion-col>
      <ion-col width-75>{{ formData.comment }}</ion-col>
    </ion-row>
  </div>
</ion-content>
```

11. Create `thankyou.scss` in the `./src/pages/thankyou` folder, as shown:

```
h6.padding {
  color: #4C555A;
  padding: 10px;
}

.my-label {
  text-align: right;
  font-weight: bold;
}

.my-table {
  ion-row {
    color: #4C555A;
    padding: 0;
    height: 30px;
  }

  ion-row + ion-row {
    margin-top: 0;
  }

  ion-row:nth-child(odd) ion-col {
    background: #F9FAFB;
  }
}
```

12. Edit the `./app/app.scss` file to ensure that you include both the `.scss` files in the two pages, as follows:

```
@import '../pages/home/home';
@import '../pages/thankyou/thankyou';
```

13. Go to your Terminal and run the app with the following command:

```
$ ionic serve
```

How it works...

Let's start with the `home.html` file, where most of the validation code is located. If you look at the structure of this page, it's very typical. You have `<ion-navbar>` with `<ion-title>`. The `<form>` element must be inside the `<ion-content>` area.

It's a requirement to use the `<form>` element for Angular 2 validation to work. Otherwise, there will be no `submit` event and you cannot catch errors for each input.

`form` has the following attributes:

```
<form #f="ngForm" novalidate (ngSubmit)="onSubmit(f)">
```

To assign a local variable *on the fly*, you use the # sign. This means that you want the `f` variable to refer to `ngForm`, which is automatically created from Angular 2. This is a special object that contains everything related to the current form. You are advised to use `novalidate` to bypass the default HTML5 validation because you are using Angular 2 for validation instead. Otherwise, the `form` will acquire conflicts. The `(ngSubmit)` is pretty much an event to trigger the `onSubmit(f)` function whenever the `button` with `type=submit` is touched or clicked. When you submit the form, it will pass the `f` variable along so that you can process the object inside the `onSubmit` method.

The `form` template consists of just `<ion-list>` and `<ion-item>`. You just need to know how to validate each input and display the error. Let's use the `Name` field as the first example. This is the `<ion-input>` for `Name`:

```
<ion-input type="text" name="name" required [(ngModel)]="data.name"></
ion-input>
```

The following is the error displayed:

```
<div [hidden]="f.controls.name && (f.controls.name.valid ||
(f.controls.name.pristine && !isSubmitted))" class="note danger">
  Name is required
</div>
```

To validate, you must assign `name` a local variable name. This is to refer to that input using `f.controls.name` in other areas. Recall that the `f` variable has been declared previously as the `ngForm` object. Here is a view of how the `ngForm` is structured:

```
▼ NgForm {ngSubmit: EventEmitter, form: ControlGroup}
  ▶ control: ControlGroup
  ▼ controls: Object
    ▶ comment: Control
    ▶ name: Control
    ▶ phone: Control
    ▶ tos: Control
    ▶ __proto__: Object
    dirty: true
    errors: null
  ▶ form: ControlGroup
  ▶ formDirective: NgForm
  ▶ ngSubmit: EventEmitter
  ▶ path: Array[0]
    pristine: false
    touched: false
    untouched: true
    valid: true
  ▶ value: Object
  ▶ __proto__: ControlContainer
```

You can view this using the Chrome Developer console because the code actually gives this output when you submit the form.

The error message `Name is required` will be hidden when either of the following conditions takes place:

- The form has not been submitted yet. Otherwise, people will see the error message right away before they even type in something. This is not a good user experience. To check for this, you have to use a temporary Boolean, called `isSubmitted`. The `f.controls.name.pristine` variable means that the input has not been modified. The opposite of this would be `f.controls.name.dirty`.
- The `f.controls.name.valid` variable is `true`. However, you cannot check this right away because, if the input is empty, the `name` object does not exist yet. That's why you need to check for the existence of `f.controls.name` before checking for the `valid` Boolean.

There is no need to check the phone requirement; so, you just need to assign `name` and a model, as shown:

```
<ion-input type="tel" name="phone" [(ngModel)]="data.phone"></ion-
input>
```

For the `Comment` field, there is a need to validate using both `required` and `minlength=4`, as follows:

```
<ion-input type="text" required minlength=4 name="comment"
[(ngModel)]="data.comment"></ion-input>
```

You may think `required` is unnecessary because, if the length is zero, Angular 2 will trigger an error flag. However, that is not true. When the user doesn't enter anything in the input, the input will have no length because the variable doesn't exist. That's why you need to check for both scenarios.

The error message for the `Comment` field is quite interesting because it shows the number of characters the user needs to enter, as shown in the following code:

```
<div *ngIf="(isSubmitted && f.controls.comment &&
f.controls.comment.pristine) || ((f.controls.comment) &&
(f.controls.comment.dirty && f.controls.comment.errors))"
class="note danger">
  Please enter {{ 4 - (f.controls.comment.errors.minlength ?
  f.controls.comment.errors.minlength.actualLength : 0) }} more
  characters
</div>
```

The main idea here is that you only want to show this `div` when the form is submitted and it's pristine via `f.controls.comment.pristine`. This means that the user has not entered anything in the form. You also want to show the message when the form is dirty and has errors via `f.controls.comment.errors`. If you inspect the console, you can see a list of many detailed errors under the `f.controls.comment.errors` object. In order to tell the user how many characters they have left to enter, you have to first check `f.controls.comment.errors.minlength` because, if that variable doesn't exist, there is no error or the `comment` input is empty. If you do not check for this, you will get a parse error later on.

In your `home.ts` file, the `onSubmit` method must toggle the `isSubmitted` Boolean to `true`, as shown in the following code snippet:

```
onSubmit(myForm) {
  this.isSubmitted = true;
  console.log('onSubmit');
  console.log(myForm);

  if ((myForm.valid) && (myForm.value.tos)) {
    this.formData.name = this.data.name;
    this.formData.phone = this.data.phone;
    this.formData.comment = this.data.comment;
    this.nav.push(ThankyouPage);
  }
}
```

Then, you have to do a general check for `myForm.valid` and `myForm.value.tos`. You may wonder why we are checking for `tos` here instead of validating it inside the template. The reason is that there is no way to validate a toggle button in Angular 2 since it doesn't make sense to do so as it cannot be `required`. Therefore, you have to do a custom validation here to make sure it's `true` in the form. This means that the user has checked the **Agree to terms and conditions** toggle.

This is a minor detail that could be a bug in Ionic 2 (currently Beta 21):

```
noSubmit(e) {
  e.preventDefault();
}
```

For each toggle button, it acts as a `type=submit` button by default since there is no `type` attribute assigned. That's why you need to cancel the `submit` event by calling `preventDefault()`.

Refer to the W3 website, at `https://www.w3.org/TR/html-markup/button.html`, for information about the default behavior of the `button` element.

The `thankyou` page is very self-explanatory because you just parse the `formData` object in the template by getting the data from the `MyFormService` service.

See also

Check out the following links for more information:

- For more information about `form` from the Angular 2 documentation, you can visit `https://angular.io/docs/ts/latest/guide/forms.html` and `https://angular.io/docs/ts/latest/api/forms/index/NgForm-directive.html`
- The Ionic documentation has its own page specifically for Ionic input components, which is `https://ionicframework.com/docs/v2/resources/forms/`
- It also has a good list of HTML5 input types that you can use for validation or keyboard enforcement, which you can find at `http://ionicframework.com/html5-input-types/`

Retrieving data via a mocked API using a static JSON file

As a frontend and app developer, you are often working with a team where someone else is responsible for the backend APIs. However, it's not always possible to have the backend available when you are developing the frontend. You have to *simulate* the backend in scenarios where the final backend APIs are not ready.

In this recipe, you will learn how to call a REST API using the `http` service. The API endpoint will be just a static JSON located on your local machine. You will also learn how to leverage placeholder images to meet design requirements. The app will show a list of image feeds and a description, as shown in the following screenshot:

Getting ready

This app example would work either in a browser or on a physical device. However, the *fake* backend server must be running on your local computer.

How to do it...

Here are the instructions to be followed:

1. First, let's quickly create the *fake* backend server. You must install `http-server` for this:

   ```
   $ sudo npm install -g http-server
   ```

2. Create a folder to store your `.json` file. Let's call it `MockRest`, as shown:

   ```
   $ mkdir MockRest
   $ cd MockRest
   ```

3. Create the `test.json` file and fill in the following content for the REST response:

   ```
   [
     {
       "title": "What a beautiful song",
       "category": "objects",
       "description": "Music is a moral law. It gives soul to the
   universe, wings to the mind, flight to the imagination, and charm
   and gaiety to life and to everything."
     },
     {
       "title": "The world we live in",
       "category": "nature",
       "description": "Look deep into nature, and then you will
       understand everything better."
     },
     {
       "title": "Life experiences",
       "category": "people",
       "description": "People who know little are usually great
       talkers, while men who know much say little."
     }
   ]
   ```

   Basically, whenever you send a REST request, you should receive the preceding content as the response. As your backend developer updates the REST response, you can always change the content of the `test.json` file accordingly.

4. Start your backend server by calling `http-server` from the Terminal in the `MockRest` folder, as shown:

   ```
   $ http-server --cors=Access-Control-Allow-Origin
   ```

5. Go to your browser and visit `http://localhost:8080/test.json` to verify that you can see the JSON content. If not, you probably have a port conflict with another web server. You need to ensure that there is no other application using port `8080`.

6. After completing your backend, open another Terminal window, create a new `MyRestBackend` app using the `blank` template, and go to the `MyRestBackend` folder, as shown:

```
$ ionic start MyRestbackend blank --v2
$ cd MyRestbackend
```

You must not stop the backend server or create an Ionic project inside the `MockRest` folder. They are two independent project folders.

7. Open the `html.html` file and replace the content with the following code:

```
<ion-header>
  <ion-navbar>
    <ion-title>
      Home
    </ion-title>
  </ion-navbar>
</ion-header>

<ion-content padding>
  <ion-card #myCard *ngFor="let item of quotes.data">
    <img [src]='"https://source.unsplash.com/category/" + item.
    category + "/600x390"' [height]="myCard.clientWidth * 390 /
    600"/>
    <ion-card-content>
      <ion-card-title>
        {{ item.title }}
      </ion-card-title>
      <p>
        {{ item.description }}
      </p>
    </ion-card-content>
  </ion-card>
</ion-content>
```

This app example uses free photos from `https://source.unsplash.com/` because you can easily query to get random photos that meet your need.

8. Open `home.ts` and edit it with the following code:

```
import { Component } from '@angular/core';
import { NavController } from 'ionic-angular';
import { QuoteService } from '../../services/quote'

@Component({
  selector: 'page-home',
  templateUrl: 'home.html'
})
export class HomePage {

  constructor(public navCtrl: NavController, public quotes:
  QuoteService) {
    this.quotes = quotes;
    this.quotes.getQuotes();
  }

}
```

   You have not created the `QuoteService` service yet. However, you probably know that this service will call the *fake* backend server to get the JSON content using the `getQuotes()` method.

9. Do a small modification of the stylesheet `home.scss`, as follows:

```
ion-card {
  img {
    background-color: #f4f4f4;
  }
}
```

10. Create the `./src/services` folder with the following command:

```
$ mkdir ./src/services
```

11. Create the `quote.ts` file in the `services` folder and copy the following code:

```
import { Injectable } from '@angular/core';
import { Http } from '@angular/http';

@Injectable()
export class QuoteService {
  private http: any;
  public data: any;

  constructor(http: Http) {
    this.http = http;
```

```
  }

  getQuotes() {
    this.http.get("http://localhost:8080/test.json")
      .subscribe(res => {
        this.data = res.json();
        console.log(this.data);
      }, error => {
        console.log(error);
      });
  }

}
```

12. Open and edit `./src/app/app.module.ts` to declare `QuoteService`, as shown:

```
import { NgModule } from '@angular/core';
import { IonicApp, IonicModule } from 'ionic-angular';
import { MyApp } from './app.component';
import { HomePage } from '../pages/home/home';
import { QuoteService } from '../services/quote'

@NgModule({
  declarations: [
    MyApp,
    HomePage
  ],
  imports: [
    IonicModule.forRoot(MyApp)
  ],
  bootstrap: [IonicApp],
  entryComponents: [
    MyApp,
    HomePage
  ],
  providers: [QuoteService]
})
export class AppModule {}
```

13. Go to your Terminal and run the app, as illustrated:

```
$ ionic serve
```

14. You will note that the page is empty and the **Console** shows the following error:

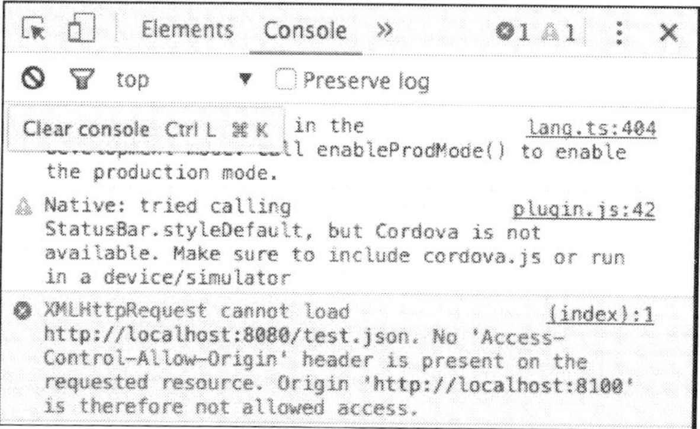

This means that your browser (in this case, Chrome) does not allow calling REST API from `http://localhost:8100` to `http://localhost:8080`. You need to install the **Allow-Control-Allow-Origin** (**CORS**) plugin, such as `https://chrome.google.com/webstore/detail/allow-control-allow-origi/nlfbmbojpeacfghkpbjhddihlkkiljbi?hl=en`, for Chrome. After that, turn on CORS, as shown in the following screenshot:

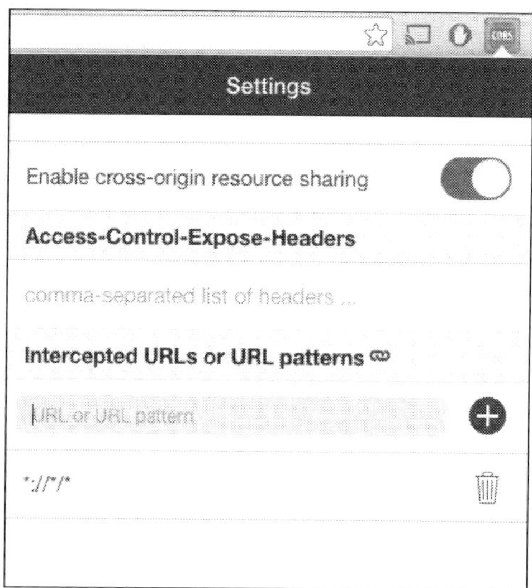

15. Refresh your browser to see the updated app.

How it works...

Your *fake* backend simply returns any file in the current `MockRest` folder. As you get more *sample* responses from the backend developer, you can copy them into this folder to provide additional backend endpoints.

This section does not provide examples of how to handle POST and complex scenarios where the responses depend on request parameters. You may want to keep the code to handle temporary cases as simple as possible since they are not production code. The recommendation is to return the same content for each POST request as well.

Let's take a look at `quote.ts`, because it's the main place where the `Http` request is made. First, you need to import `Injectable` and `Http`, which you can do as follows:

```
import {Injectable} from '@angular/core';
import {Http} from '@angular/http';
```

The `@Injectable` decorator is used to allow other pages and components to use `QuoteService` as a dependency. The `Http` service (or class) is provided by Angular 2 (not Ionic 2) and this is similar to the `$http` provider in Angular 1. However, instead of returning a promise, `Http` will return an **observable** object so that you can *subscribe* to it. The `getQuotes()` method, shown as follows, is the most important part of this file:

```
getQuotes() {
  this.http.get("http://localhost:8080/test.json")
    .subscribe(res => {
      this.data = res.json();
      console.log(this.data);
    }, error => {
      console.log(error);
    });
}
```

The `this.http` object must be injected from the constructor. Then, it will trigger GET via `this.http.get()`, just like the `$http` provider. However, there is no `.then()` function but in Angular 2; you have to `subscribe` to the object. A new feature of ES6 is the *arrow* function, as you see via `res => {}`. This is similar to the lambda function in other languages (for example, Python). There is no need to declare the name of the function and you don't have to type *function* each time. In addition, it automatically passes the parameter (`res` in this case) and the `this` context inside the function.

You can read more about the arrow function from TypeScript documentation at `https://www.typescriptlang.org/docs/handbook/functions.html`.

The REST response from your *fake* backend will be assigned to `this.data` of the `QuoteService` service, as shown:

```
this.data = JSON.parse(res._body);
```

If you see the browser console, it will look similar to the following screenshot:

```
                                                                                     quote.ts:17
▼ [Object, Object, Object]
  ▼ 0: Object
      category: "objects"
      description: "Music is a moral law. It gives soul to the universe, wings to the mind, flight to the imagination,
      title: "What a beautiful song"
    ▶ __proto__: Object
  ▼ 1: Object
      category: "nature"
      description: "Look deep into nature, and then you will understand everything better."
      title: "The world we live in"
    ▶ __proto__: Object
  ▼ 2: Object
      category: "people"
      description: "People who know little are usually great talkers, while men who know much say little."
      title: "Life experiences"
    ▶ __proto__: Object
    length: 3
  ▶ __proto__: Array[0]
```

Another nice trick in the `home.html` template is to display a gray placeholder for the photos instead of pushing down the content when the photos are downloaded and rendered, as shown in the following code snippet:

```
<ion-card #myCard *ngFor="let item of quotes.data">
    <img [src]='"https://source.unsplash.com/category/" + item.
    category + "/600x390"' [height]="myCard.clientWidth * 390 / 600"/>
```

The following screenshot shows a quick example before the photos are loaded:

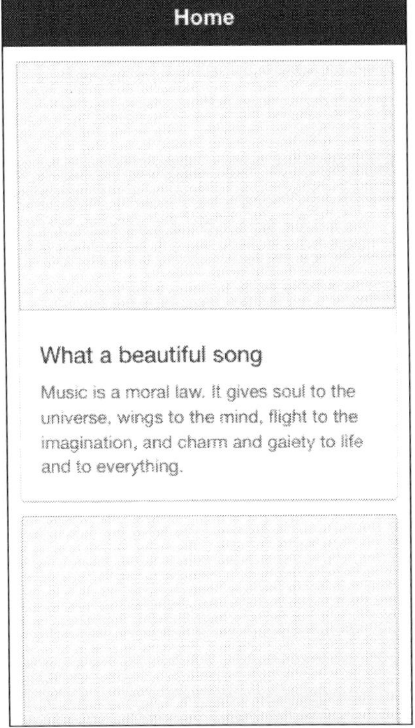

In order to tell the `<img>` tag to have an exact size, you have to do a height calculation using `[height]="myCard.clientWidth * 390 / 600"`. This is because the photo is 600 x 390. The `myCard` object is a local object created from `ion-card`. This `myCard` object will have access to all properties of the `ion-card` DOM, including the width via `clientWidth`. You have probably noted that this is just pure JavaScript and has nothing to do with Ionic or Angular itself.

See also

- For more information about the Angular 2 `Http` provider, you can visit the official documentation at `https://angular.io/docs/ts/latest/api/http/index/HttpModule-class.html`

Integrating with Stripe for online payment

In this section, you will learn how to integrate with a real backend service for the payment process. Earning revenue is an important aspect of creating an app. While there are many other methods of collecting payment, Stripe is a common payment system and can integrate very well with Ionic. In addition, there is no need to provide a high level of security and compliance (that is, PCI) since you will not be *storing* the credit card information.

Your app will not process via a real payment method because you can use a public test key from Stripe. The app will ask for a few fields to create a token. Observe the following screenshot of the app:

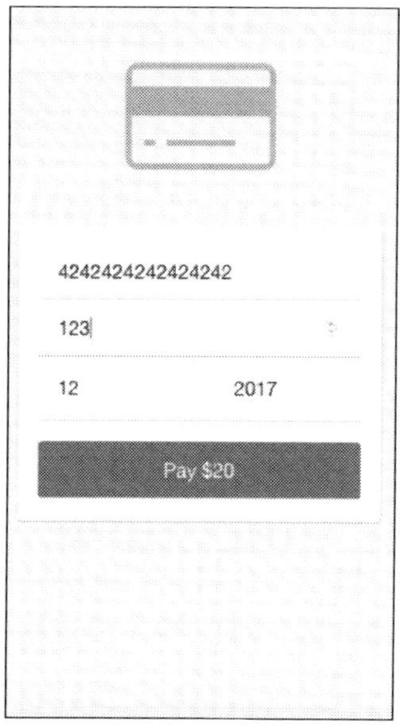

If you touch the **Pay $20** button, it will take you to the next screen where you will get the payment token, as shown in the following screenshot:

Actually, there are additional steps for your backend to call Stripe to authorize and process the transaction. However, it's not within the scope of this section. The Stripe document has a good tutorial page on Node.js at `https://stripe.com/docs/api/node#authentication`.

Getting ready

There is no need to test in a physical device because Ionic 2 and Stripe will work just fine in the web browser.

How to do it...

Observe the following instructions:

1. If you don't have a Stripe account, you need to register on `https://stripe.com`.
2. Log in and go to `https://dashboard.stripe.com/test/dashboard`.
3. Click on your username on the top right and select **Account Settings**, as illustrated in the following screenshot:

4. Select the **API Keys** tab.
5. Copy your **Test Publishable Key**, shown as follows, somewhere because you need to use it for your JavaScript code later:

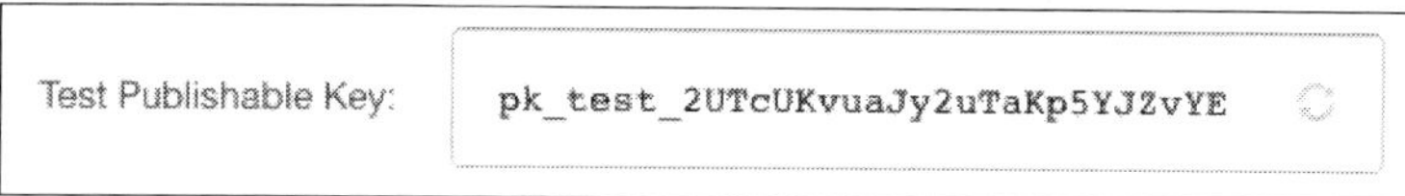

Now, go back to the Terminal.

6. Create a new `StripePayment` app using the `blank` template, as follows, and go into the `StripePayment` folder:

```
$ ionic start StripePayment blank --v2
$ cd StripePayment
```

7. Open the `./src/index.html` file and insert the line shown somewhere in the `<body>` tab as follows:

```
<script type="text/javascript"
src="https://js.stripe.com/v2/"></script>
```

> This is to load the `Stripe` object globally in your app. This is not the recommended method with Angular 2 because anything that is used within a component must be imported via the `import` instruction. However, at the time of writing this book, angular-stripe is unavailable for Angular 2. So, there is no way to do this properly. The preceding method will work just fine.

8. Open the `./src/pages/home/home.html` file and modify the content with the following code:

```
<ion-content class="gray-bg">
  <p class="center">
    <ion-icon class="icon-large" name="card"></ion-icon>
  </p>

  <ion-card>
    <ion-card-content>
      <ion-list>

        <ion-item>
          <ion-input type="number" name="cc"
          [(ngModel)]="ngForm.cc"
          placeholder="Number"></ion-input>
```

```
        </ion-item>

        <ion-item>
          <ion-input type="number" name="cvc"
          [(ngModel)]="ngForm.cvc" placeholder="CVC"></ion-
          input>
        </ion-item>

        <ion-item>
          <ion-input item-left type="number" name="month"
          [(ngModel)]="ngForm.month"
          placeholder="Month"></ion-input>
          <ion-input item-right type="number" name="year"
          [(ngModel)]="ngForm.year"
          placeholder="Year"></ion-input>
        </ion-item>

        <button type="button" ion-button bottom block
        (click)="onSubmit()">Pay $20</button>

      </ion-list>
    </ion-card-content>
  </ion-card>

</ion-content>
```

Stripe only needs the credit card number, CVC, and expiration to create a token for charging. The customer name and address are optional; so, you don't need to include them here.

9. Then, replace the content of `./src/pages/home/home.ts` with the following code:

```
import { Component } from '@angular/core';
import { NavController } from 'ionic-angular';
import { ThankyouPage } from '../thankyou/thankyou'
declare var Stripe: any;

@Component({
  selector: 'page-home',
  templateUrl: 'home.html'
})
export class HomePage {
  private token: string = '';
  private ngForm: any = {
      cc: '',
      cvc: '',
```

```
      month: '',
      year: '',
      amount: 2000
    };

    constructor(public nav: NavController) {
      this.nav = nav;
      console.log(Stripe);
      Stripe.setPublishableKey('YOUR STRIPE PUBLIC KEY
      HERE');
    }

    onSubmit() {
      console.log(this.ngForm);
      Stripe.card.createToken({
        number: this.ngForm.cc, //'4242424242424242',
        cvc: this.ngForm.cvc, //'123',
        exp_month: this.ngForm.month, //12,
        exp_year: this.ngForm.year, //2017,
        amount: 2000
      }, (status, response) =>
      this.stripeResponseHandler(status, response));
    }

    stripeResponseHandler(status, response) {

      if (response.error) {
        // Show the errors on the form
        console.log('error');
        console.log(response.error.message);
      } else {
        // response contains id and card, which contains
        additional card details
        this.token = response.id;
        // Insert the token into the form so it gets
        submitted to the server
        console.log('success');
        console.log('Sending token param:');
        console.log(this.token);
        this.nav.push(ThankyouPage, {token: this.token});
      }
    }

}
```

You need to change your **Test Publishable Key** here by replacing **YOUR STRIPE PUBLIC KEY HERE** with your own key that you copied earlier.

10. Edit `./src/pages/home/home.scss` with the following code:

```
.center {
  text-align: center;
}

.gray-bg {
  background-color: #f4f4f7;
}

.icon-large {
  font-size: 150px;
  color: #387ef5;
  opacity: 0.5;
}

.list-ios > .item-block:first-child {
  border-top: 0;
}

ion-card ion-list .item {
  border-bottom: 1px solid #c8c7cc;
}

ion-list .item-inner {
  border-bottom: 0;
}

ion-card-content .button-block {
  margin-top: 16px;
    }
```

11. Create the `thankyou` page that shows the token ID by making a new folder, called `./src/pages/thankyou`, as shown:

```
$ mkdir ./src/pages/thankyou
```

12. Create the `thankyou.html` file in the `thankyou` folder and copy the following code:

```
<ion-content class="green-bg">
  <h4 class="center">
    Your token is
  </h4>
```

```
    <p class="center">
      <code>
        {{ token }}
      </code>
    </p>
</ion-content>
```

In reality, there is no need to show the token ID to the user. This is just an example to get the token ID to charge.

13. Create the `thankyou.ts` file in the `thankyou` folder and copy the following code:

```
import { Component } from '@angular/core';
import { NavController, NavParams } from 'ionic-angular';

@Component({
  selector: 'thank-you',
  templateUrl: 'thankyou.html'
})
export class ThankyouPage {
  private token: string = '';

  constructor(public nav: NavController, public params:
  NavParams) {
    this.token = this.params.get('token');
    console.log('Getting token param:');
    console.log(this.token);
  }

}
```

14. Create the `thankyou.scss` file to modify the theme using the following code:

```
.green-bg {
  color: black;
  background-color: #32db64;
}

h4.center {
  padding-top: 150px;
}

.center {
  text-align: center;
}
```

15. Since the `thankyou.scss` file is new in the project, you need to include it in `./src/app/app.scss`. Insert this line at the bottom of the code:

```
@import '../pages/thankyou/thankyou';
```

16. Open and edit `./src/app/app.module.ts` to declare `ThankyouPage` as follows:

```
import { NgModule } from '@angular/core';
import { IonicApp, IonicModule } from 'ionic-angular';
import { MyApp } from './app.component';
import { HomePage } from '../pages/home/home';
import { ThankyouPage } from '../pages/thankyou/thankyou'

@NgModule({
  declarations: [
    MyApp,
    HomePage,
    ThankyouPage
  ],
  imports: [
    IonicModule.forRoot(MyApp)
  ],
  bootstrap: [IonicApp],
  entryComponents: [
    MyApp,
    HomePage,
    ThankyouPage
  ],
  providers: []
})
export class AppModule {}
```

17. Go to your Terminal and run the app:

```
$ ionic serve
```

18. For the purpose of testing, you can use `4242424242424242` as the credit card number, `123` as `cvc`, and `12/2017` as the expiration.

How it works...

This is the Stripe charging process:

1. The user fills in the payment form and clicks on the **Submit** button.
2. The frontend (your Ionic app) will call API to Stripe using the `Stripe` object and send along all the payment information.

3. Stripe will return a token ID, which is basically a way to confirm that everything is correct and you can charge the card now.
4. The frontend will use the token ID to send to its backend (without the credit card information) to authorize the charge.
5. The backend will call another Stripe API to say *I'm going to charge now*. Stripe will return the `success` event to the backend at this point.
6. The backend will then return the `success` event to the frontend.
7. The frontend should render a new page, such as the `thankyou` page.

As discussed previously, this chapter will not cover the backend portion of this app because it doesn't focus on Ionic. You can build the backend using any language, such as Node.js, PHP, or Python.

Let's take a look at `home.ts` because the majority of Stripe API processing is located there. First, you need to do a `declare`, as illustrated, because `Stripe` is a global object that was included in the `index.html`:

```
declare var Stripe: any;
```

If you don't do a `declare`, the app will still run but you will get an error from TypeScript.

When the user submits the form, it will trigger the following method:

```
onSubmit() {
  console.log(this.ngForm);
  Stripe.card.createToken({
    number: this.ngForm.cc, //'4242424242424242',
    cvc: this.ngForm.cvc, //'123',
    exp_month: this.ngForm.month, //12,
    exp_year: this.ngForm.year, //2017,
    amount: 2000
  }, (status, response) => this.stripeResponseHandler(status,
  response));
}
```

When you call `Stripe.card.createToken`, the Stripe object will trigger an API call in the background to `https://stripe.com/` with the JSON submitted. You may realize that this example does not use `ngModel` at all, but you can get the form values directly from within `ngForm`. This functionality is accomplished by the following code in your `home.html`:

```
<button type="button" ion-button bottom block
(click)="onSubmit()">Pay $20</button>
```

Once Stripe returns your token ID, it will call the following arrow function:

```
(status, response) => this.stripeResponseHandler(status, response)
```

The reason for using the arrow function here is because your code within the `stripeResponseHandler` method needs the `this` context of the `HomePage` class. This is a nice way to access the token variable. Observe the following code:

```
stripeResponseHandler(status, response) {

  if (response.error) {
    // Show the errors on the form
    console.log('error');
    console.log(response.error.message);
  } else {
    // response contains id and card, which contains additional
    card details
    this.token = response.id;
    // Insert the token into the form so it gets submitted to
    the server
    console.log('success');
    console.log('Sending token param:');
    console.log(this.token);
    this.nav.push(ThankyouPage, {token: this.token});
  }
}
```

The `response.id` will have your token ID from Stripe. Otherwise, you can handle the error using `response.error.message`. In this example, since it only passes the token ID to the next page, you can simply send it as a parameter `{token: this.token}`:

```
this.nav.push(ThankyouPage, {token: this.token});
```

In your `thankyou.ts`, you can access the parameter `token` using the following code:

```
this.params.get('token');
```

See also

- To understand more about Stripe API, you can check out the official documentation at `https://stripe.com/docs/stripe.js`
- There are more examples from other languages that you can experiment with at `https://stripe.com/docs/examples`

5
Adding Animation

In this chapter, we will cover the following tasks related to adding animation and interaction to the app:

- Embedding fullscreen inline video as background
- Creating physics-based animation using Dynamics.js
- Animating the slide component by binding gesture to animation state
- Adding background CSS animation to the login page

Introduction

User experience is crucial for the initial traction of users. When your early adopters use the app for the first time, they will have a better impression, which creates trust and increases retention. App animation will also provide interactive feedback for the users so that they know what to do or take action based on very gentle visual hints.

Native apps used to have an advantage over web-based hybrid apps because of animation performance. However, frameworks like Ionic and Angular have closed the gap in performance a lot in the recent years. Web animation is also easier to learn and code since many frontend developers are already familiar with JavaScript and CSS.

In this chapter, you will learn how to do basic animation using video and CSS. Then, you will start utilizing physics-based animation to create interesting interactivity. Moreover, you could even bind the gesture frame by frame so that your animation happens instantly during a swipe event.

Embedding full screen inline video as background

Today, there are many apps leveraging video as an animated background for the introduction screen. This makes the app more interesting and creative. The users feel that they are welcomed to the app. This tactic is great to impress new users and encourage them to come back.

This section will teach you how to add a video with autoplay in the background:

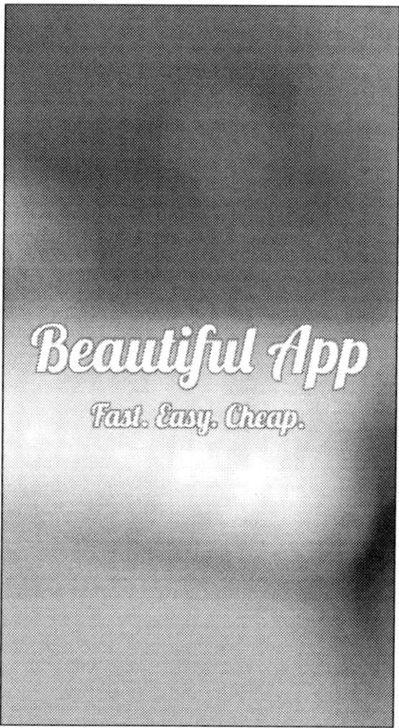

You will also learn how to use `animate.css` to add custom animation to the app header text.

Getting ready

This app example could work either in the browser or on a physical device. However, it's optional that you connect your physical device to verify that the animation is playing correctly in the background.

How to do it...

Here are the instructions:

1. Create a new `VideoIntro` app using the `blank` template, as shown, and go into the `VideoIntro` folder:

   ```
   $ ionic start VideoIntro blank --v2
   $ cd VideoIntro
   ```

2. You need to have your video ready at this point. However, for this example, let's download a free video from a public website that does not require a license. Navigate to `http://www.coverr.co`.
3. You can download any video. The example in this app uses the `Blurry-People.mp4` clip. Download it to your computer:

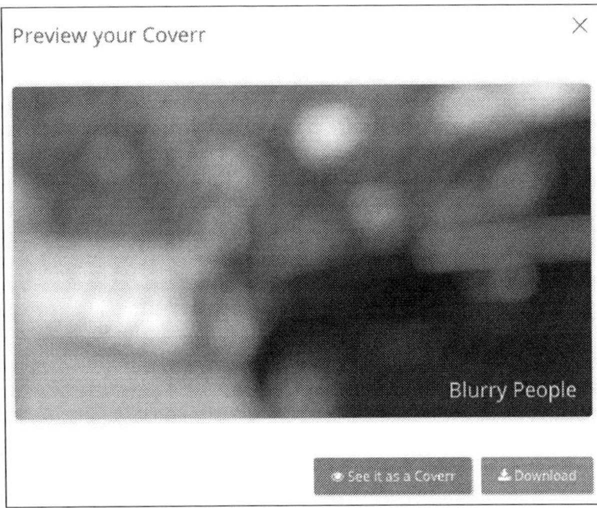

4. Save the videos in `./src/assets/`:

5. Open the `./src/index.html` file and replace the content with the following code:

```
<!DOCTYPE html>
<html lang="en" dir="ltr">
<head>
  <meta charset="UTF-8">
  <title>Ionic App</title>
  <meta name="viewport" content="width=device-width,
  initial-scale=1.0, minimum-scale=1.0, maximum-scale=1.0,
  user-scalable=no">
  <meta name="format-detection" content="telephone=no">
  <meta name="msapplication-tap-highlight" content="no">

  <link rel="icon" type="image/x-icon"
  href="assets/icon/favicon.ico">
  <link rel="manifest" href="manifest.json">
  <meta name="theme-color" content="#4e8ef7">

  <!-- Google Fonts -->
  <link href='https://fonts.googleapis.com/css?family=Lobster'
  rel='stylesheet' type='text/css'>

  <!-- cordova.js required for cordova apps -->
  <script src="cordova.js"></script>

  <!-- un-comment this code to enable service worker
  <script>
    if ('serviceWorker' in navigator) {
      navigator.serviceWorker.register('service-worker.js')
        .then(() => console.log('service worker installed'))
        .catch(err => console.log('Error', err));
    }
  </script>-->

  <link href="build/main.css" rel="stylesheet">
  <link rel="stylesheet"
  href="https://cdnjs.cloudflare.com/ajax/libs/
  animate.css/3.5.2/animate.min.css">

</head>
<body>

  <!-- Ionic's root component and where the app will
  load -->
```

```
    <ion-app></ion-app>

    <!-- The polyfills js is generated during the build
    process -->
    <script src="build/polyfills.js"></script>

    <!-- The bundle js is generated during the build
    process -->
    <script src="build/main.js"></script>

  </body>
  </html>
```

Basically, the main difference with the original `index.html` file is that you want to include the `Google Lobster` font for the heading text and `animate.css` for animation.

6. For the main template, you can modify the `./src/pages/home.html` file and replace it with the following code:

```
<ion-content class="home">
  <div class="fullscreen-bg">
    <video class="fullscreen-bg__video" autoplay loop
    muted webkit-playsinline>
      <source src="assets/Blurry-People.mp4"
      type='video/mp4; codecs="h.264"' >
      <source src="assets/Blurry-People.webm"
      type="video/webm">
    </video>
  </div>
  <div class="center animated zoomIn">
    <h1>Beautiful App</h1>
    <h2>Fast. Easy. Cheap.</h2>
  </div>
</ion-content>
```

   There are only two important items on this page: the video and the header with subheader.

7. Open and edit the `./src/pages/home/home.scss` file in the same folder using the following code:

```
.home {
  font-family: 'Lobster', cursive;
  color: white;
```

```
    text-shadow: 1px 0 0 gray, -1px 0 0 gray, 0 1px 0 gray,
    0 -1px 0 gray, 1px 1px gray, -1px -1px 0 gray, 1px -1px 0
    gray, -1px 1px 0 gray;

    h1 {
      font-size: 5rem;
    }

  }

  .fullscreen-bg {
    position: fixed;
    top: 0;
    right: 0;
    bottom: 0;
    left: 0;
    overflow: hidden;
    z-index: -100;
  }

  .fullscreen-bg__video {
    position: absolute;
    top: 0;
    left: 0;
    height: 100%;
  }

  .center {
    top: 50%;
    transform: translateY(-50%);
    position: absolute !important;
    text-align: center;
    width:100%;
  }
```

All animation is done using CSS; thus, you don't need to write any code for the JavaScript file.

8. Open the `config.xml` file and add the following line within the `<widget>` tag:

```
<preference name="AllowInlineMediaPlayback" value="true"/>
```

9. Go to your terminal and run the app with the following command:

```
$ ionic serve
```

How it works...

Let's start with the `home.html` file because that is the only page where you added the animation:

```
<video class="fullscreen-bg__video" autoplay loop muted
webkit-playsinline>
  <source src="assets/Blurry-People.mp4"
  type='video/mp4; codecs="h.264"' >
  <source src="assets/Blurry-People.webm" type="video/webm">
</video>
```

This is just a typical `<video>` tag in HTML5. However, there is a new attribute, called `webkit-playsinline`. This means that you want the video to play where it is on the HTML page and not open it up fullscreen with the play control. The reason is that you want this video to play in the background, while you can animate text on top of it. This is the reason you need to enable this feature by setting `AllowInlineMediaPlayback` in `config.xml`.

The second item in this template is your header and subheader:

```
<div class="center animated zoomIn">
  <h1>Beautiful App</h1>
  <h2>Fast. Easy. Cheap.</h2>
</div>
```

Note that there are `animated` and `zoomIn` classes included. These are the required classes for `animate.css` to kick in. If you run the app, you will see the text starting to appear from a smaller size to a bigger size (that is, a zoom-in effect).

The `home.scss` file is important because it has a lot of animation logic. Let's take a look at the header text first:

```
.home {
  font-family: 'Lobster', cursive;
  color: white;
  text-shadow: 1px 0 0 gray, -1px 0 0 gray, 0 1px 0 gray,
  0 -1px 0 gray, 1px 1px gray, -1px -1px 0 gray, 1px -1px
  0 gray, -1px 1px 0 gray;

  h1 {
    font-size: 5rem;
  }

}
```

One interesting thing here is the use of the `text-shadow` attribute. This is because you want to create a thin border line around the text so that your white text can be easily seen on top of a light background.

To set the video to fullscreen, you need it to have a negative index so that it's below the other layers. Also, the height must be 100%. This is shown as follows:

```
.fullscreen-bg {
  position: fixed;
  top: 0;
  right: 0;
  bottom: 0;
  left: 0;
  overflow: hidden;
  z-index: -100;
}

.fullscreen-bg__video {
  position: absolute;
  top: 0;
  left: 0;
  height: 100%;
}
```

Finally, in order to position the text vertically in the center, you have to create this class:

```
.center {
  top: 50%;
  transform: translateY(-50%);
  position: absolute !important;
  text-align: center;
  width:100%;
}
```

The `center` class forces the element to have top of 50% but then push the Y position -50% to reset the vertical pivot of the `<div>` tag in the middle area. You will rarely need to customize such classes; thus, it's good to keep the `center` class handy for future use.

Creating a physics-based animation using Dynamics.js

Using physics-based animations can make your app more interactive and lively, which helps attract and retain more users. There are many methods to add physics to your component animation. For example, you could even use the CSS `animation-timing` function to add property values, such as `ease-in`, `ease-out`, or `cubic-bezier`. However, it's easier and better to use an existing JavaScript-based physic animation. `Dynamics.js` is one of those JavaScripts that comes with utilities and performance. Using native CSS physic features is actually not a good practice as it comes with a frame-per-second penalty on mobile devices.

The app will show a bouncing button, which can show and hide a top quote box, as follows, it also uses physics animation:

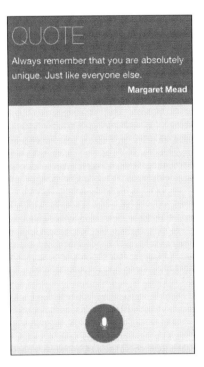

Getting ready

This app example could work either in a browser or on a physical device. However, it's recommended that you run the app via your physical device to test for performance.

How to do it...

Here are the instructions:

1. Open a terminal window, create a new `SpinningButton` app using the `blank` template, and go into the `SpinningButton` folder:

   ```
   $ ionic start SpinningButton blank --v2
   $ cd SpinningButton
   ```

2. Visit `http://dynamicsjs.com/` and download the `dynamics.min.js` file to your `./src/assets` folder, as follows:

   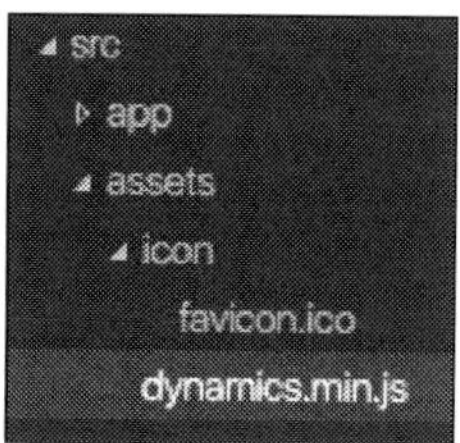

3. Open the `./src/index.html` file and replace the code with the following:

   ```
   <!DOCTYPE html>
   <html lang="en" dir="ltr">
   <head>
     <meta charset="UTF-8">
     <title>Ionic App</title>
     <meta name="viewport" content="width=device-width,
     initial-scale=1.0, minimum-scale=1.0, maximum-scale=1.0,
     user-scalable=no">
     <meta name="format-detection" content="telephone=no">
     <meta name="msapplication-tap-highlight" content="no">

     <link rel="icon" type="image/x-icon" href="assets/icon/favicon.
     ico">
     <link rel="manifest" href="manifest.json">
     <meta name="theme-color" content="#4e8ef7">

     <!-- cordova.js required for cordova apps -->
     <script src="assets/dynamics.min.js"></script>
     <script src="cordova.js"></script>

     <!-- un-comment this code to enable service worker
   ```

```
  <script>
    if ('serviceWorker' in navigator) {
      navigator.serviceWorker.register('service-worker.js')
        .then(() => console.log('service worker
        installed'))
        .catch(err => console.log('Error', err));
    }
  </script>-->

  <link href="build/main.css" rel="stylesheet">

</head>
<body>

  <!-- Ionic's root component and where the app will
  load -->
  <ion-app></ion-app>

  <!-- The polyfills js is generated during the build
  process -->
  <script src="build/polyfills.js"></script>

  <!-- The bundle js is generated during the build
  process -->
  <script src="build/main.js"></script>

</body>
</html>
```

The key part of this file is to ensure that `dynamics.min.js` is included.

4. Open and edit the `./src/pages/home/home.html` file to replace the content with the following:

```
<ion-content class="home">
  <div class="my-card" #myCard>
    <h1>QUOTE</h1>
    <p class="body">Always remember that you are
    absolutely unique. Just like everyone else.</p>
    <p class="name">Margaret Mead</p>
  </div>
</ion-content>

<ion-fab center bottom>
  <button ion-fab #thisEl (click)="animateMe(thisEl)">
```

```
    <ion-icon name="mic"></ion-icon>
  </button>
</ion-fab>
```

There is no need to have header navigation in this app because it will just be a single page.

5. Open the `home.ts` file for editing in the same folder as Step 2, with the following code:

```
import { Component, ViewChild } from '@angular/core';
import { NavController } from 'ionic-angular';
declare var dynamics: any;

@Component({
  selector: 'page-home',
  templateUrl: 'home.html'
})

export class HomePage {
  private isAnimating: Boolean = false;
  private isQuoteShown: Boolean = false;
  @ViewChild('myCard') myCard;

  constructor(public navCtrl: NavController) {
    console.log(dynamics);
  }

  animateMe(el) {

    if (!this.isAnimating) {
      this.isAnimating = true;

      dynamics.animate(el._elementRef.nativeElement, {
        translateY: -50
      }, {
        type: dynamics.bounce,
        duration: 1300,
        complete: () => {
          console.log('Done animating button.');
          this.isAnimating = false;
        }
      });

      if (!this.isQuoteShown) {
        dynamics.animate(this.myCard.nativeElement, {
```

```
          translateY: 0
        }, {
          type: dynamics.spring,
          duration: 1300,
          complete: () => {
            console.log('Done animating drop down.');
            this.isAnimating = false;
          }
        });

        this.isQuoteShown = true;
      } else {
        dynamics.animate(this.myCard.nativeElement, {
          translateY: -150
        }, {
          type: dynamics.easeOut,
          duration: 900,
          friction: 50,
          complete: () => {
            console.log('Done animating drop down.');
            this.isAnimating = false;
          }
        });

        this.isQuoteShown = false;
      }

    }
  }

}
```

Note that you must import the `dynamics` object in this file.

6. Modify the `home.scss` stylesheet, as follows:

```
ion-content.home {
  background-color: #ecf0f1;
}

.my-card {
  color: white;
  transform: translate(0,-150px);
  background: #9b59b6;
  height: 150px;
```

```
    padding: 10px;

    h1 {
      font-size: 4rem;
      font-weight: 100;
      margin: 0;
    }

    p {
      color: white;
    }

    p.body {
      font-size: 16px;
      line-height: 1.5em;
      margin-bottom: 0;
      margin-top: 5px;
    }

    p.name {
      font-size: 14px;
      font-weight: bold;
      text-align: right;
      margin-top: 5px;
    }
  }
```

7. Go to your terminal and run the app with the following command:

```
$ ionic serve
```

How it works...

The main concept behind the physics animation in this app is the `dynamics.animate` method from the `Dynamics.js` library. Let's start with the button in the template, as shown:

```
<ion-fab center bottom>
  <button ion-fab #thisEl (click)="animateMe(thisEl)">
    <ion-icon name="mic"></ion-icon>
  </button>
</ion-fab>
```

This is your floating button that you can click to create a nice bouncing effect by calling the `animateMe()` method.

To learn more about Ionic 2's floating button, you can refer to the Ionic documentation at http://ionicframework.com/docs/v2/components/#floating-action-buttons.

The simple logic here is as follows:

- If the button is animated, `isAnimating` must be `True`. Once it's `True`, any additional click will not trigger the animation since we don't want the physics to kick in multiple times.
- If the top quote bar is displayed, `isQuoteShown` must be `True`. Otherwise, it will call a different animation to hide it.

You can pass many options in the `dynamics.animate` method. For example, the button will use `dynamics.bounce` as the type; thus, it will bounce up and down on each click. You can also specify the duration to be applied to the animation process itself. After the animation is done, it will trigger the callback in the `complete` function, as illustrated:

```
dynamics.animate(el._elementRef.nativeElement, {
  translateY: -50
}, {
  type: dynamics.bounce,
  duration: 1300,
  complete: () => {
    console.log('Done animating button.');
    this.isAnimating = false;
  }
});
```

An important thing to keep in mind is that `Dynamics.js` must refer to the DOM JavaScript object itself and not the DOM node or Ionic object. That's why you have to use `el._elementRef.nativeElement` to point to the native element object instead.

For the quote box, it creates a local variable, called `myCard`, in the template, as shown:

```
<div class="my-card" #myCard>
  <h1>QUOTE</h1>
  <p class="body">Always remember that you are absolutely unique.
  Just like everyone else.</p>
  <p class="name">Margaret Mead</p>
</div>
```

You must refer to this variable using the `ViewChild` decorator, as shown, so that `@Page` knows to include it as a dependency:

```
@ViewChild('myCard') myCard;
```

See also

- If you are interested in learning more about native CSS physics-based animation, visit `https://developer.mozilla.org/en-US/docs/Web/CSS/animation-timing-function`.

Animating the slide component by binding a gesture to the animation state

Another way to get a *wow* experience from users is to have great-looking introduction slides. A typical app would have three to five slides to describe what the app does and how it will benefit the users. Today, many apps even add videos or interactive screens so that the users can get a *feel* for how the app may work. Such an interactive animation will require some internal development to bind touch gestures to the animation state. Animating based on a specific state is very difficult because you really have to get granular gesture data. On the other hand, it's a lot easier to just animate at the beginning or ending of a state. For example, you could animate an object inside a slide when the slide completely shows up on the screen after a left swipe. However, this animation effect is not as interesting or attractive as binding the animation during the touch movement.

The app you will build in this section will have three slides that will animate when you swipe left or right:

You will see fade in and fade out animation effects between slides. The following Angular logo also moves up when you swipe left from the second slide:

Getting ready

There is no need to test the app in a physical device because the animation is done via HTML and JavaScript. However, it's recommended to test the app in your device to evaluate to animation performance.

How to do it...

Here are the instructions:

1. Create a new `SliderAnimation` app using the `blank` template, as follows, and go to the `SliderAnimation` folder:

   ```
   $ ionic start SliderAnimation blank --v2
   $ cd SliderAnimation
   ```

2. Open the `./src/pages/home/home.html` file and modify its content with the following code:

   ```
   <ion-content class="home">
     <div class="slides-float">

       <div class="slide-float" #slidefloat1>
   ```

```
      <ion-icon name="ios-ionic"></ion-icon>
      <h1>Ionic 2</h1>
    </div>

    <div class="slide-float" #slidefloat2>
      <ion-icon name="logo-angular"></ion-icon>
      <h1>Angular 2</h1>
    </div>

    <div class="slide-float" #slidefloat3>
      <ion-icon name="logo-javascript"></ion-icon>
      <h1>Both</h1>
    </div>

  </div>

  <ion-slides #myslides pager (ionDrag)="onMove()">

    <ion-slide>
      <h2>is Beautiful</h2>
    </ion-slide>

    <ion-slide>
      <h2>is Fast</h2>
    </ion-slide>

    <ion-slide>
      <h2>are Awesome</h2>
    </ion-slide>

  </ion-slides>
</ion-content>
```

This template mainly uses the `<ion-slides>` tag. However, there are some layers to float on top of the `<ion-slide>` tag in order to animate them separately.

3. After this, replace the content of `./src/pages/home/home.ts` with the following:

```
import { Component, ViewChild } from '@angular/core';
import { NavController } from 'ionic-angular';

@Component({
  selector: 'page-home',
  templateUrl: 'home.html'
})
```

```
export class HomePage {
  @ViewChild('myslides') myslides;
  @ViewChild('slidefloat1') slidefloat1;
  @ViewChild('slidefloat2') slidefloat2;
  @ViewChild('slidefloat3') slidefloat3;
  private rAf: any;
  private bindOnProgress: boolean = false;

  constructor(public navCtrl: NavController) {
    this.rAf = (function(){
      return  (window as any).requestAnimationFrame || (window as
      any).webkitRequestAnimationFrame || (window as
      any).mozRequestAnimationFrame ||
        function( callback ){
          window.setTimeout(callback, 1000 / 60);
        };
    })();
  }

  onMove() {
    if (!this.bindOnProgress) {
      this.bindOnProgress = true;

      this.myslides.slider.on('onProgress', (swiper,
      progress) => {

        // (0, 1) - (0.25, 0) ==> (0-1)/(0.25-0) => -1/0.25
        * x + 1
        let firstQuarter = () => {
          let slidefloat1Opacity = -1/0.25 * progress + 1;
          console.log('slidefloat1Opacity: ' +
          slidefloat1Opacity);
          this.slidefloat1.nativeElement.style.opacity =
          slidefloat1Opacity;
          this.slidefloat2.nativeElement.style.opacity = 0;
        }

        // (0.25, 0) - (0.5, 1) ==> (1-0)/(0.5-0.25) =>
        1/0.25 * x - 1 = 4*x - 1
        let secondQuarter = () => {
          let slidefloat2Opacity = 4 * progress - 1;
          console.log('slidefloat2Opacity: ' +
          slidefloat2Opacity);
          this.slidefloat2.nativeElement.style.opacity =
          slidefloat2Opacity;
          this.slidefloat2.nativeElement.style.transform =
          'translateY(0px)';
```

```
      this.slidefloat1.nativeElement.style.opacity = 0;
    }

    // (0.5, 0) - (0.75, -250) ==> (-250-0)/(0.75-0.5)
    = -250/0.25 => -1000*x + 500
    let thirdQuarter = () => {
      let slidefloat2transform = -1000 * progress +
      500;
      console.log('slidefloat2transform: ' +
      slidefloat2transform);
      this.slidefloat2.nativeElement.style.transform =
      'translateY(' + slidefloat2transform + 'px)';
      this.slidefloat3.nativeElement.style.opacity = 0;
    }

    // (0.75, 0) - (1, 1) ==> (1-0)/(1-0.75) => 1/0.25
    * x - 0.75*4 = 4*x - 3
    let fourthQuarter = () => {
      let slidefloat3Opacity = 4 * progress - 3;
      console.log('slidefloat3Opacity: ' +
      slidefloat3Opacity);
      this.slidefloat3.nativeElement.style.opacity =
      slidefloat3Opacity;
      this.slidefloat2.nativeElement.style.transform =
      'translateY(-250px)';
    }

    // Animate per quarter of the total 3 slides
    if (progress <= 0.25) {
      this.rAf(firstQuarter);
    } else if ((progress > 0.25) && (progress <= 0.5 )) {
      this.rAf(secondQuarter);
    } else if ((progress > 0.5) && (progress <= 0.75 )) {
      this.rAf(thirdQuarter);
    } else if ((progress > 0.75) && (progress <= 1 )) {
      this.rAf(fourthQuarter);
    }

  });

 }

}
}
```

Note that the comments are useful to calculate an animation formula for each object.

4. Edit `./app/pages/home/home.scss` with the following:

```
.slides-float {
  .slide-float {
    top: 0;
    position: fixed;
    width: 100%;
    margin-top: 20px;
  }
}

.home {
  background-color: DarkSlateBlue;

  h2 {
    font-size: 3rem;
  }

  ion-slide {
    color: white;
    background-color: transparent;
  }

  .slides-float {
    color: white;
    text-align: center;

    > .slide-float:nth-child(2), > .slide-float:nth-
    child(3) {
      opacity: 0;
    }
  }

  .slide-float {
    ion-icon {
      font-size: 150px;
    }

    h1 {
      font-weight: lighter;
      font-size: 60px;
      margin-top: 0;
    }
  }
}
```

5. Go to your Terminal and run the app with the following command:

```
$ ionic serve
```

How it works...

This is the general process for animation:

1. Since there are three slides, the user has to swipe twice to reach the end. This means that the first swipe will be at 50% progress.
2. When a user swipes left to 25%, the Ionic logo will fade out.
3. When a user swipes to 50%, the Angular logo will fade in for the second slide.
4. When a user swipes to 75%, the Angular logo will move up to disappear instead of fading out.
5. Finally, in the last 75% to 100%, the JavaScript logo will fade in.

You probably noted that the amount of fade or movement will depend on the progress percentage. Thus, if you swipe left and right a little bit, you can see the animation responding to the gesture right away. There are two *layers* in the template. The *floating* static layer, as illustrated, must be on top and it must stay at the same position regardless of which slide is current:

```
<div class="slides-float">

  <div class="slide-float" #slidefloat1>
    <ion-icon name="ios-ionic"></ion-icon>
    <h1>Ionic 2</h1>
  </div>

  <div class="slide-float" #slidefloat2>
    <ion-icon name="logo-angular"></ion-icon>
    <h1>Angular 2</h1>
  </div>

  <div class="slide-float" #slidefloat3>
    <ion-icon name="logo-javascript"></ion-icon>
    <h1>Both</h1>
  </div>

</div>
```

The bottom layer is your typical `<ion-slides>`, as shown:

```
<ion-slides #myslides pager (ionDrag)="onMove()">

  <ion-slide>
    <h2>is Beautiful</h2>
  </ion-slide>

  <ion-slide>
    <h2>is Fast</h2>
  </ion-slide>

  <ion-slide>
    <h2>are Awesome</h2>
  </ion-slide>

</ion-slides>
```

When you swipe, it's actually moving `<ion-slide>`. However, it also triggers the `onMove()` method because you bind it with the `move` event. The `onMove()` method will access `#slidefloat1`, `#slidefloat2`, and `#slidefloat3` from the floating `<div>` layer. The `home.ts` file is where you have to animate these individual floating slides.

There are several variables that you need to declare in the `home.ts` file. You need to be able to access the `<ion-slides>` object in order to call the *native* Swiper methods:

```
@ViewChild('myslides') myslides;
```

According to the Ionic documentation, the `<ion-slides>` object is written based on the Swiper library at `http://ionicframework.com/docs/v2/api/components/slides/Slides/`.

You need to bind it with the swiping event natively in order to get the correct progress data.

The following three variables are necessary to access each floating slide:

```
@ViewChild('slidefloat1') slidefloat1;
@ViewChild('slidefloat2') slidefloat2;
@ViewChild('slidefloat3') slidefloat3;
```

You need to leverage `requestAnimationFrame`, as follows, for the best animation performance:

```
private rAf: any;
```

Otherwise, users will sense a *jerky* movement during a swipe because your animation is not at 60 FPS.

Lastly, you need to bind the swipe event only once; thus, it's necessary to have a Boolean toggle to detect the binding event:

```
private bindOnProgress: boolean = false;
```

The following code shows how to create a `requestAnimationFrame` object to call whichever function is to be rendered later:

```
this.rAf = (function(){
  return  (window as any).requestAnimationFrame || (window as
  any).webkitRequestAnimationFrame || (window as
  any).mozRequestAnimationFrame ||
    function( callback ){
      window.setTimeout(callback, 1000 / 60);
    };
})();
```

The `onMove()` method is where you put all the animation logic, which must bind with the `onProgress` event, as follows:

```
this.myslides.slider.on('onProgress', {})
```

First, let's take a look at the code at the bottom of `onMove()`, as shown:

```
if (progress <= 0.25) {
  this.rAf(firstQuarter);
} else if ((progress > 0.25) && (progress <= 0.5 )) {
  this.rAf(secondQuarter);
} else if ((progress > 0.5) && (progress <= 0.75 )) {
  this.rAf(thirdQuarter);
} else if ((progress > 0.75) && (progress <= 1 )) {
  this.rAf(fourthQuarter);
}
```

Basically, you want to have four quarters (or segments) of animation. When you swipe from slide 1 to slide 2, it will trigger the `firstQuarter` and `secondQuarter` methods. That is, you want to fade out the first floating slide and fade in the second floating slide at the end of the process. The concept is similar for the `thirdQuarter` and `fourthQuarter` methods. Note that you don't want to call the method directly but just pass the function reference inside `this.rAf` to have the rendering engine manage the frame rate. Otherwise, the rendered function may end up blocking other processes in the UI, which causes jerky movement.

For each of the quarters, you only have to change the `style` property, given a known **progress value**, as shown:

```
let firstQuarter = () => {
  let slidefloat1Opacity = -1/0.25 * progress + 1;
  console.log('slidefloat1Opacity: ' + slidefloat1Opacity);
  this.slidefloat1.nativeElement.style.opacity =
  slidefloat1Opacity;
  this.slidefloat2.nativeElement.style.opacity = 0;
}
```

It's important to use the arrow function here so that you can access the `this` context. You have to call `this.slidefloat2.nativeElement` to get to the `<div>` DOM object. It's really up to you to write your own math function to calculate the position or opacity during the slide movement with the progress value. In this example, the `slidefloat1Opacity` variable is just a linear function based on the `progress` input value.

The `secondQuarter` follows the same approach. However, the `thirdQuarter` uses the `transform` property instead of `opacity`, as illustrated:

```
let thirdQuarter = () => {
  let slidefloat2transform = -1000 * progress + 500;
  console.log('slidefloat2transform: ' + slidefloat2transform);
  this.slidefloat2.nativeElement.style.transform = 'translateY(' +
  slidefloat2transform + 'px)';
  this.slidefloat3.nativeElement.style.opacity = 0;
}
```

There are many ways to make a DOM object change its position. However, it's best to leverage the `transform` property instead of using the `left` and `top` properties. You want to achieve the highest Frame Per Second. In the `thirdQuarter` method, your `slidefloat2transform` will be calculated and it will update a new Y position using `translateY()`.

Note that you must use `this.bindOnProgress` to disable another event binding to `onProgress` because, for each swipe, it will continue to add more events.

See also

- To understand more about `requestAnimationFrame`, you can check out the official documentation at `https://developer.mozilla.org/en-US/docs/Web/API/window/requestAnimationFrame`
- The Swiper API is located at `http://idangero.us/swiper/api/`

- Ionic 2 has an official usage example at `http://ionicframework.com/docs/v2/components/#slides`
- Ionic 2 also provides a limited number of API for slides at `http://ionicframework.com/docs/v2/api/components/slides/Slides/`

Adding a background CSS animation to the login page

Animation can also be completely done in CSS. In many cases, you will probably run into some interesting demos online and would like to incorporate the CSS-only code for animation. If the animation is not as critical to the user experience, you could just use to add additional effects to the app. CSS animation is great because you don't have to write JavaScript code to manage the animation and just leave the browser to process it.

In this section, you will build an app to show some floating squares in the background of your login page, as shown:

Getting ready

There is no need to test in a physical device because CSS animation will work just fine in the Ionic app.

How to do it...

Here are the instructions:

1. Create a new `BubbleLogin` app using the `blank` template, as follows, and go to the `BubbleLogin` folder:

   ```
   $ ionic start BubbleLogin blank --v2
   ```

   ```
   $ cd BubbleLogin
   ```

2. Open the `./src/pages/home/home.html` file and modify the content with the following code:

   ```
   <ion-content #myContent class="home">
     <ul class="bg-bubbles">
       <li></li>
       <li></li>
       <li></li>
       <li></li>
       <li></li>
       <li></li>
       <li></li>
       <li></li>
       <li></li>
       <li></li>
     </ul>

     <ion-list>

       <ion-item>
         <ion-label>Username</ion-label>
         <ion-input type="text"></ion-input>
       </ion-item>

       <ion-item class="input-password">
         <ion-label>Password</ion-label>
         <ion-input type="password" ></ion-input>
       </ion-item>

     </ion-list>

     <div padding>
       <button ion-button block round color="secondary">LOGIN</
       button>
   ```

```
    </div>

    <p class="logo">
      <ion-icon name="ios-chatbubbles"></ion-icon>
    </p>
</ion-content>
```

The `bg-bubbles` class will convert a list of `<li>` into floating squares pieces.

3. Edit `./src/pages/home/home.scss` with the following:

```
.home {
  background-color: SeaGreen;

  .logo {
    margin: 0;
    color: white;
    font-size: 100px;
    text-align: center;
  }

  scroll-content {
    overflow-y: hidden;
  }

  .item {
    background-color: transparent;
  }

  .item-input ion-label, .item-select ion-label,
   input.text-input {
    color: white;
  }

  ion-list > .item:first-child {
    border-top: 0;
    border-bottom: 1px solid white;
  }

  ion-list > .item:first-child .item-inner {
    margin-right: 8px;
  }

  ion-list .item-inner {
    border-bottom: 0;
```

```
    }

    .input-password {
      border-bottom: 1px solid white!important;

      item-inner {
        border-bottom: 1px solid white;
        margin-right: 8px;
      }
    }

  }

  .bg-bubbles {
    position: absolute;
    top: 0;
    left: 0;
    width: 100%;
    height: 100%;

    z-index: 0;

    li {
      position: absolute;
      list-style: none;
      display: block;
      width: 40px;
      height: 40px;
      background-color: black;
      opacity: 0.2;
      bottom: -160px;

      -webkit-animation: square 25s infinite;
      animation:         square 25s infinite;

      -webkit-transition-timing-function: linear;
      transition-timing-function: linear;

      &:nth-child(1) {
        left: 10%;
      }

      &:nth-child(2) {
```

```
    left: 20%;

    width: 80px;
    height: 80px;

    animation-delay: 2s;
    animation-duration: 17s;
  }

  &:nth-child(3) {
    left: 25%;
    animation-delay: 4s;
  }

  &:nth-child(4) {
    left: 40%;
    width: 60px;
    height: 60px;

    animation-duration: 22s;

    background-color: black;
  }

  &:nth-child(5) {
    left: 70%;
  }

  &:nth-child(6) {
    left: 80%;
    width: 120px;
    height: 120px;

    animation-delay: 3s;
    background-color: black;
  }

  &:nth-child(7) {
    left: 32%;
    width: 160px;
    height: 160px;

    animation-delay: 7s;
```

```
        }

        &:nth-child(8) {
          left: 55%;
          width: 20px;
          height: 20px;

          animation-delay: 15s;
          animation-duration: 40s;
        }

        &:nth-child(9) {
          left: 25%;
          width: 10px;
          height: 10px;

          animation-delay: 2s;
          animation-duration: 40s;
          background-color: black;
        }

        &:nth-child(10) {
          left: 90%;
          width: 160px;
          height: 160px;

          animation-delay: 11s;
        }
      }
    }

    @-webkit-keyframes square {
      0%   { transform: translateY(0); }
      100% { transform: translateY(-700px) rotate(600deg); }
    }
    @keyframes square {
      0%   { transform: translateY(0); }
      100% { transform: translateY(-700px) rotate(600deg); }
       }
```

4. Go to your terminal and run the app with the following command:

```
$ ionic serve
```

How it works...

Since this app does not use JavaScript for animation, you will not need to modify anything in `home.ts`.

The CSS will drive the animation infinitely with the following code:

```
animation: square 25s infinite;
transition-timing-function: linear;
```

You will also be using two points in the `square` keyframe:

```
@keyframes square {
  0%   { transform: translateY(0); }
  100% { transform: translateY(-700px) rotate(600deg); }
}
```

So, for a 0% to 100% loop, it will move 700 px vertically and rotate 600 degrees in the duration.

The reason that each square has a different size and speed is because you can customize the CSS as per the `<li>` tag further. Consider the following example:

```
&:nth-child(2) {
  left: 20%;

  width: 80px;
  height: 80px;

  animation-delay: 2s;
  animation-duration: 17s;
}
```

Since this animation does not generate a random number of square objects and there are a limited number of objects, you could write a customization for each `<li>` tag in the CSS.

Note that you have to put the animation with `z-index: 0` because it will stay above other layers, such as form and button.

See also

- To understand more about CSS keyframes, you can check out the Mozilla documentation at `https://developer.mozilla.org/en-US/docs/Web/CSS/@keyframes`

6

User Authentication and Push Notification Using Ionic Cloud

In this chapter, we will cover the following tasks related to authenticating users and registering and receiving push notification messages:

- Registering and authenticating users using Ionic Cloud
- Building an iOS app to receive push notifications
- Building an Android app to receive push notifications

Introduction

Tracking and engaging users are key features necessary for your app to grow. That means you should be able to register and authenticate users. Once the users start using the app, you also need to segment the users so that you can customize their interactions. Then, you can send push notifications to encourage users to revisit the app.

There are three components that you need to use for your project, as follows:

- **Ionic Cloud**: This is a cloud service that helps save user information and coordinate push notifications between you, Apple, or Google and the end users' devices.
- **Ionic Cloud Angular module**: This is just an Angular module to import to your local project. It provides some simple utilities for your code to interface with Ionic Cloud. Otherwise, directly calling Ionic Cloud API would be very complex.
- **Cordova Push Notification and InAppBrowser**: Since your code is in JavaScript, you need to communicate with the device's native features, such as push notification.

Registering and authenticating users using Ionic Cloud

Ionic Cloud can provide all of the user management and authentication capabilities out of the box. The following providers are supported by Ionic Cloud:

- E-mail/password
- Custom authentication
- Facebook
- Google
- Twitter
- Instagram
- LinkedIn
- GitHub

Depending on the app, you may not need to use all of these authentication methods. For example, it would make more sense to use a LinkedIn authentication for an app focusing on a working professional to narrow down the audiences who fit the user profile of the app. If you have your own authentication server where you maintain your own user database, you can still use the custom authentication of Ionic Cloud to create a custom token.

This chapter will try to simplify the authentication concept as much as possible. You will learn how to do the following things:

- Register a new user
- Log in and logging out a user
- Change user profile data using custom fields

Observe the following screenshot of the app:

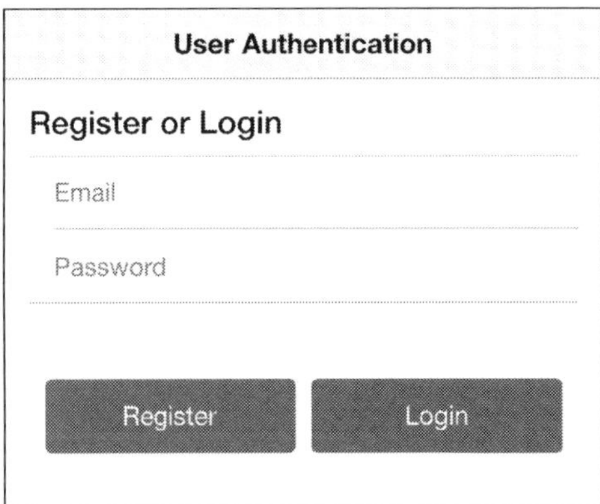

Getting ready

You can run this app via a browser. There is no need to test user authentication using a physical device.

How to do it...

Observe the following instructions:

1. Create a new `MySimpleAuth` app using the `blank` template, as shown, and go to the `MySimpleAuth` folder:

   ```
   $ ionic start MySimpleAuth blank --v2
   $ cd MySimpleAuth
   ```

2. Install Ionic Cloud Angular using the following command:

   ```
   $ npm install @ionic/cloud-angular --save
   ```

3. Initialize your Ionic Cloud setting so that an app ID can be created in your account, as follows:

   ```
   $ ionic io init
   ```

You will be prompted to log in to your Ionic Cloud account for this command line. The initialization process will save the `app_id` and `api_key` values to your project's `ionic.io.bundle.min.js`. This means you cannot change the project in your Ionic Cloud account after this (or you will have to manually remove the IDs and reinitialize). Your app ID is also recorded in the `ionic.config.json` file.

4. Log in to your Ionic Cloud at `https://apps.ionic.io`.
5. Identify the new app that you initialized and copy the app ID (that is, `7588ce26`), as shown in the following screenshot:

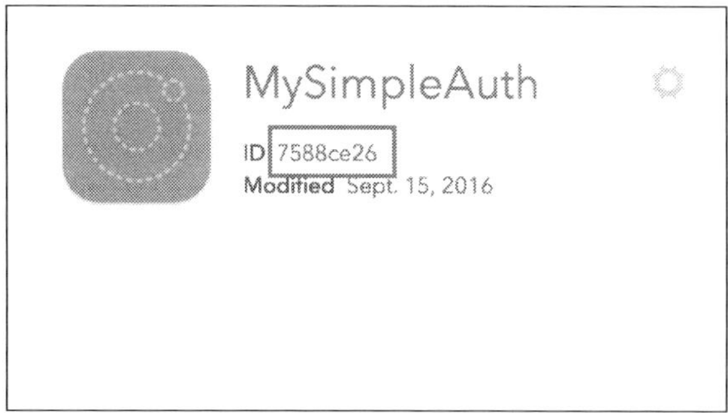

6. Open and edit `./src/app/app.module.ts` with the following code:

```
import { NgModule } from '@angular/core';
import { IonicApp, IonicModule } from 'ionic-angular';
import { CloudSettings, CloudModule } from '@ionic/cloud-angular';
import { MyApp } from './app.component';
import { HomePage } from '../pages/home/home';

const cloudSettings: CloudSettings = {
  'core': {
    'app_id': '288db316'
  }
};

@NgModule({
  declarations: [
    MyApp,
    HomePage
  ],
  imports: [
    IonicModule.forRoot(MyApp),
    CloudModule.forRoot(cloudSettings)
  ],
  bootstrap: [IonicApp],
  entryComponents: [
    MyApp,
    HomePage
  ],
  providers: []
})
export class AppModule {}
```

You need to ensure that the `app_id` has the correct value in your case.

7. Edit and replace ./src/pages/home/home.html with the following code:

```
<ion-header>
  <ion-navbar>
    <ion-title>
      User Authentication
    </ion-title>
  </ion-navbar>
```

```
</ion-header>

<ion-content padding>

  <div *ngIf="!auth.isAuthenticated()">

    <h4>
      Register or Login
    </h4>

    <ion-list>

      <ion-item>
        <ion-label fixed>Email</ion-label>
        <ion-input type="text" [(ngModel)]="email"></ion-
        input>
      </ion-item>

      <ion-item>
        <ion-label fixed>Password</ion-label>
        <ion-input type="password"
        [(ngModel)]="password"></ion-input>
      </ion-item>

    </ion-list>

    <ion-grid>
      <ion-row>
        <ion-col width-50>
          <button ion-button block
          (click)="register()">Register</button>
        </ion-col>
        <ion-col width-50>
          <button ion-button block
          (click)="login()">Login</button>
        </ion-col>
      </ion-row>
    </ion-grid>

  </div>

  <div *ngIf="auth.isAuthenticated()">

    <h4>
      User Profile
```

```
      </h4>

      <ion-list *ngIf="auth.isAuthenticated()">

        <ion-item>
          <ion-label fixed>Name</ion-label>
          <ion-input class="right" type="text"
          [(ngModel)]="name"></ion-input>
        </ion-item>

        <ion-item>
          <ion-label>Birthday</ion-label>
          <ion-datetime displayFormat="MM/DD/YYYY"
          [(ngModel)]="birthday"></ion-datetime>
        </ion-item>

      </ion-list>

      <ion-grid>
        <ion-row>
          <ion-col width-50>
            <button ion-button color="secondary" block
            (click)="save()">Save</button>
          </ion-col>
          <ion-col width-50>
            <button ion-button color="dark" block
            (click)="logout()">Logout</button>
          </ion-col>
        </ion-row>
      </ion-grid>

    </div>

  </ion-content>
```

These are just your basic `login` and `logout` templates. It's all in a single page to keep things simple.

8. Open and edit `./src/pages/home/home.ts` with the following code:

```
import { Component } from '@angular/core';
import { NavController, LoadingController, ToastController
} from 'ionic-angular';
```

```
import { Auth, User, UserDetails, IDetailedError } from
'@ionic/cloud-angular';

@Component({
  templateUrl: 'home.html'
})
export class HomePage {
  public email: string = "";
  public password: string = "";
  public name: string = "";
  public birthday: string = "";

  constructor(public navCtrl: NavController, public auth:
  Auth, public user: User, public loadingCtrl:
  LoadingController, public toastCtrl: ToastController) {
    this.initProfile();
  }

  private initProfile() {
    if (this.auth.isAuthenticated()) {
      this.name = this.user.get('name', '');
      this.birthday = this.user.get('birthday', '');
    }
  }

  register() {
    let details: UserDetails = {'email': this.email,
    'password': this.password};

    let loader = this.loadingCtrl.create({
      content: "Registering user..."
    });
    loader.present();

    this.auth.signup(details).then(() => {
      console.log('User is now registered');
      console.log(this.user);
      loader.dismiss();
      return this.auth.login('basic', {'email': this.email,
      'password': this.password});

    }, (err: IDetailedError<string[]>) => {
      loader.dismiss();

      for (let e of err.details) {
```

```
        if (e === 'conflict_email') {
          alert('Email already exists.');
        } else {
          alert('Error creating user.');
        }
      }
    });
  }

  login() {
    let details: UserDetails = {'email': this.email,
    'password': this.password};

    let loader = this.loadingCtrl.create({
      content: "Logging in user..."
    });
    loader.present();

    this.auth.login('basic', details).then((data) => {
      console.log('Finished login');
      this.initProfile();

      loader.dismiss();

      console.log(data);
      console.log(this.user);
    }, (err) => {
      loader.dismiss();
      alert('Login Error');
    } );
  }

  save() {
    let toast = this.toastCtrl.create({
      message: 'User profile was saved successfully',
      position: 'bottom',
      duration: 3000
    });
    toast.present();

    this.user.set('name', this.name);
    this.user.set('birthday', this.birthday);
    this.user.save();
```

```
    }

    logout() {
      this.auth.logout();
      this.email = '';
      this.password = '';
      this.name = '';
      this.birthday = '';
    }

  }
```

The preceding code provides four methods to register, save data, log in, and log out a user.

9. Finally, add a minor `input` field alignment in `./src/pages/home/home.scss`, as follows:

```
.home-page {
  ion-input.right > input {
    text-align: right;
  }
}
```

10. Go to your Terminal and run the app:

```
$ ionic serve
```

How it works...

In a nutshell, Ionic Cloud acts as a backend server for your app. It allows you to create a new user record in its database. Through the `user` class, you can interact with the Ionic Cloud authentication system. The first step is to register the user. This takes an **Email** and **Password** as shown in the following screenshot:

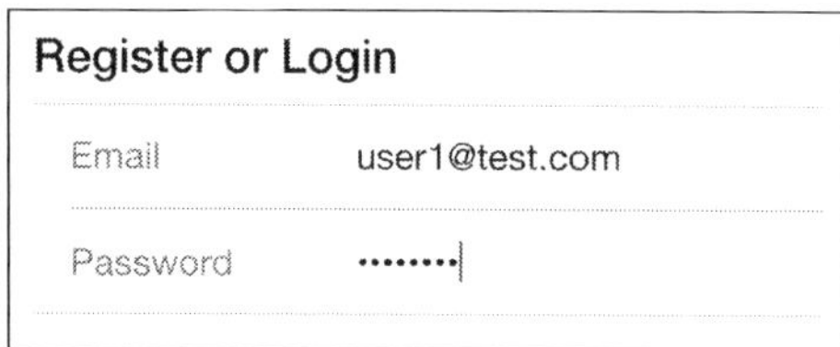

When you click on **Register**, the following code will be executed:

```
this.auth.signup(details).then(() => {
  console.log('User is now registered');
  console.log(this.user);
  loader.dismiss();
  return this.auth.login('basic', {'email': this.email,
  'password': this.password});
}
```

The `details` object has the e-mail and password from the form. Once it has successfully completed, it will automatically log in the user via `this.auth.login`.

Note that this piece of code here is just to show the loading screen to prevent the user from clicking on the Register button multiple times:

```
let loader = this.loadingCtrl.create({
  content: "Registering user..."
});
loader.present();
```

This example app only has **Name** and **Birthday** as custom user data, as illustrated in the following screenshot:

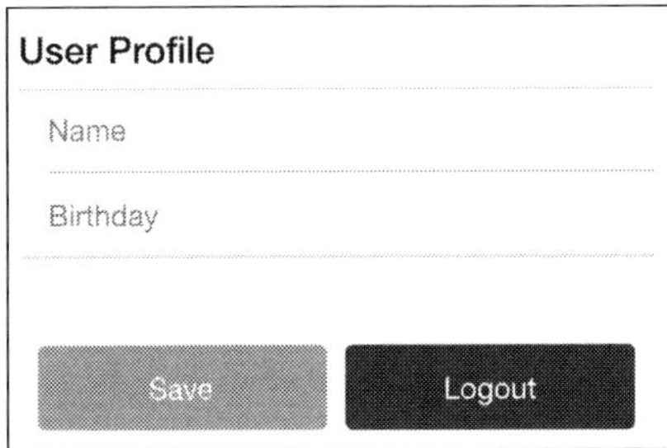

To save the **User Profile**, you call the `save()` method as shown in the following code:

```
save() {
  let toast = this.toastCtrl.create({
    message: 'User profile was saved successfully',
    position: 'bottom',
    duration: 3000
  });
  toast.present();

  this.user.set('name', this.name);
```

```
        this.user.set('birthday', this.birthday);
        this.user.save();
    }
```

If you look into the console log, the user token and custom data are also available, as shown in the following screenshot:

```
                                                                                          home.ts:66
▼Object {token: "eyJ0eXAiOiJKV1QiLCJhbGciOiJIUzI1NiJ9.eyJqdGkiOiIwN…TEifQ.7HqhtNd-8rE3WWUD1lfRgXiTyTW2i6MXMt8G77JMAJ8"}
    token: "eyJ0eXAiOiJKV1QiLCJhbGciOiJIUzI1NiJ9.eyJqdGkiOiIwNjUwMTliYS02ZjFhLTRlNDctOGU3Mi1hMTFiZDFlZWRkZTEifQ.7HqhtNd-8rE3WWUD1lfRgX
  ▶__proto__: Object
▼User {details: Object, social: Object, service: SingleUserService, fresh: false, _unset: Object…}        home.ts:67
  ▶_unset: Object
  ▼data: UserData
    ▼data: Object
       birthday: "2012-01-01"
       name: "Test User 1"
     ▶__proto__: Object
    ▶__proto__: Object
  ▶details: Object
   fresh: false
   id: "2f3b545d-1b3f-4738-92ff-23acfc3f9149"
  ▶service: SingleUserService
  ▶social: Object
  ▶__proto__: Object
```

You can also view the **UserData** in the Ionic Cloud portal. Log in to your account and navigate to your app's **Auth** menu.

Click on the **VIEW** button of the user you created, as shown in the following screenshot:

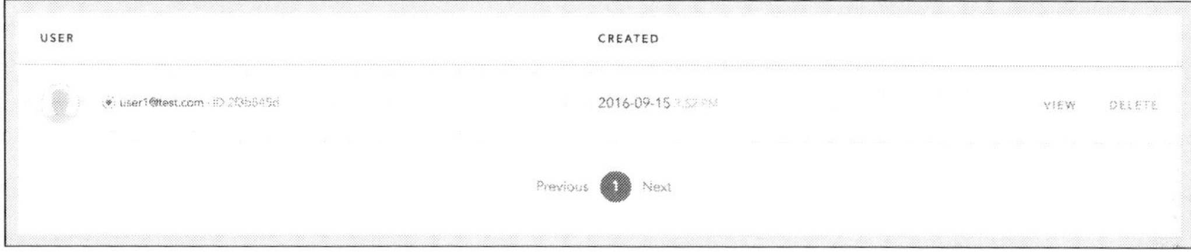

Select the **CUSTOM DATA** tab and you can see the same information stored for the user, as illustrated in the following screenshot:

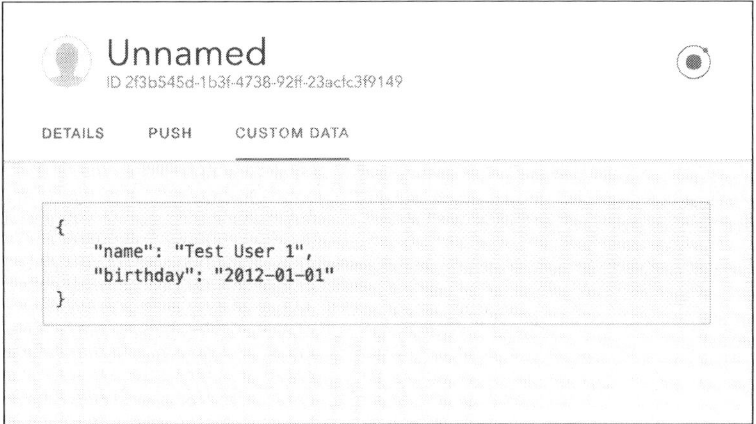

For more information about user authentication, you may want to refer the official Ionic documentation at `http://docs.ionic.io/services/users/`.

Building an iOS app to receive push notifications

Push notification is an important feature to engage users frequently, especially when the users are not using the app. Many people download an app but only open it a few times. If you send them a push notification message, it will encourage them to open the app to get involved in a new activity. Implementing push notifications is very complex if you have to build everything from scratch. However, Ionic makes it very simple by leveraging the Cordova Push Notification plugin and Ionic Cloud as the providers. A push notification provider is a server that can communicate with the **Apple Push Notification service** (**APNs**) or Google's **Firebase Cloud Messaging** (**FCM**). You can set up your own provider server using existing open sources, but you have to maintain this server separately and keep up with potential changes from the APN APIs.

In this section, you will learn how to do the following things:

- Set up Ionic Cloud for iOS Push Notification
- Configure iOS app, certificates (App and Push), and provisioning profile
- Write code to receive push notifications

The following is a screenshot of the app after receiving a couple of notification messages:

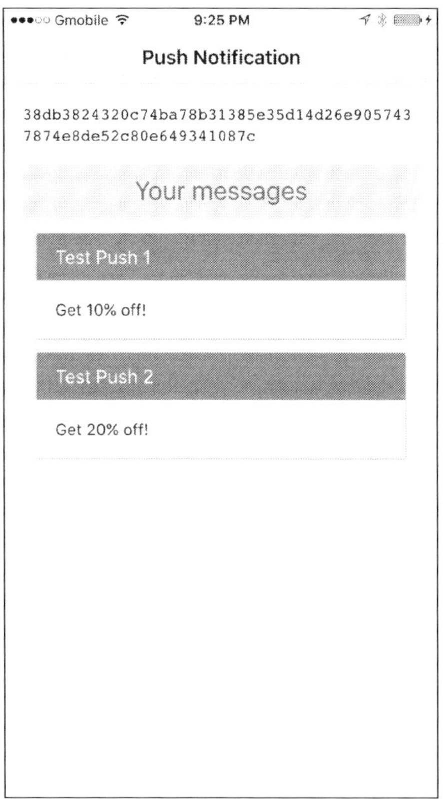

Getting ready

It's required to have a physical iOS device available in order to test for notification messages.

You must also register for the **Apple Developer Program** (**ADP**) in order to access `https://developer.apple.com` and `https://itunesconnect.apple.com` because these websites will require an approved account.

In addition, the following instructions use the specific version of these components:

- Mac OSX El Capitan 10.11.4
- Xcode 7.3.1
- Ionic CLI 2.1.8
- Cordova 6.4.0
- Node 6.8.1
- NPM 3.10.8

How to do it...

Observe the following instructions:

1. Create a new `MyiOSPush` app using the `blank` template, as shown, and go to the `MyiOSPush` folder:

   ```
   $ ionic start MyiOSPush blank --v2
   $ cd MyiOSPush
   ```

2. Install the Ionic `cloud-angular` client, which is a library to interact with the `push` object, as follows:

   ```
   $ npm install @ionic/cloud-angular --save
   ```

   You need to have Node version 4.x or later and NPM version 3.x or later.

3. Initialize your Ionic Cloud setting, as illustrated, so that an app ID can be created in your account:

   ```
   $ ionic io init
   ```

   You will be prompted to log in to your Ionic Cloud account for this command line. The initialization process will save the `app_id` and `api_key` values to your project's `ionic.io.bundle.min.js`. This means you cannot change the project in your Ionic Cloud account after this (or you will have to manually remove the IDs and reinitialize). Your app ID is also recorded in the `ionic.config.json` file.

4. You need to install the Cordova Push Notification plugin and provide some value as `SENDER_ID`. Since you are only using iOS Push Notification, you can just provide a fake value, temporarily, here, as shown in the following code:

   ```
   $ cordova plugin add phonegap-plugin-push --variable
   SENDER_ID=12341234 --save
   ```

5. Open your `./ionic.config.json` file in the project folder and copy the `app_id` value. In this case, the value is `00f293c4` from the following code:

   ```
   {
     "name": "MyiOSPush",
     "app_id": "00f293c4",
     "v2": true,
     "typescript": true
   }
   ```

6. Open and edit `./src/app/app.module.ts` with the following content:

```
import { NgModule } from '@angular/core';
import { IonicApp, IonicModule } from 'ionic-angular';
import { CloudSettings, CloudModule } from '@ionic/cloud-
angular';
import { MyApp } from './app.component';
import { HomePage } from '../pages/home/home';

const cloudSettings: CloudSettings = {
  'core': {
    'app_id': '00f293c4'
  },
  'push': {
    'sender_id': 'SENDER_ID',
    'pluginConfig': {
      'ios': {
        'badge': true,
        'sound': true
      },
      'android': {
        'iconColor': '#343434'
      }
    }
  }
};

@NgModule({
  declarations: [
    MyApp,
    HomePage
  ],
  imports: [
    IonicModule.forRoot(MyApp),
    CloudModule.forRoot(cloudSettings)
  ],
  bootstrap: [IonicApp],
  entryComponents: [
    MyApp,
    HomePage
  ],
  providers: []
})
export class AppModule {}
```

You must replace `'app_id': '00f293c4'` with your own app ID.

7. Visit the Apple Developer website at `https://developer.apple.com` and log in with your credentials.
8. Click on **Certificates, Identifiers & Profiles**, as illustrated in the following screenshot:

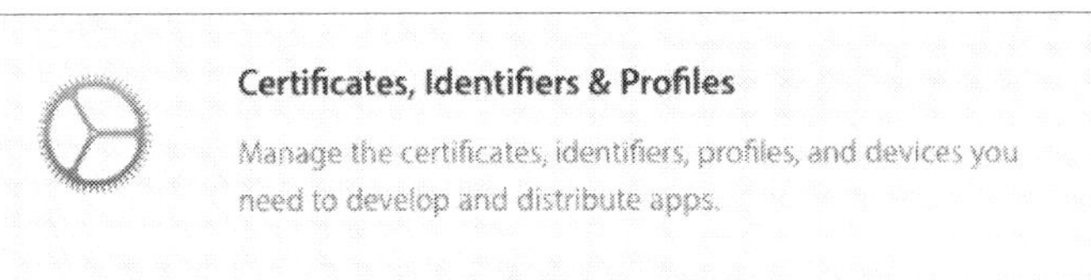

9. Select the correct device platform you are targeting. In this case, it will be **iOS, tvOS, watchOS** as shown in the following screenshot:

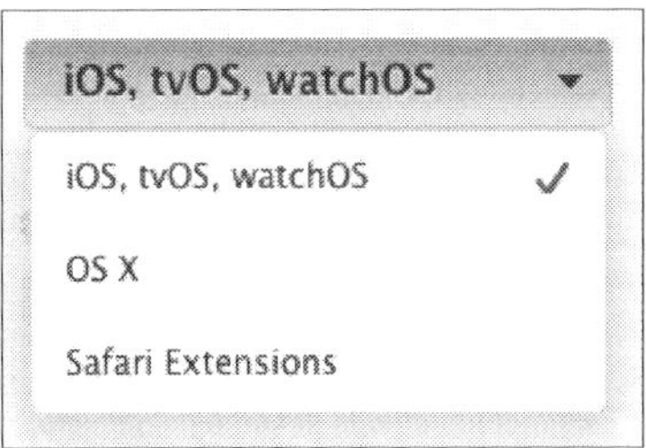

10. Navigate to **Identifiers** > **App IDs** to create an app ID, as illustrated in the following screenshot:

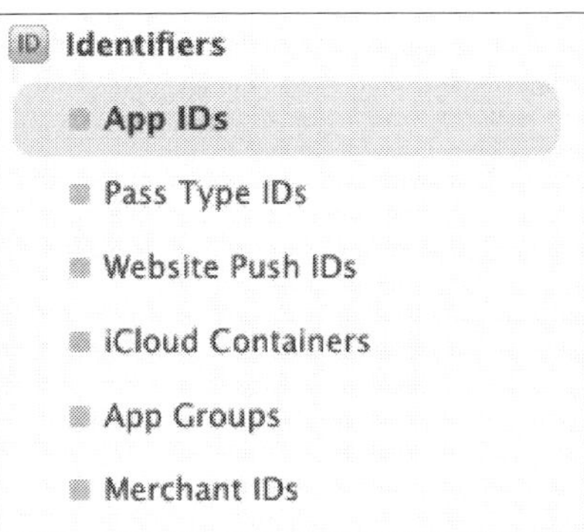

11. Click on the plus(**+**) button in the top right corner of the screen, as shown in the following screenshot:

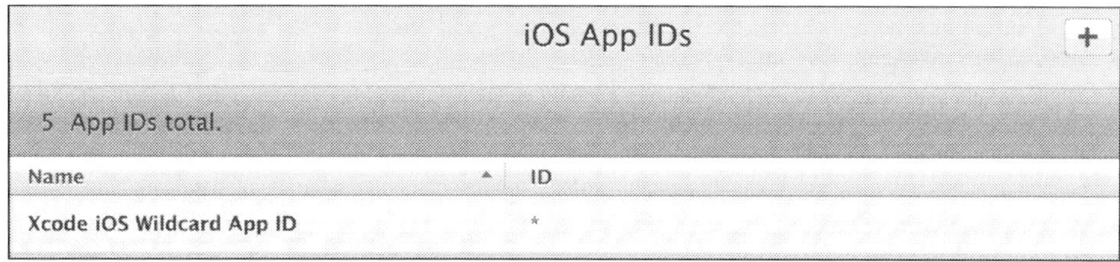

12. Fill in the form to register your **App ID**. The **Name** field could be anything and it's not the same Ionic Cloud's app ID. You can provide the name of your project (that is, `MyiOSPush`) to keep things simple, as shown:

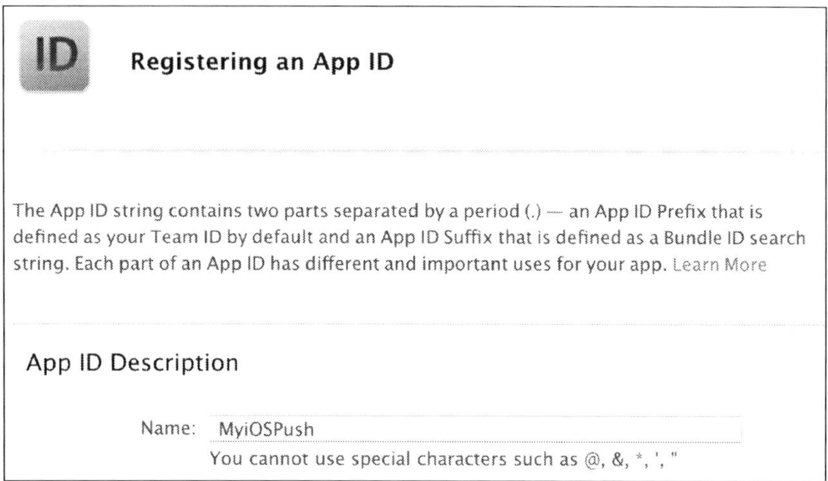

13. The important part that you need to do correctly here is the **Bundle ID** because it must match your bundle identifier in the `./config.xml` file or Xcode, as illustrated:

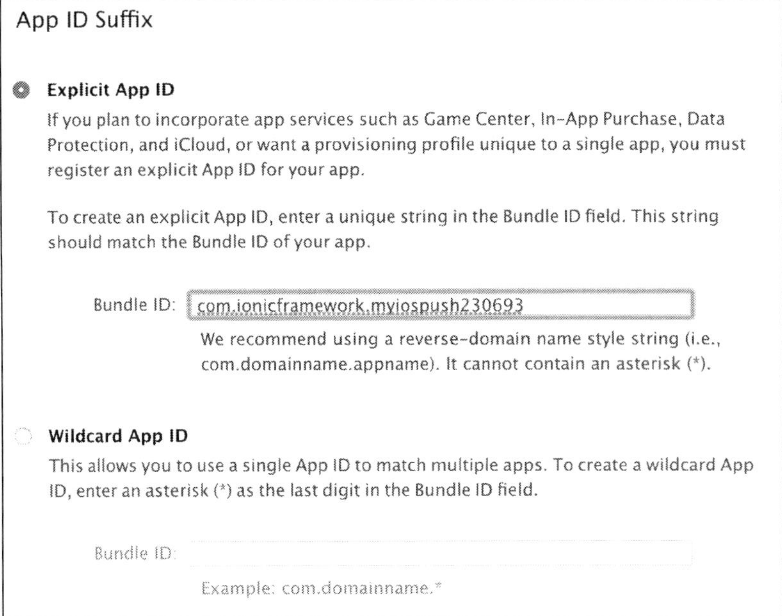

App ID Suffix
Explicit App ID
If you plan to incorporate app services such as Game Center, In-App Purchase, Data Protection, and iCloud, or want a provisioning profile unique to a single app, you must register an explicit App ID for your app.
To create an explicit App ID, enter a unique string in the Bundle ID field. This string should match the Bundle ID of your app.
Bundle ID:
com.ionicframework.myiospush230693
We recommend using a reverse-domain name style string (i.e., com.domainname.appname). It cannot contain an asterisk (*).
Wildcard App ID
This allows you to use a single App ID to match multiple apps. To create a wildcard App ID, enter an asterisk (*) as the last digit in the Bundle ID field.
Bundle ID:
Example: com.domainname.*

14. To enable push notifications, you need to check the **Push Notification** service on the following page:

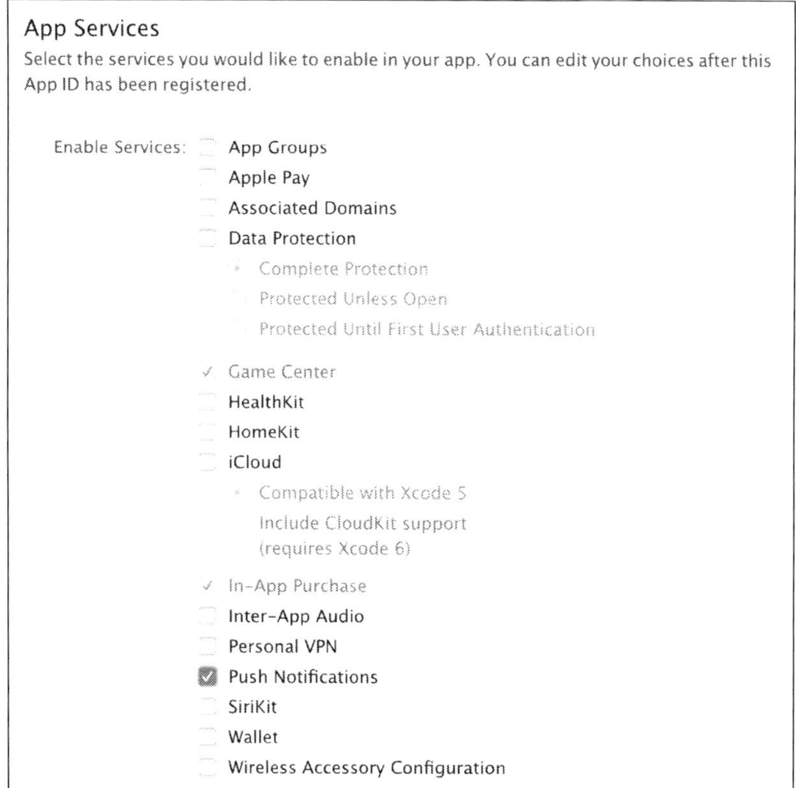

15. Select **Register**, as shown:

16. Select **Done** to complete the step to create **App ID**, as follows:

17. To start with certificate creation, you will need to generate a certificate signing request file locally on your Mac OSX using **Keychain Access**. Navigate to the **Keychain Access** top left menu and navigate to **Certificate Assistant** > **Request a Certificate From a Certificate Authority...**, as illustrated:

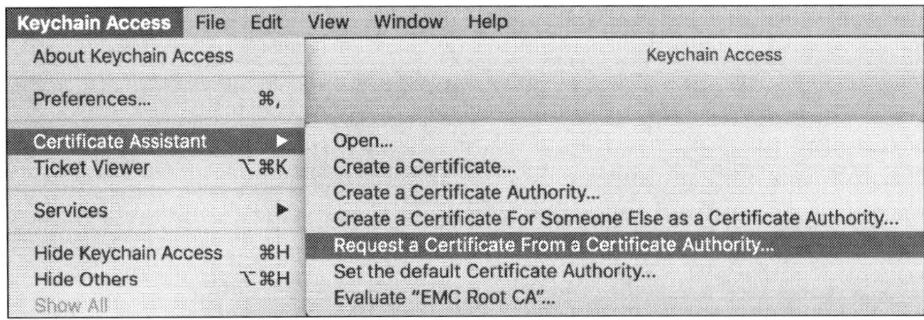

18. Enter your **User Email Address** and **Common Name**. Leave the **CA Email Address** field blank and check **Saved to disk**, as shown:

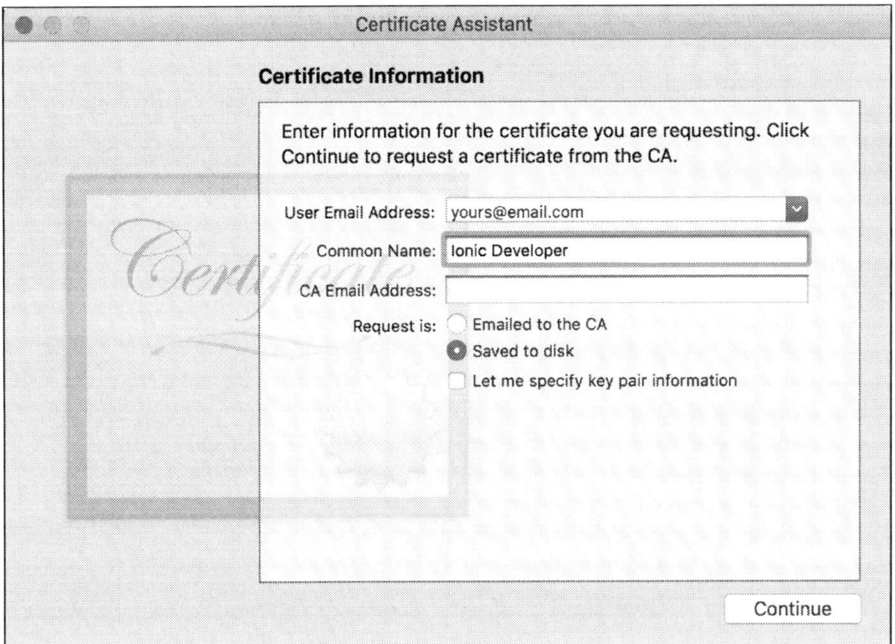

19. Save your `CertificateSigningRequest.certSigningRequest` file, as follows:

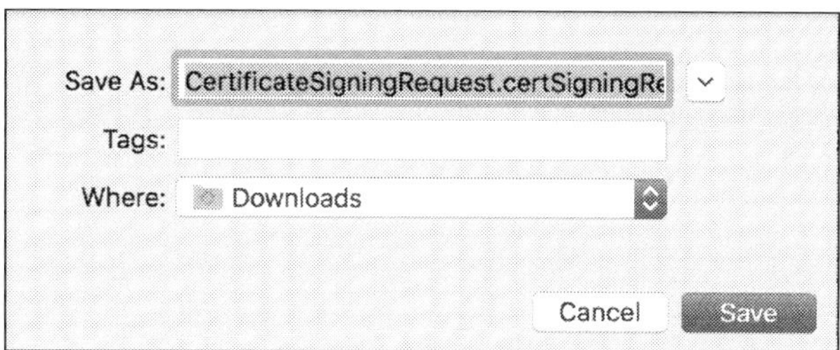

20. Navigate to the Apple Developer website and navigate to **Certificates** > **All**, as shown:

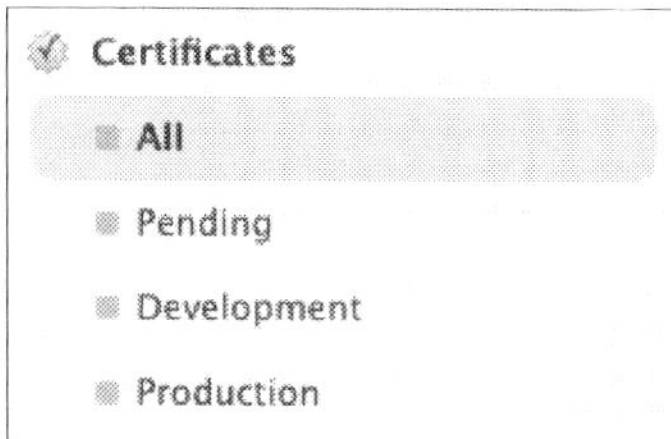

21. Click on the plus button in the top right corner to start creating a certificate, as follows:

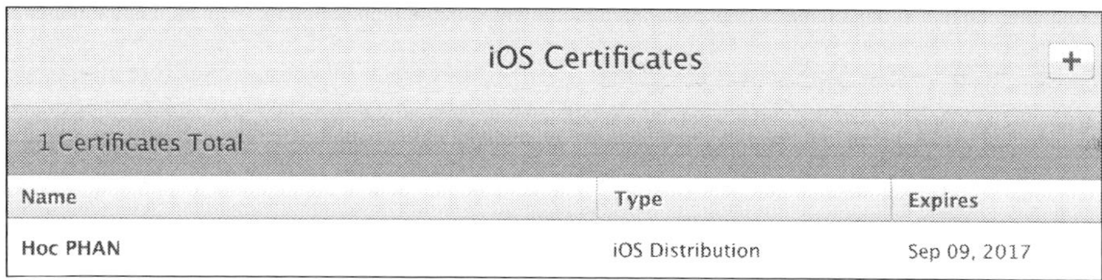

22. You just have to go through the steps on the website to fill out the necessary information. In this example, you will select the **Development** version instead of **Production**, as illustrated:

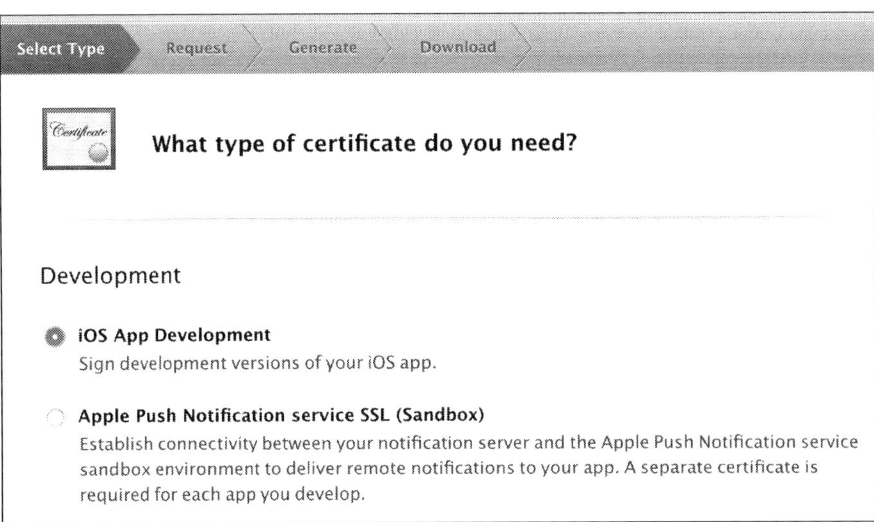

23. Click on the **Continue** button, as follows, to proceed:

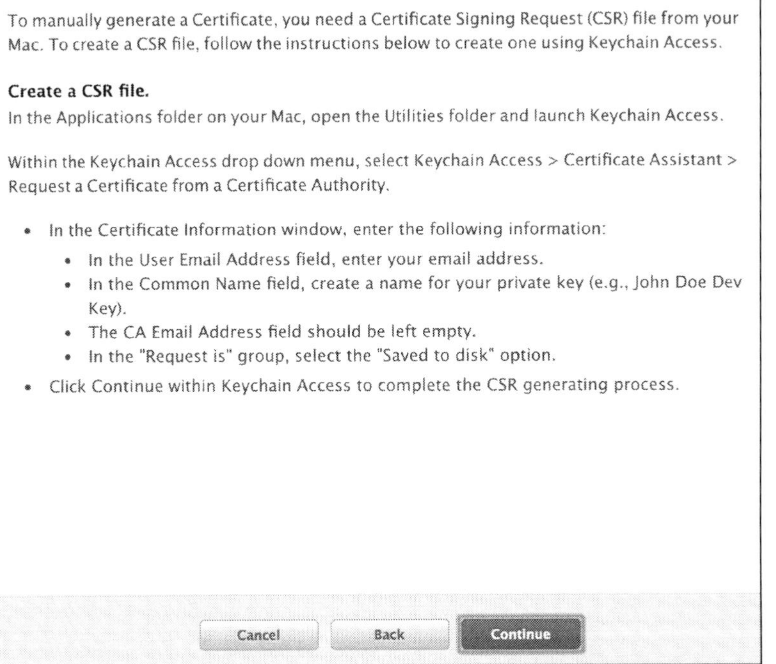

24. Click on the **Choose File...** button, as shown in the following screenshot, to upload your signing request file that you saved earlier:

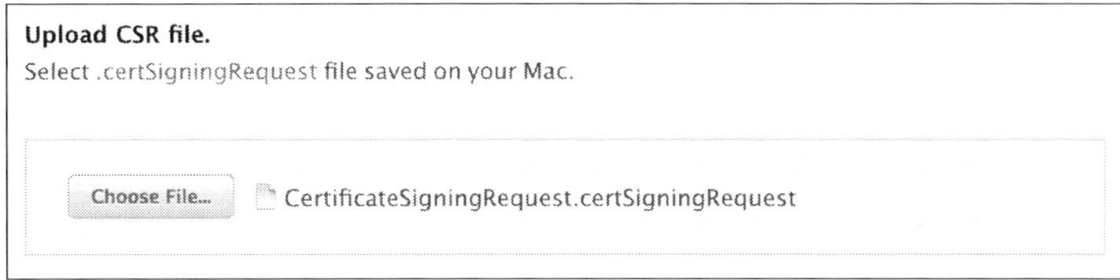

25. Click on the **Continue** button, as illustrated, to proceed:

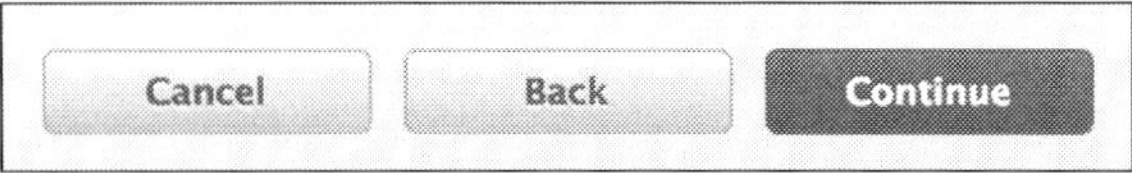

26. Click on the **Download** button to download your iOS Development certificate file:

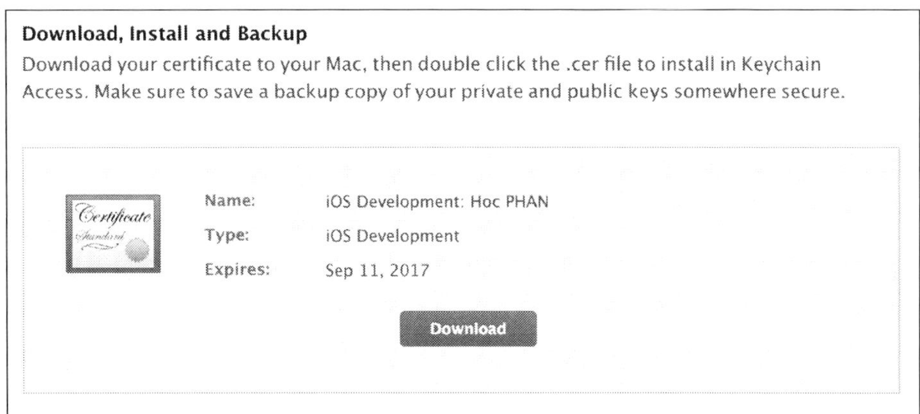

27. Click on the `.cer` file you downloaded, as shown, so that it can be imported to **Keychain Access**:

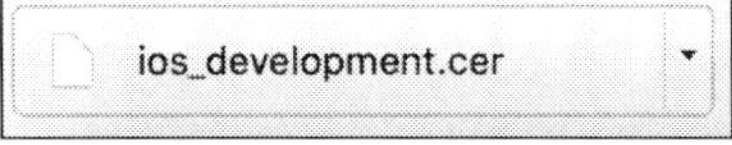

28. Locate your certificate in **Keychain Access** because you need to export this to the `.p12` file format. Ionic Cloud will need this file later in order to generate a push token and send push notifications to the app. Observe the following screenshot:

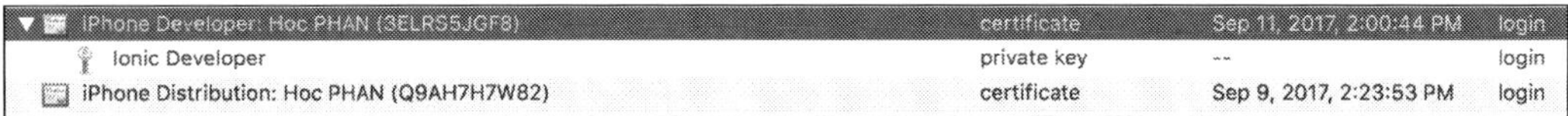

29. Right click and select **Export** from the drop-down menu:

30. Save your `Certificates.p12` file, as illustrated, so that you can import it to Ionic Cloud later:

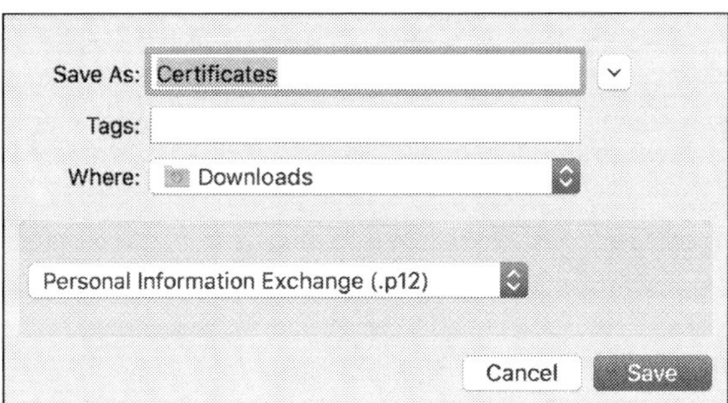

31. As illustrated in the following screenshot, provide a password to protect this file:

You must provide a password in this step although it's optional in **Keychain Access**. The reason is that Ionic Cloud cannot import a `.p12` file without a password.

32. If you need to push the app to a specific device, you must register the device. Go to **Devices** > **All**:

33. Click on the plus button:

34. Provide the device **UDID** and save to register the device. Observe the following screenshot:

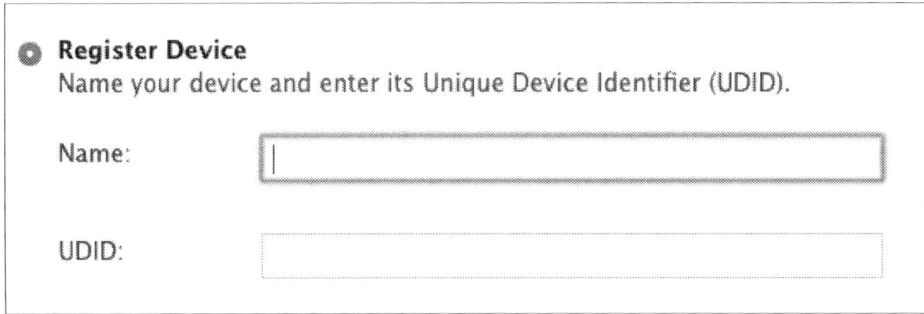

35. You'll need a provisioning profile. Navigate to **Provisioning Profiles** > **All**:

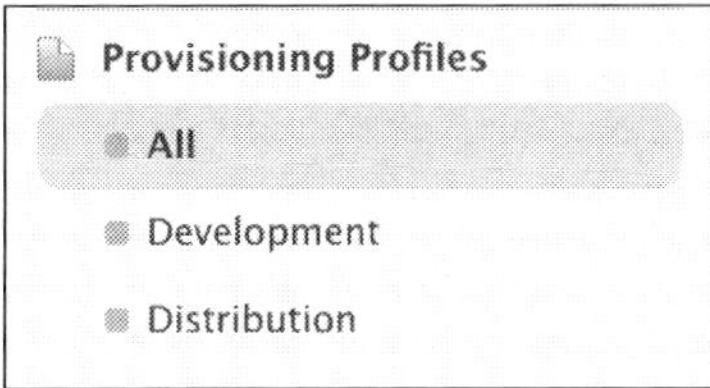

36. Click on the plus button:

37. Select **iOS App Development** as your provisioning profile since this example is for the development version only:

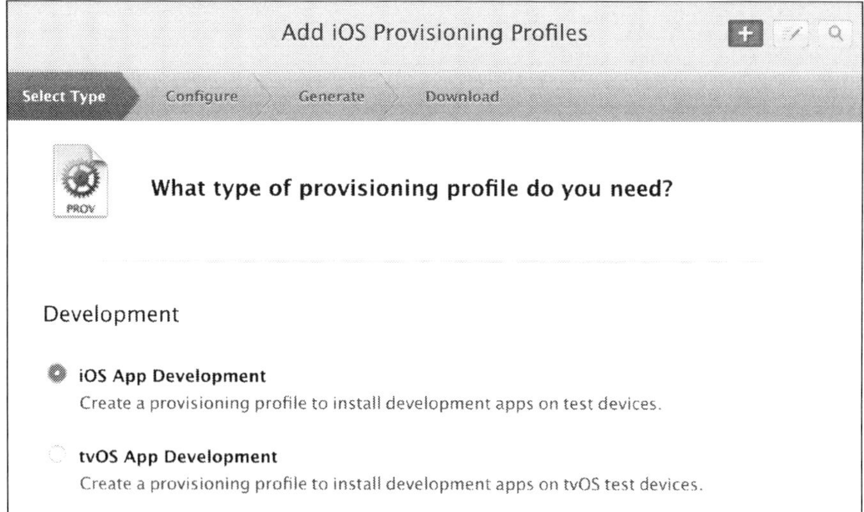

38. Click on the **Continue** button:

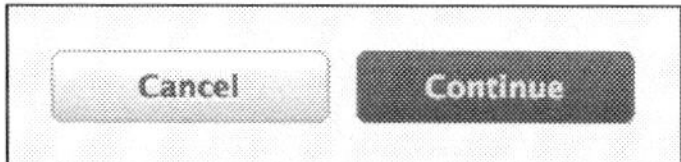

39. Select the correct **App ID** in the drop-down menu and save to finalize your provisioning profile creation:

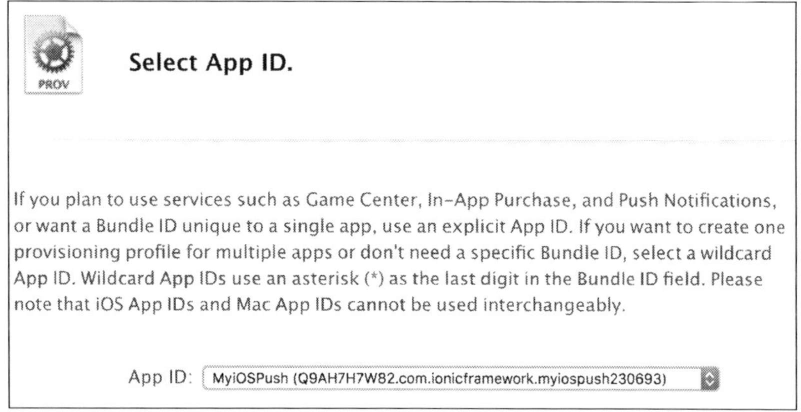

40. Click on the **Continue** button:

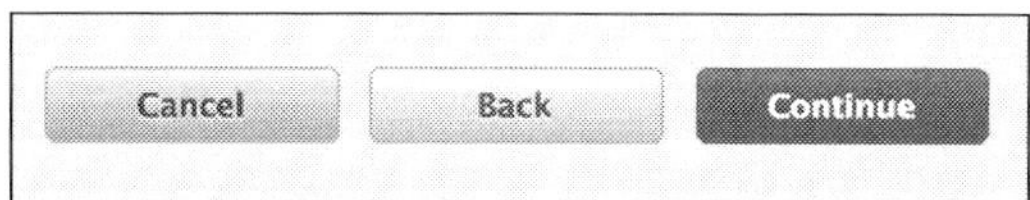

41. Select the iOS Development certificate you created earlier, as shown in the following screenshot:

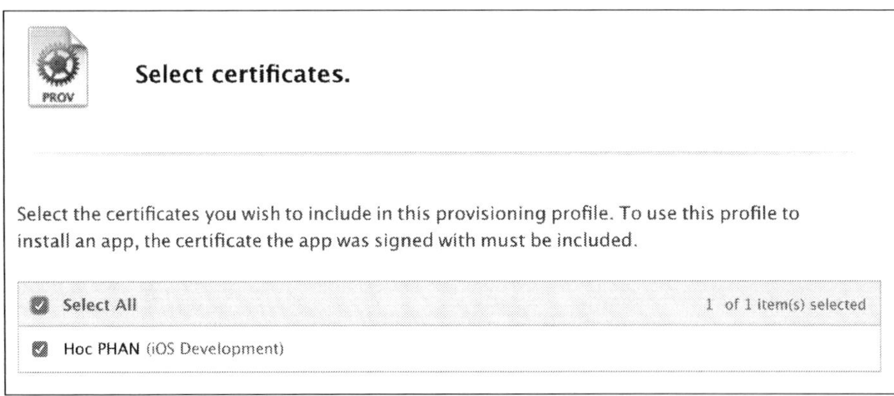
Select certificates.
Select the certificates you wish to include in this provisioning profile. To use this profile to install an app, the certificate the app was signed with must be included.
Select All
1 of 1 item(s) selected
Hoc PHAN (iOS Development)

42. As illustrated, select at least one device that you want to be able to install the app for testing:

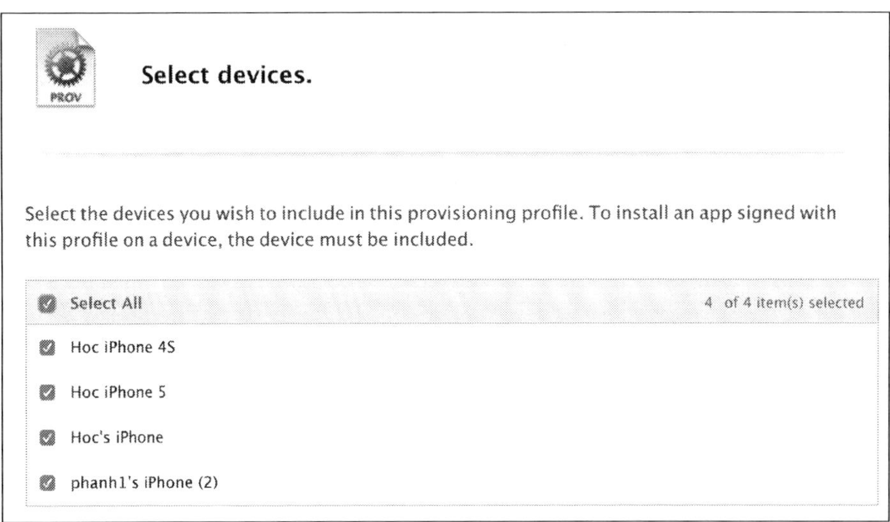
Select devices.
Select the devices you wish to include in this provisioning profile. To install an app signed with this profile on a device, the device must be included.
Select All
4 of 4 item(s) selected
Hoc iPhone 4S
Hoc iPhone 5
Hoc's iPhone
phanh1's iPhone (2)

43. Provide a **Profile Name** to your provisioning profile, as shown:

44. Click on the **Download** button to download the provisioning profile file (that is, `MyiOSPush_Provisioning_Profile.mobileprovision`):

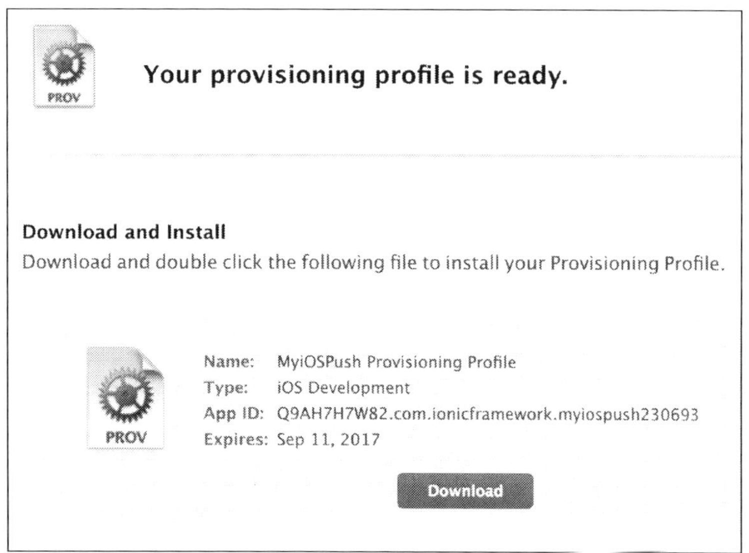

45. Click on `MyiOSPush_Provisioning_Profile.mobileprovision`, which you just downloaded, in order to import it into Xcode:

This step is very important because if you don't import it into Xcode, your app cannot be built successfully. If your app failed to build because of an invalid provisioning profile, it's best to check the provisioning profile status in the Developer console.

46. To enable the **Push Notification** feature, you must request a **Push Certificate**, which is different from the app certificate. Select the **App ID** that you created earlier (that is, `MyiOSPush`):

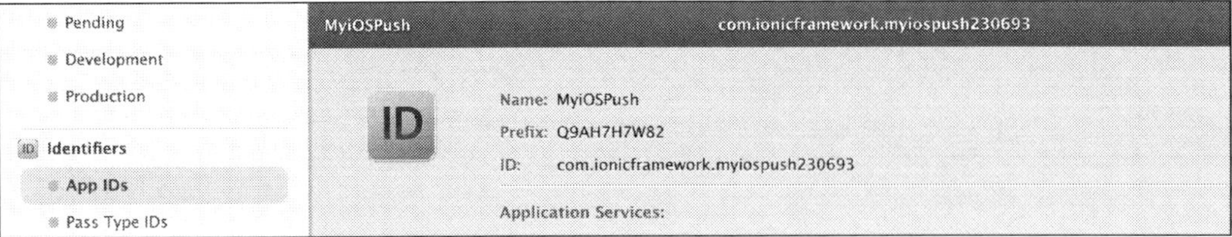

47. Click on the **Edit** button at the bottom of the page:

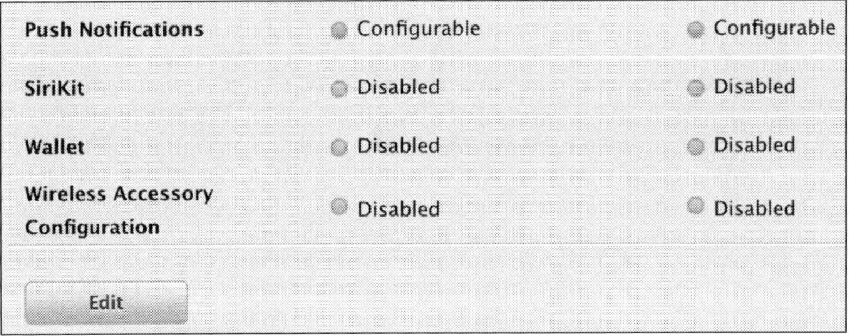

The **Push Notifications** must show the **Configurable** state. Otherwise, your app is not available for **Push Notifications**.

48. Click on the **Create Certificates...** button under the **Push Notifications** > **Development SSL Certificate** section:

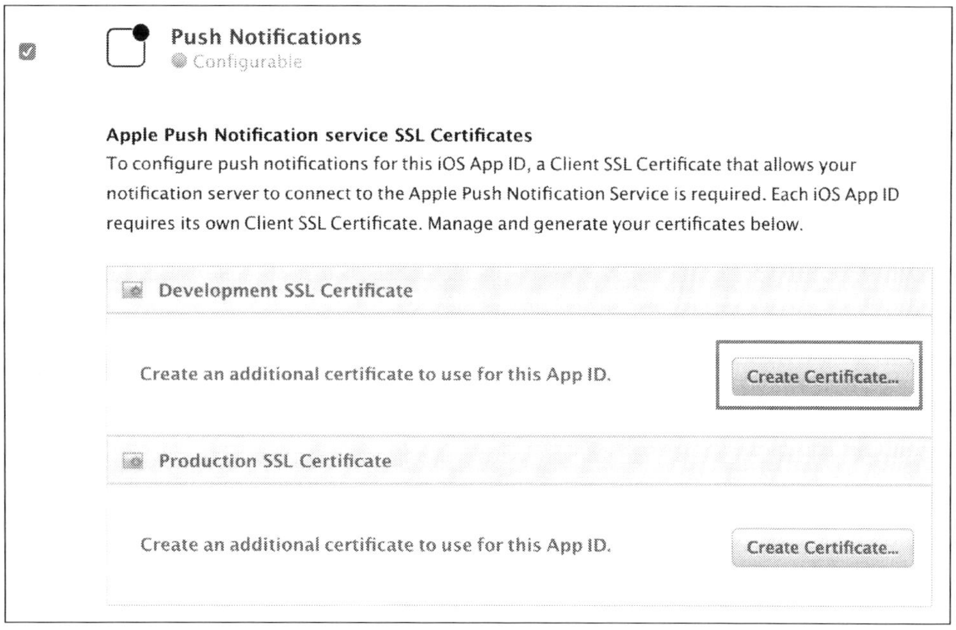

49. You will be taken to a new page to create your CSR file. Click on the **Continue** button:

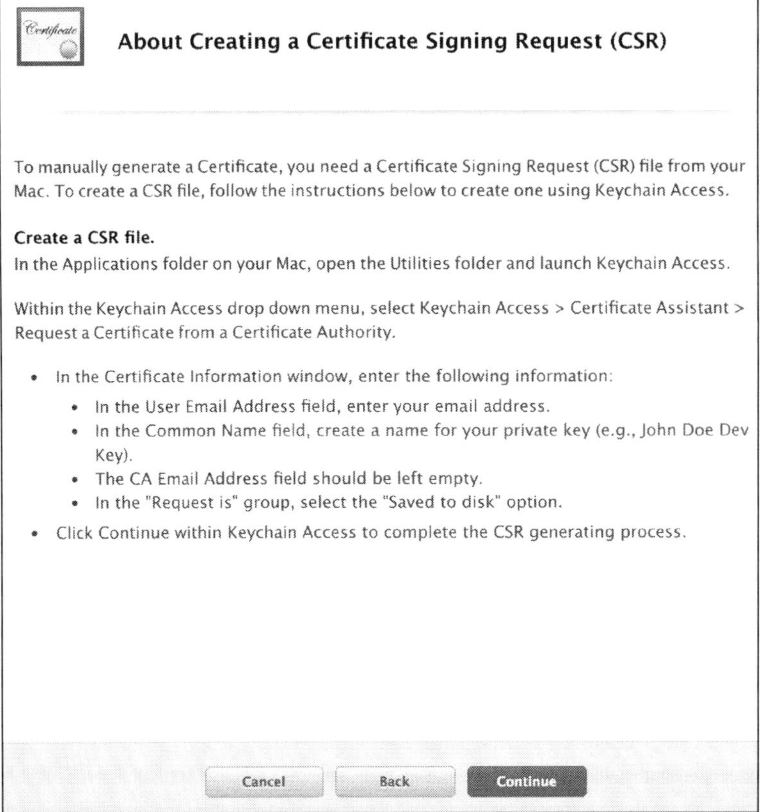

50. Click on the **Choose File...** button:

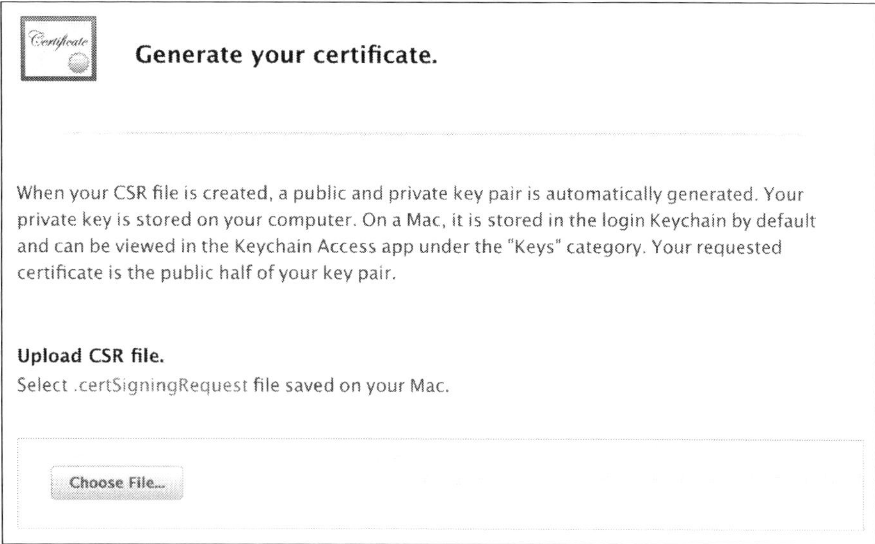

51. Locate the `CertificateSigningRequest.certSigningRequest` file that you created earlier:

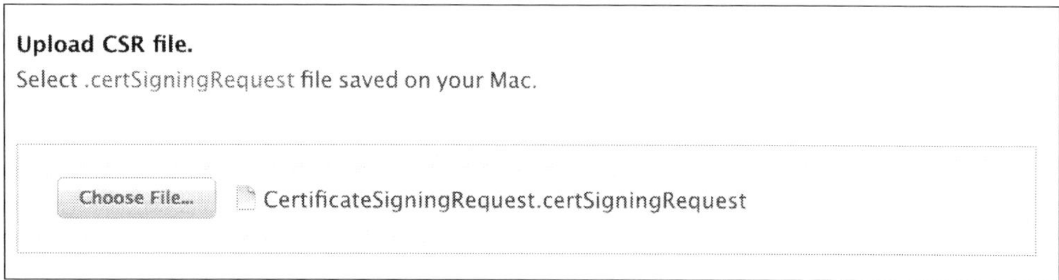

[You must upload the same, `.certSigningRequest` file as you did for the app certificate. Otherwise, your app will not receive push notifications and it's very hard to debug.]

52. Click on the **Continue** button:

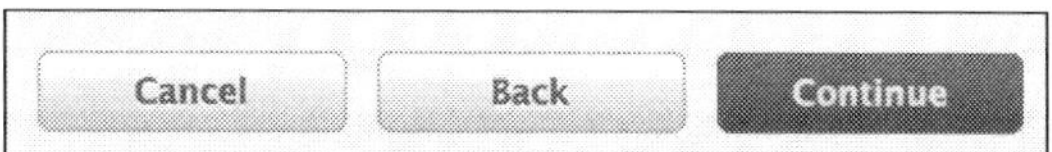

53. Click on the **Download** button to download the certificate file. You can name it `aps_certificate.cer` to avoid overwriting to the earlier `.cer` file:

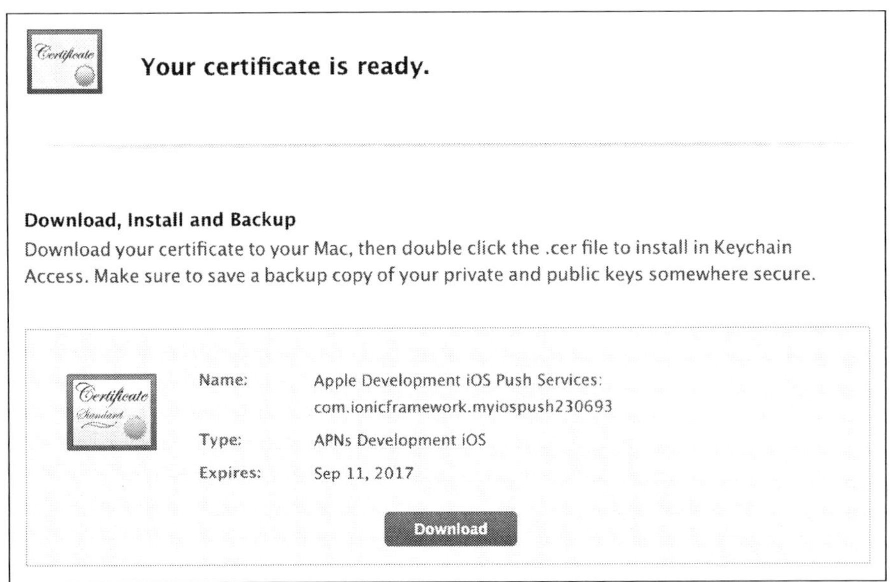

54. Once your `.cer` file is downloaded, you need to click on it to import it to **Keychain Access**:

55. Locate the new push services certificate in **Keychain Access** and select it, as illustrated in the following screenshot:

56. Right click on the certificate and select **Export**:

57. Give it a new name to avoid overwriting it to the app certificate. This process is, basically, converting a `.cer` to `.p12` file for Ionic Cloud:

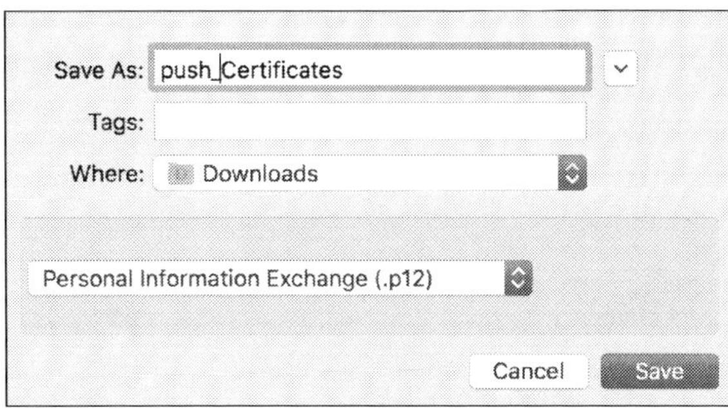

58. Provide a password for this `.p12` file to protect it:

Password for the `.p12` file is required because Ionic Cloud will not import a `.p12` file for APN without password.

59. Once you have completed the setup on the Apple Developer website, you need to upload the provisioning profile and two certificates (app and push) to Ionic Cloud. Navigate to `https://apps.ionic.io` and log in with your credentials.
60. Select the app generated for this project (that is, `MyiOSPush`):

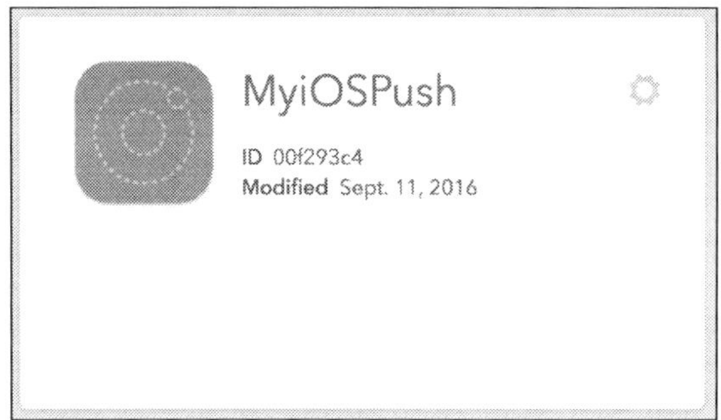

61. Navigate to **Settings** > **Certificates**:

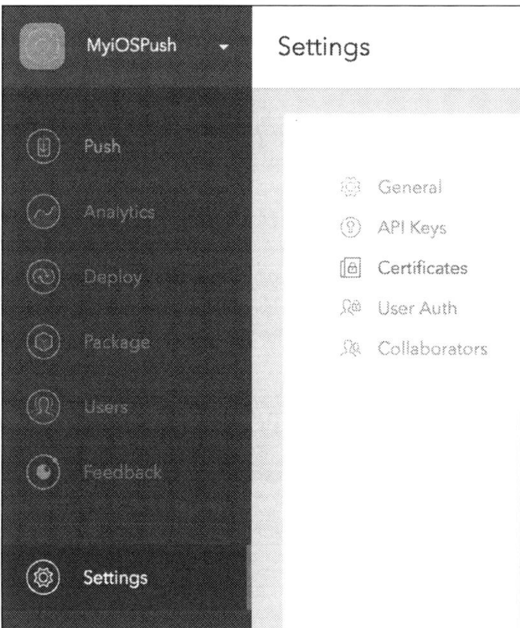

62. Select **New Security Profile**:

63. Provide a **Profile Name** and click on the **Create** button to save the profile:

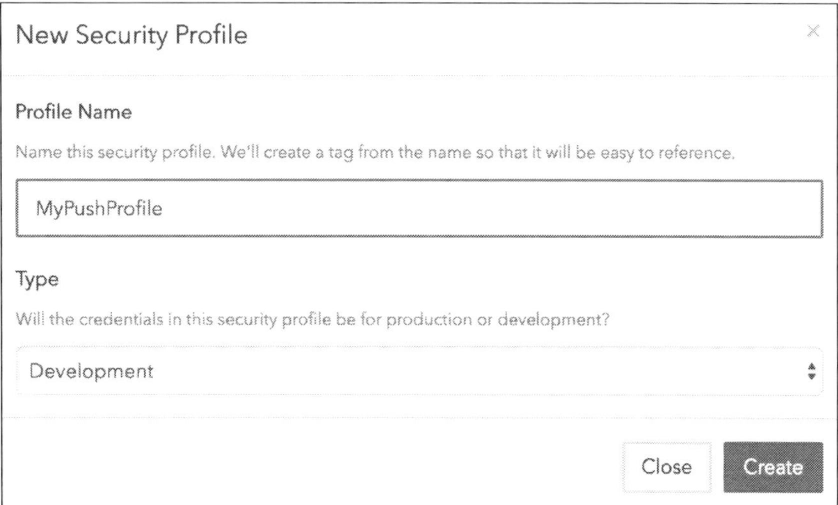

64. Select **EDIT** next to the `MyPushProfile` that you just created to edit the settings:

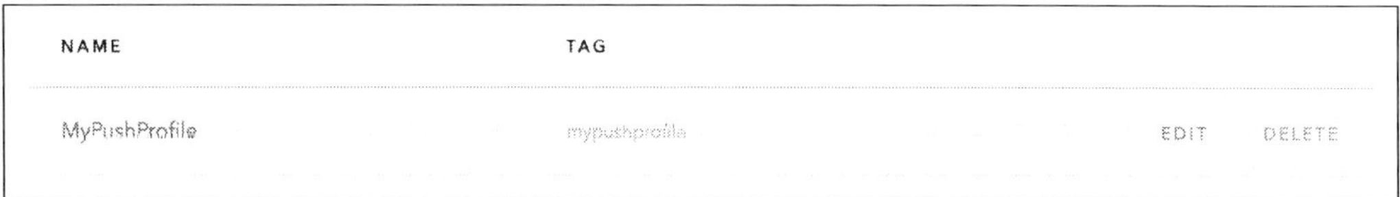

65. You will need to upload three files: a provisioning profile, and app development certificate for the app itself, and an APN certificate for push notification. Let's start with the app requirements. Click on **Choose File** under **Build Credentials** and upload two files: `Certificates.p12` (from Step 30) and `MyiOSPush_Provisioning_Profile.mobileprovision` (from Step 44). Ensure that you provide the same password that you used to protect the `.p12` file earlier:

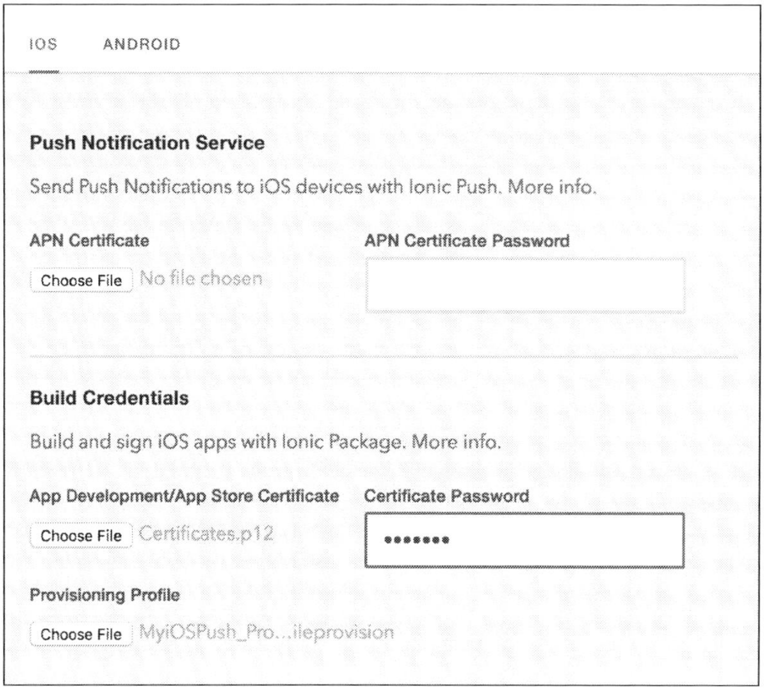

66. Click on **Choose File** under **Push Notification Service** and upload the `push_Certificates.p12` file (from Step 58). Ensure that you provide the same password that protects this file:

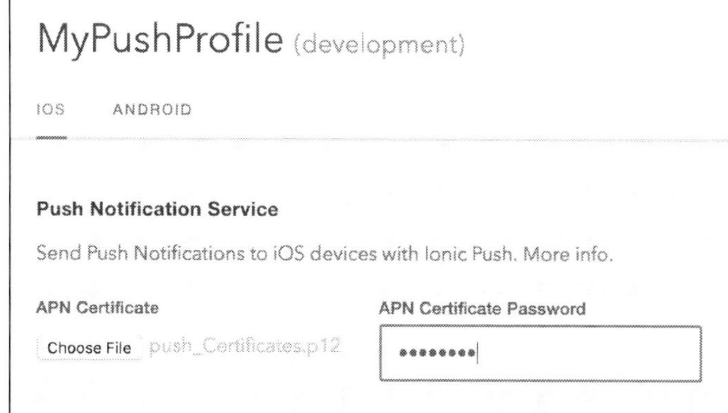

You should not get confused between the two `.p12` files as one is for your app and one is for your push notification feature.

67. Click on the **Save** button to save your security profile. This completes your Ionic Cloud setup for push notification.
68. You need to modify your home page code in order to receive notification messages. Open and edit `./src/pages/home/home.html` and paste the given code:

```
<ion-header>
  <ion-navbar>
    <ion-title>
      Push Notification
    </ion-title>
  </ion-navbar>
</ion-header>

<ion-content padding>

  <code class="center">{{ pushToken }}</code>
  <button ion-button block [disabled]="clicked"
  [hidden]="pushToken" (click)="registerPush()">
    <span [hidden]="clicked">Register Push</span>
    <span [hidden]="!clicked">Registering...</span>
  </button>

  <h2 class="big-square" *ngIf="!pushToken">
    You have no message
  </h2>

  <h3 class="sub-title" *ngIf="pushToken">
```

```
    Your messages
  </h3>

  <ion-card *ngFor="let msg of messages">
    <ion-card-header>
      {{ msg.title }}
    </ion-card-header>
    <ion-card-content>
      {{ msg.text }}
    </ion-card-content>
  </ion-card>
</ion-content>
```

69. Replace the content of the `home.ts` file, in the same folder, with the following code:

```
import { Component, ApplicationRef } from '@angular/core';
import { NavController } from 'ionic-angular';
import { Push, PushToken } from '@ionic/cloud-angular';

@Component({
  templateUrl: 'home.html'
})
export class HomePage {
  public push: any;
  public pushToken: string;
  public messages = [];
  public clicked: Boolean = false;
  constructor(public navCtrl: NavController, push: Push,
  private applicationRef: ApplicationRef) {
    this.push = push;
  }

  private processPush(msg, that) {
    console.log('Push notification message received');
    console.log(msg);
    this.messages.push({
      title: msg.title,
      text: msg.text
    })
    this.applicationRef.tick();
  }

  registerPush() {
```

```
      this.clicked = true;

      this.push.register().then((t: PushToken) => {
        return this.push.saveToken(t);
      }).then((t: PushToken) => {

        this.push.rx.notification().subscribe(msg =>
        this.processPush(msg, this));

        console.log('Token saved:', t.token);
        this.pushToken = t.token;
      }, (err) => {
        alert('Token error');
        console.log(err);
      });

    }
  }
```

70. Replace `home.scss`, also in the `/home` folder, with the given code:

```
.home-page {
  .center {
    text-align: center;
  }

  h2.big-square {
    text-align: center;
    padding: 50px;
    color: #D91E18;
    background: #F9BF3B;
  }

  h3.sub-title {
    text-align: center;
    padding: 10px;
    color: #446CB3;
    background: #E4F1FE;
  }

  ion-card ion-card-header {
    padding: 10px 16px;
    background: #F9690E;
```

```
    color: white;
  }

  ion-card ion-card-header + ion-card-content, ion-card .item +
  ion-card-content {
    padding-top: 16px;
  }
}
```

71. Connect your physical iPhone to the Mac via a USB connection.
72. Ensure that you are in the app folder and build for the iOS platform, as follows:

```
$ ionic run ios --device
```

You may need to include the `--device` parameter at the end due to an existing bug with Ionic 2.

73. The OS will prompt to allow codesign to sign using the iOS Developer certificate. You must accept this to allow access in order to build the app and upload it to your device:

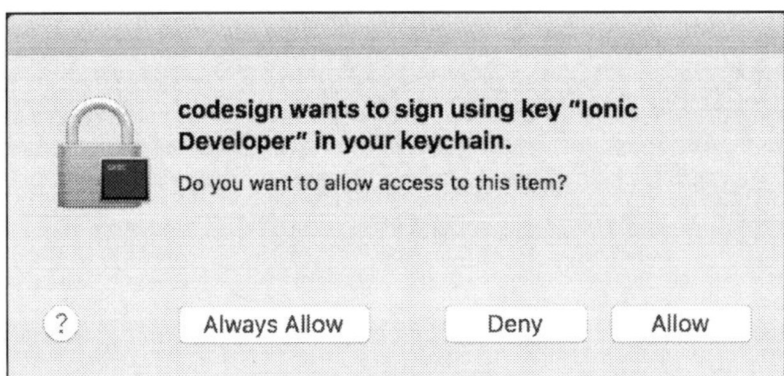

74. Verify that the app has been running successfully on the device. The initial screen should look as illustrated:

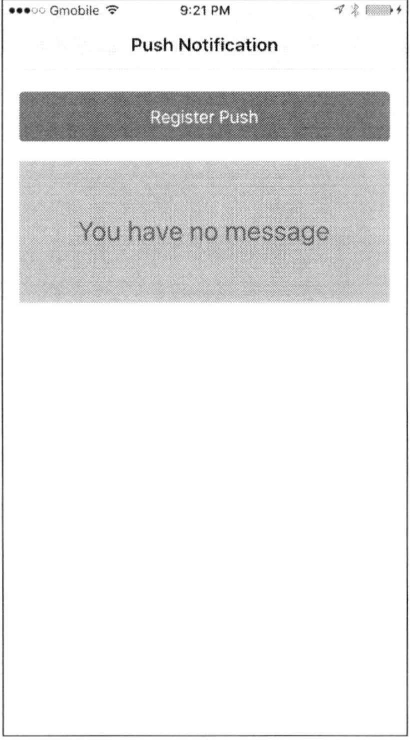

At this point, you have completed the push notification setup and coding. The next step is to verify that you receive notifications via the app. Here are the instructions:

1. Click on the **Register Push** button in the mobile app to register for push notification to the Ionic Cloud provider server to acquire a token. Click on **OK** to accept permission to receive push notifications, as follows:

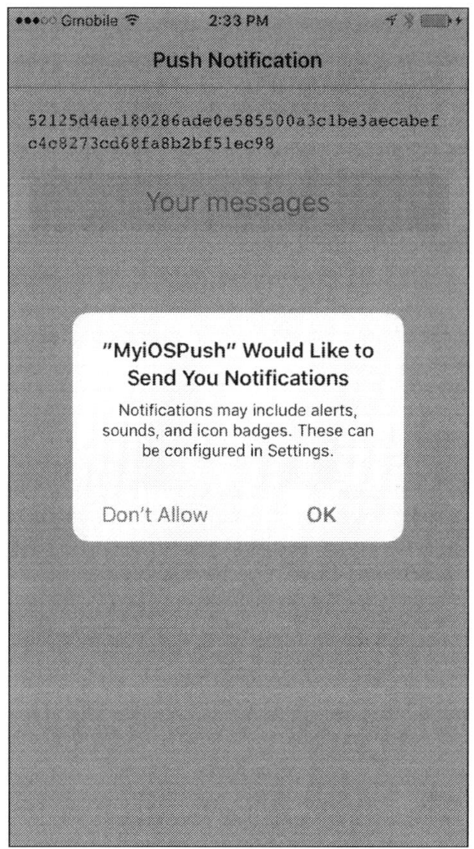

2. Navigate to **Ionic Cloud** > your app (**MyiOSPush**) > **Push**:

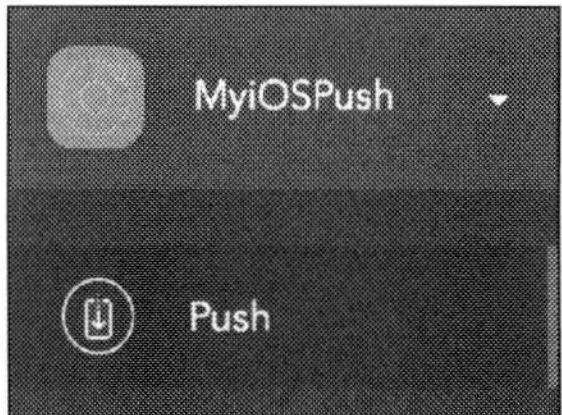

3. Click on the **CREATE YOUR FIRST PUSH** button:

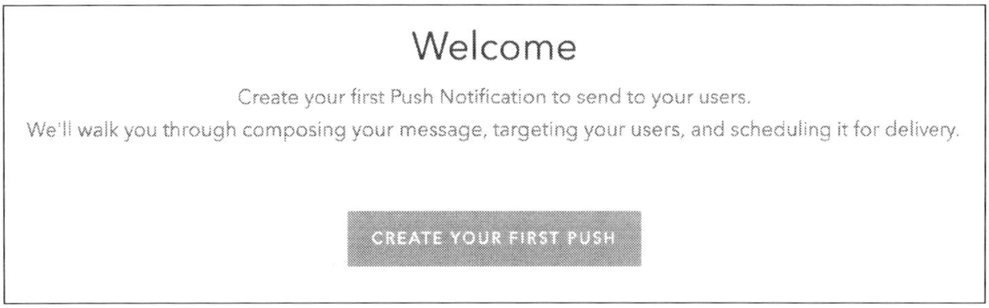

Welcome

Create your first Push Notification to send to your users.

We'll walk you through composing your message, targeting your users, and scheduling it for delivery.

CREATE YOUR FIRST PUSH

4. Fill in the push notification form to create your first push message:

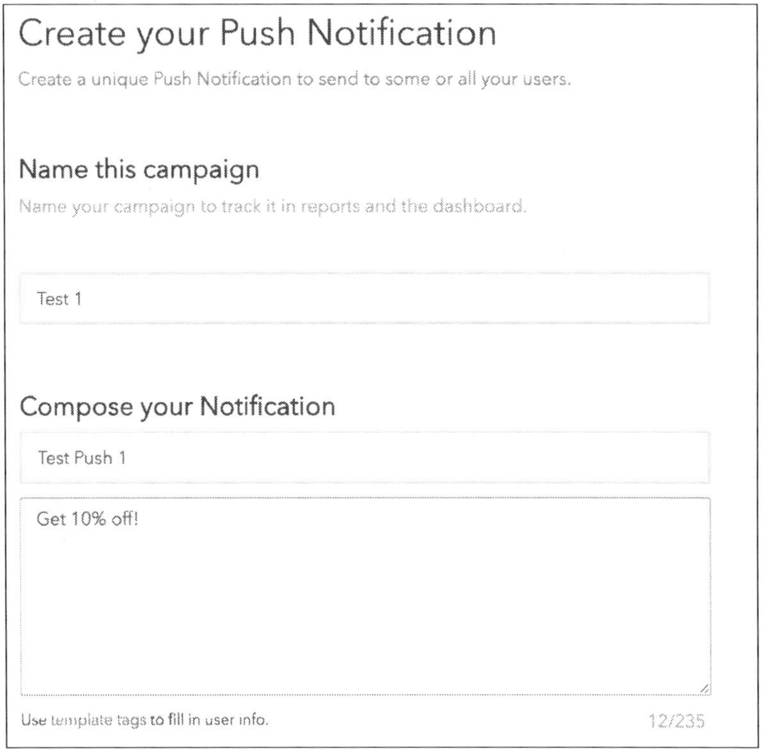

Create your Push Notification

Create a unique Push Notification to send to some or all your users.

Name this campaign

Name your campaign to track it in reports and the dashboard.

Test 1

Compose your Notification

Test Push 1

Get 10% off!

Use template tags to fill in user info. 12/235

5. Verify on the right screen to ensure that the push message is displayed as desired:

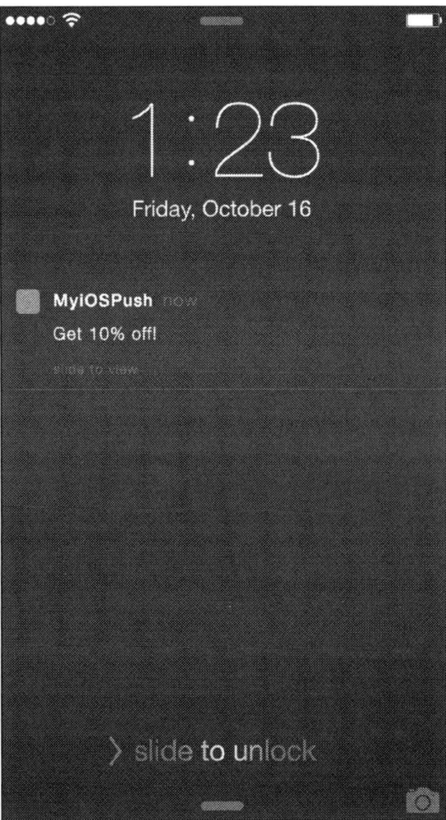

6. Leave the segment as **All users** so that anyone can get the push:

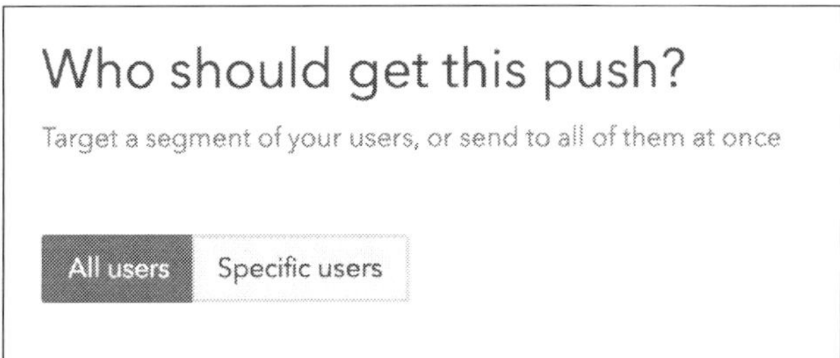

7. Select the security profile (that is, `mypushprofile`) that you created earlier. Then, click on the **Send this Push** button:

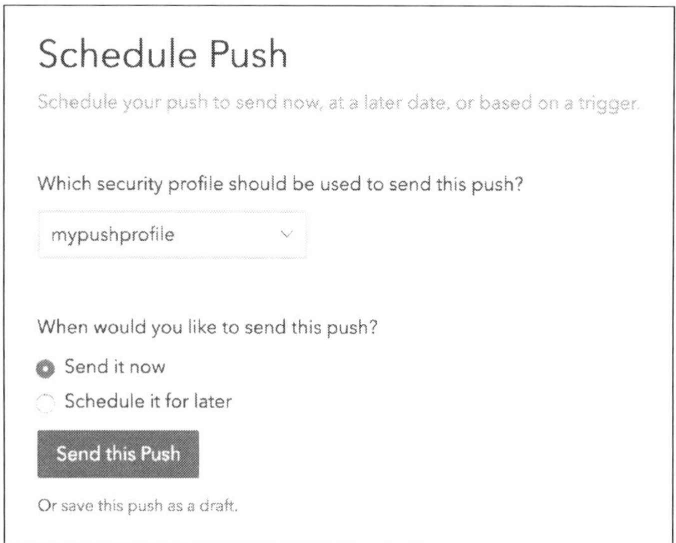

8. Verify that the push notification has been sent successfully from Ionic Cloud. It should have the **Sent** status, as shown:

9. In the app on your mobile device, verify that the push message has appeared as illustrated:

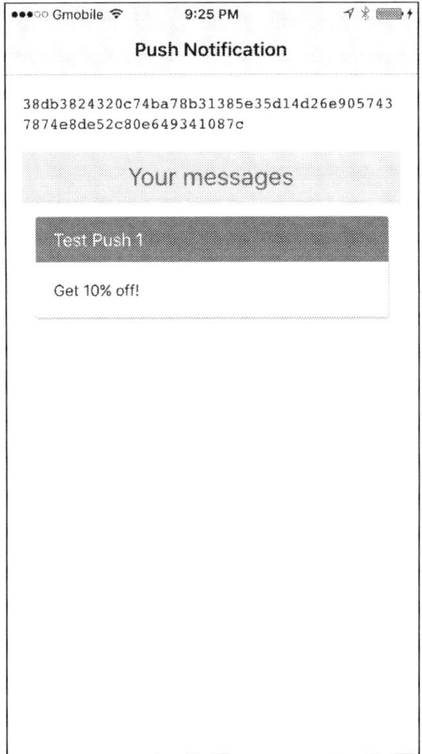

You have successfully completed the verification steps.

How it works...

To understand how the entire process works, let's summarize what you have done, as shown in the following section:

- Created an Ionic project and initialized it to create an Ionic Cloud project:
  - Your Ionic project on the local computer must sync with the Ionic Cloud project for push notifications and other management, such as user authentication
- Set up your Apple Developer account by doing the following things:
  - Created an app ID
  - Created app certificate (after creating a signing request locally via **Keychain Access**)

- Created a provisioning profile
- Created a push certificate

- Set up your Ionic Cloud account:
  - Created a security profile.
  - Imported three files from Apple Developer: an app certificate, a provisioning profile, and a push certificate. These files are needed so that Ionic Cloud can be a trusted provider to communicate with Apple's APN server to trigger push notifications.

- Wrote code in your app to receive notifications:
  - You need to install the Ionic Cloud Angular library and the Cordova Push Notification plugin. The basic idea is to make the `push` object available for the app to use. This `push` object has been configured with your Ionic Cloud push provider.

Now, let's focus on the coding portion itself to understand how this works.

You need to change how the app bootstraps in `app.module.ts`. This requires the importing of the `provideCloud` and `CloudSettings` providers, as shown:

```
import { provideCloud, CloudSettings } from '@ionic/cloud-angular';
```

Besides setting the `app_id` to match with your project `app_id` in Ionic Cloud, you need to specify the `push` object with the parameters you want for both iOS and Android, as follows:

```
const cloudSettings: CloudSettings = {
  'core': {
    'app_id': '00f293c4'
  },
  'push': {
    'sender_id': 'SENDER_ID',
    'pluginConfig': {
      'ios': {
        'badge': true,
        'sound': true
      },
      'android': {
        'iconColor': '#343434'
      }
    }
  }
};
```

Then, inside `NgModule`, you need to insert the following line so that Ionic knows that it needs to initialize Ionic Cloud as well:

```
CloudModule.forRoot(cloudSettings)
```

In your `home.html` template, there is a button to trigger the registration of push notification by calling `registerpush()`:

```
<code class="center">{{ pushToken }}</code>
<button ion-button block [disabled]="clicked" [hidden]="pushToken"
(click)="registerPush()">
  <span [hidden]="clicked">Register Push</span>
  <span [hidden]="!clicked">Registering...</span>
</button>
```

This registration process must be intervened manually by the user because the user will have to accept permission in the next step. It's not recommended to require the users to accept a push notification request when they open the app right away. The main reason is because they are not familiar with your app and don't know what to expect (that is, whether they will get bombarded with notifications later on).

The messages will be displayed via the `messages` object, as shown in the following code:

```
<ion-card *ngFor="let msg of messages">
  <ion-card-header>
    {{ msg.title }}
  </ion-card-header>
  <ion-card-content>
    {{ msg.text }}
  </ion-card-content>
</ion-card>
```

Here, each `message` item has the `title` and `text` fields.

In `home.ts`, there are two critical imports that you must be aware of: `Push` and `PushToken` are required to register and receive push notifications. `ApplicationRef` will be discussed later as you need to trigger re-render the Angular template manually, as illustrated:

```
import { Component, ApplicationRef } from '@angular/core';
import { NavController } from 'ionic-angular';
import { Push, PushToken } from '@ionic/cloud-angular';
The registerPush() method is the key to acquire the PushToken from
Ionic Cloud, as shown:
registerPush() {
  this.clicked = true;

  this.push.register().then((t: PushToken) => {
```

```
      return this.push.saveToken(t);
    }).then((t: PushToken) => {

      this.push.rx.notification().subscribe(msg =>
      this.processPush(msg, this));

      console.log('Token saved:', t.token);
      this.pushToken = t.token;
    }, (err) => {
      alert('Token error');
      console.log(err);
    });
  }
```

All you need to call is the `this.push.register()` function. This will return a `PushToken` object as you can see in the following screenshot of the console log:

```
Ionic Push: saved push token: 38db3824320c74ba78b31385e35d14d26e9057437874e8de52c80e649341087c
Token saved: – "38db3824320c74ba78b31385e35d14d26e9057437874e8de52c80e649341087c"
```

To receive notifications, you need to subscribe by using the following code:

```
this.push.rx.notification().subscribe()
```

This will call `processPush()` each time there is a new notification message, as follows:

```
private processPush(msg, that) {
  console.log('Push notification message received');
  console.log(msg);
  this.messages.push({
    title: msg.title,
    text: msg.text
  })
  this.applicationRef.tick();
}
```

When the user receives a push message, this function will append to the `messages` array. If you don't call `this.applicationRef.tick()`, the UI will not get updated since this process is outside Angular cycle. If you look into the console log, the `PushMessage` looks as follows, with the `text` and `title` fields:

```
Push notification message received
▼ PushMessage
  ▶ app: {asleep: false, closed: false}
    count: undefined
    image: undefined
    payload: undefined
  ▶ raw: {title: "Test Push 1", additionalData: {foreground: true, coldstart: false}, message: "Get 10% off!"}
    sound: undefined
    text: "Get 10% off!"
    title: "Test Push 1"
  ▶ PushMessage Prototype
```

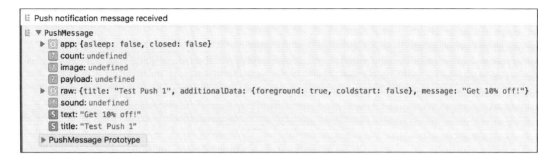

If the user doesn't open the app, you will see that the notification appears in the notification area.

There's more...

Ionic has its own iOS setup instructions pages, as follows:

- `http://docs.ionic.io/setup.html`
- `http://docs.ionic.io/services/profiles/#ios-setup`
- `http://docs.ionic.io/services/push/`

The Cordova Push Notification plugin is available directly at `https://github.com/phonegap/phonegap-plugin-push`.

For more information about the Apple Push Notification service, you can visit the official documentation at `https://developer.apple.com/library/ios/documentation/NetworkingInternet/Conceptual/RemoteNotificationsPG/Chapters/ApplePushService.html`.

Building an Android app to receive push notifications

Push notification works in the same way as iOS for Google. However, instead of using the Apple Notification Service, you will be working through the Firebase Cloud Messaging server, which is a new replacement for **Google Cloud Messaging** (**GCM**). However, Ionic Cloud abstracts this process so that you don't have to code using a different API. You will be using the same `push` object as for the iOS app.

For more information about the differences between FCM and GCM, visit the FAQ at `https://firebase.google.com/support/faq`.

In this section, you will learn how to do the following things:

- Set up Ionic Cloud for Android push notification
- Configure the Firebase project for the push API
- Write code to receive push notifications in Android

You will be using the same code base as your iOS Push Notification example. The main difference is the process to set up in your Firebase and Ionic Cloud account.

Getting ready

You can test the Android push notification using the Android emulator. So, there is no need to have a physical Android device available.

You must also register for Firebase in order to access `https://console.firebase.google.com`.

In addition, the following instructions use the specific version of these components:

- Mac OSX El Capitan 10.11.4
- Ionic CLI 2.1.8
- Cordova 6.4.0
- Node 6.8.1
- NPM 3.10.8

- Android Studio 2.x, with at least Android 5.1 (Lollipop) installed.

  Observe the following screenshot:

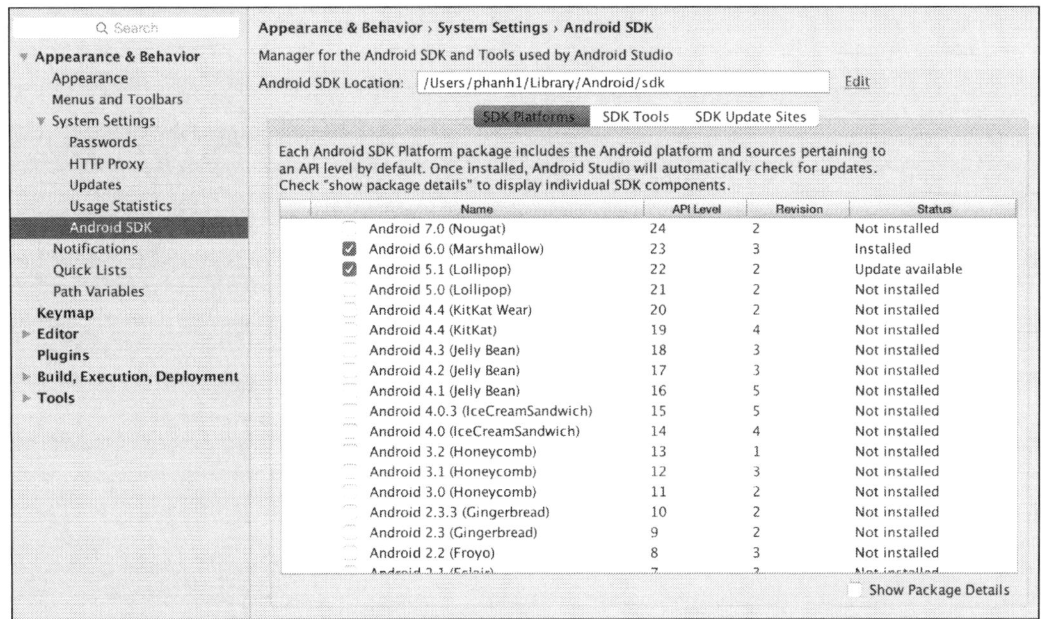

- Android SDK Tools, Build Tools, Platform Tools and Intel **Hardware Accelerated Execution Manager** (**HAXM**) (`https://software.intel.com/en-us/android/articles/installation-instructions-for-intel-hardware-accelerated-execution-manager-windows`).

Observe the following screenshot:

SDK Platforms | SDK Tools | SDK Update Sites

Below are the available SDK developer tools. Once installed, Android Studio will automatically check for updates. Check "show package details" to display available versions of an SDK Tool.

	Name	Version	Status
☑	Android SDK Build Tools		Installed
☑	Android Auto API Simulators	1.0.0	Installed
☐	Android Auto Desktop Head Unit emulator	1.1	Not installed
☑	Android SDK Platform-Tools 24.0.3	24.0.3	Installed
☑	Android SDK Tools 25.2.2	25.2.2	Installed
⊟	Android Support Repository, rev 17	17.0.0	Update Available: 3...
☐	CMake 3.6.3155560	3.6.3155560	Not installed
☐	ConstraintLayout for Android 1.0.0-alpha5	1	Not installed
☐	ConstraintLayout for Android 1.0.0-alpha6	1	Not installed
☐	ConstraintLayout for Android 1.0.0-alpha7	1	Not installed
☐	ConstraintLayout for Android 1.0.0-alpha8	1	Not installed
☐	Documentation for Android SDK	1	Not installed
☐	GPU Debugging tools	1.0.3	Not installed
☑	Google Play APK Expansion Library, rev 3	3.0.0	Installed
☐	Google Play APK Expansion library	1	Not installed
☑	Google Play Billing Library, rev 5	5.0.0	Installed
☐	Google Play Licensing Library	1	Not installed
☑	Google Play Licensing Library, rev 2	2.0.0	Installed
⊟	Google Play services, rev 26	26.0.0	Update Available: 32
☑	Google Repository	32	Installed
☑	Google Web Driver, rev 2	2.0.0	Installed
☑	Intel x86 Emulator Accelerator (HAXM installer), rev 6.0.3	6.0.3	Installed
☐	LLDB 2.0	2.0.2558144	Not installed

- At least one **Android Virtual Device** (**AVD**) has been created (use the `$ android avd` command line to open AVD Manager). Observe the following screenshot:

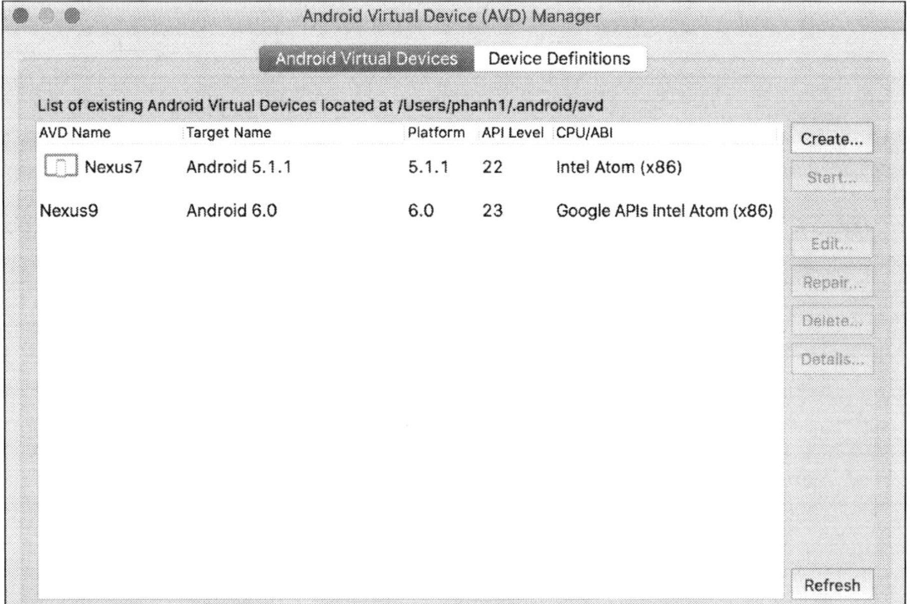

How to do it...

Here are the instructions:

1. Create a new `MyAndroidPush` app using the `blank` template, as follows, and go to the `MyAndroidPush` folder:

```
$ ionic start MyAndroidPush blank --v2
$ cd MyAndroidPush
```

2. Install the Ionic Cloud Angular client, which is a library, to interact with the `push` object, as illustrated:

```
$ npm install @ionic/cloud-angular --save
```

You need to have Node version 4.x or later and NPM version 3.x or later.

3. Initialize your Ionic Cloud setting so that an app ID can be created in your account, as shown:

```
$ ionic io init
```

You will be prompted to log in to your Ionic Cloud account for this command line.

4. You will need a Firebase project number and a Firebase server ID in order to set up your `app.ts` file correctly. First, let's log in to the Firebase console at `https://console.firebase.google.com`.
5. Click on the **CREATE NEW PROJECT** button and fill in a project name (that is, `MyAndroidPush`):

6. Navigate to **Grow** > **Notifications** in the left navigation menu:

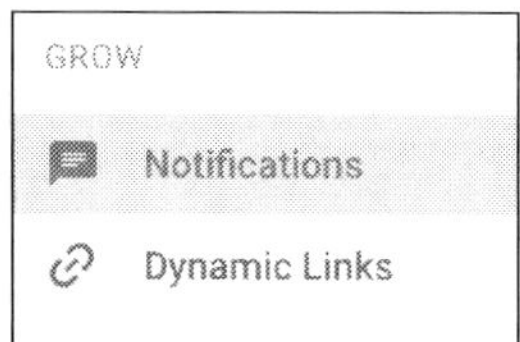

7. Select the Android icon:

The Firebase Cloud Messaging service also supports the iOS app. So, it's possible that you can use FCM for both the iOS and Android projects.

8. Provide **Package name** in the form. You can copy and paste the **Package name** from your app project at `./config.xml`:

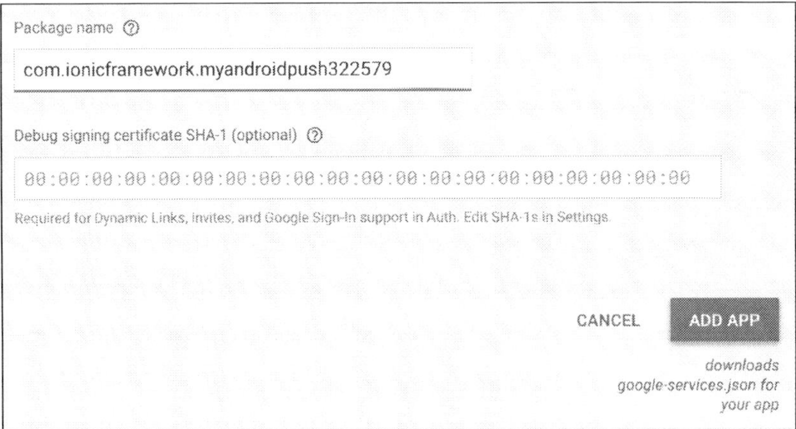

9. Select **CONTINUE** and save the JSON file somewhere. You will not need this JSON file for Ionic project:

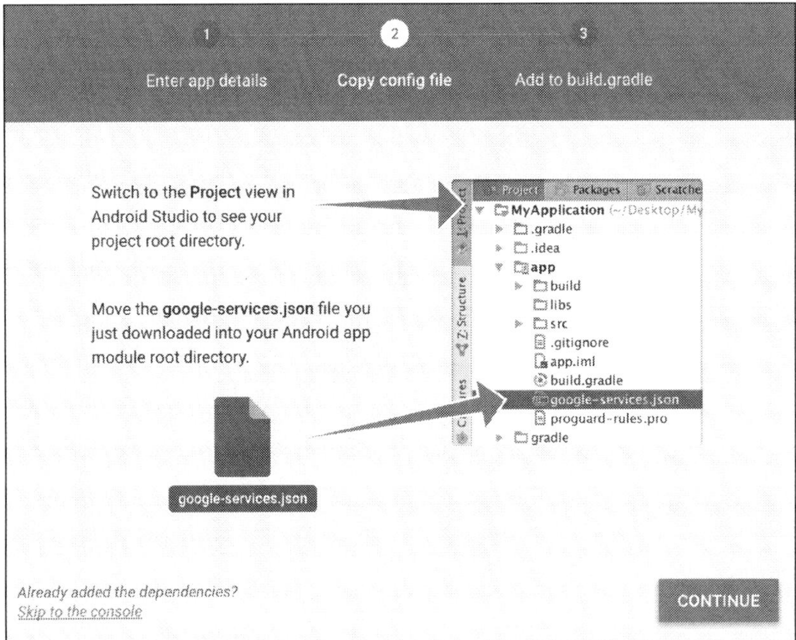

10. Click on the **FINISH** button to complete setting up the notification service:

11. Now, you will need the **Server key** and **Sender ID**. Navigate to the gear icon in the top left corner and select the **Project settings** menu item:

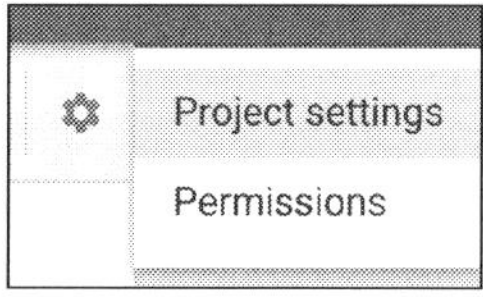

12. Select the **CLOUD MESSAGING** tab:

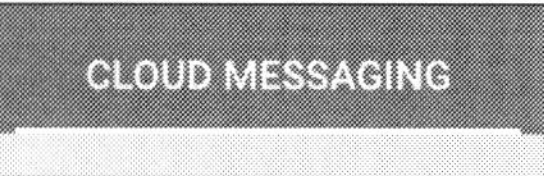

13. Copy both the **Server key** and **Sender ID** (the same as **Project ID** if using Google Cloud Messaging):

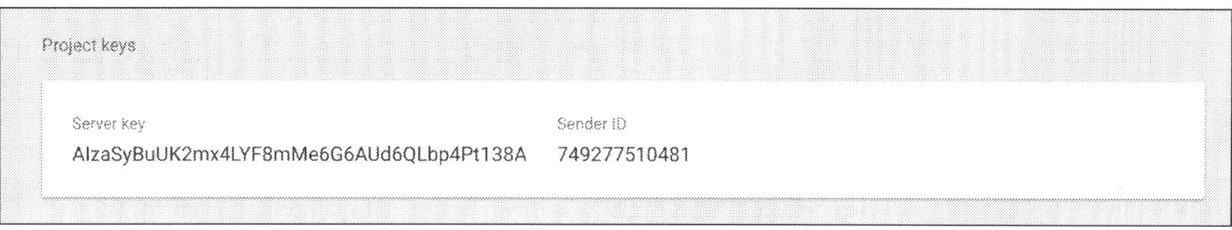

14. Navigate back to the Terminal and ensure that you are in the Ionic project folder.
15. You need to install the Cordova Push Notification plugin and provide the same **Sender ID** value as the `SENDER_ID` value in the command line previously, as shown:

```
$ cordova plugin add phonegap-plugin-push --variable
SENDER_ID=749277510481 --save
```

16. Open your `./ionic.config.json` file in the project folder and copy the `app_id` value (in this case, the value is `e546b9f6`) from the following code:

```
{
  "name": "MyAndroidPush",
  "app_id": "e546b9f6",
  "v2": true,
  "typescript": true
}
```

17. Open and edit `./src/app/app.module.ts` with the following content:

```
import { NgModule } from '@angular/core';
import { IonicApp, IonicModule } from 'ionic-angular';
import { MyApp } from './app.component';

import { CloudSettings, CloudModule } from '@ionic/cloud-
angular';

import { HomePage } from '../pages/home/home';

const cloudSettings: CloudSettings = {
  'core': {
    'app_id': 'e546b9f6'
  },
  'push': {
    'sender_id': '749277510481',
    'pluginConfig': {
      'ios': {
        'badge': true,
        'sound': true
      },
      'android': {
        'iconColor': '#343434'
      }
    }
  }
};


@NgModule({
  declarations: [
    MyApp,
    HomePage
  ],
  imports: [
    IonicModule.forRoot(MyApp),
    CloudModule.forRoot(cloudSettings)
  ],
  bootstrap: [IonicApp],
  entryComponents: [
    MyApp,
    HomePage
  ],
  providers: []
})
export class AppModule {}
```

> You must replace `'app_id': '00f293c4'` with your own app ID. Also, you have to provide **Sender ID** here one more time.

18. The code for your home page is very similar to the iOS push example. Open and edit `./src/pages/home/home.html`, and paste the following code:

```
<ion-header>
  <ion-navbar>
    <ion-title>
      Push Notification
    </ion-title>
  </ion-navbar>
</ion-header>

<ion-content padding>

  <code class="center">{{ pushToken }}</code>
  <button ion-button block [disabled]="clicked"
  [hidden]="pushToken" (click)="registerPush()">
    <span [hidden]="clicked">Register Push</span>
    <span [hidden]="!clicked">Registering...</span>
  </button>

  <h2 class="big-square" *ngIf="!pushToken">
    You have no message
  </h2>

  <h3 class="sub-title" *ngIf="pushToken">
    Your messages
  </h3>

  <ion-card *ngFor="let msg of messages">
    <ion-card-header>
      {{ msg.title }}
    </ion-card-header>
    <ion-card-content>
      {{ msg.text }}
    </ion-card-content>
  </ion-card>
</ion-content>
```

19. Replace the content of the `home.ts` file, in the same folder, with the following code:

```
import { Component, ApplicationRef } from '@angular/core';
import { NavController } from 'ionic-angular';
import { Push, PushToken } from '@ionic/cloud-angular';

@Component({
  templateUrl: home.html'
})
export class HomePage {
  public push: any;
  public pushToken: string;
  public messages = [];
  public clicked: Boolean = false;
  constructor(public navCtrl: NavController, push: Push,
  private applicationRef: ApplicationRef) {
    this.push = push;
  }

  private processPush(msg, that) {
    console.log('Push notification message received');
    console.log(msg);
    this.messages.push({
      title: msg.title,
      text: msg.text
    })
    this.applicationRef.tick();
  }

  registerPush() {
    this.clicked = true;

    this.push.register().then((t: PushToken) => {
      return this.push.saveToken(t);
    }).then((t: PushToken) => {

      this.push.rx.notification().subscribe(msg =>
      this.processPush(msg, this));

      console.log('Token saved:', t.token);
      this.pushToken = t.token;
    }, (err) => {
      alert('Token error');
      console.log(err);
```

```
    });

  }
}
```

20. Replace home.scss, also in the /home folder, with the following code:

    ```
    .home-page {
      .center {
        text-align: center;
      }

      h2.big-square {
        text-align: center;
        padding: 50px;
        color: #D91E18;
        background: #F9BF3B;
      }

      h3.sub-title {
        text-align: center;
        padding: 10px;
        color: #446CB3;
        background: #E4F1FE;
      }

      ion-card ion-card-header {
        padding: 10px 16px;
        background: #F9690E;
        color: white;
      }

      ion-card ion-card-header + ion-card-content, ion-card
      .item + ion-card-content {
        padding-top: 16px;
      }
    }
    ```

21. If this is the first time you create this app, you must have a keystore file. This file is used to identify your app for push and publishing. If you lose it, you cannot update your app later on. To create a keystore, type the following command line and ensure that it's the same keytool version of the SDK (that is, check your PATH environment variable):

    ```
    $ keytool -genkey -v -keystore MyAndroidPushKey.keystore -alias
    MyAndroidPushKey -keyalg RSA -keysize 2048 -validity 10000
    ```

22. Once you fill out the information in the command line, make a copy of this file somewhere safe because you will need it later. Observe the following code:

```
Enter keystore password:
Re-enter new password:
What is your first and last name?
  [Unknown]:  Hoc Phan
What is the name of your organizational unit?
  [Unknown]:
What is the name of your organization?
  [Unknown]:
What is the name of your City or Locality?
  [Unknown]:
What is the name of your State or Province?
  [Unknown]:
What is the two-letter country code for this unit?
  [Unknown]:
Is CN=Hoc Phan, OU=Unknown, O=Unknown, L=Unknown, ST=Unknown,
C=Unknown correct?
  [no]:  yes

Generating 2,048 bit RSA key pair and self-signed certificate
(SHA256withRSA) with a validity of 10,000 days
       for: CN=Hoc Phan, OU=Unknown, O=Unknown, L=Unknown,
ST=Unknown, C=Unknown
Enter key password for <MyAndroidPushKey>
       (RETURN if same as keystore password):
[Storing MyAndroidPushKey.keystore]
```

You must provide a password for this step. Otherwise, Ionic Cloud won't let you upload the `keystore` file.

23. Now, log in to your Ionic Cloud at `https://apps.ionic.io` to configure the security profile next.

24. Navigate to your project (that is, `MyAndroidPush`) and select the **Settings** menu:

25. Select **Certificates**, as follows:

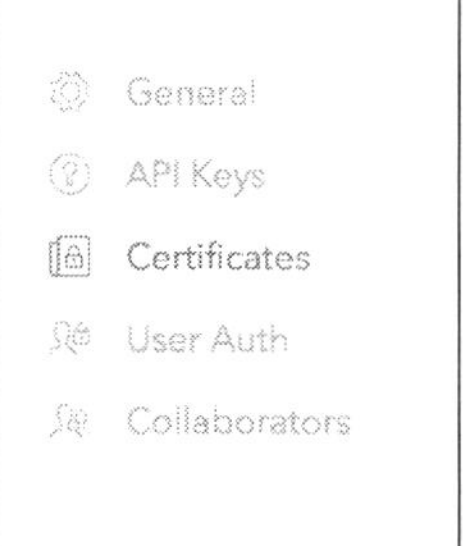

26. Create a **New Security Profile** and provide a name (for example, `MyAndroidPush`):

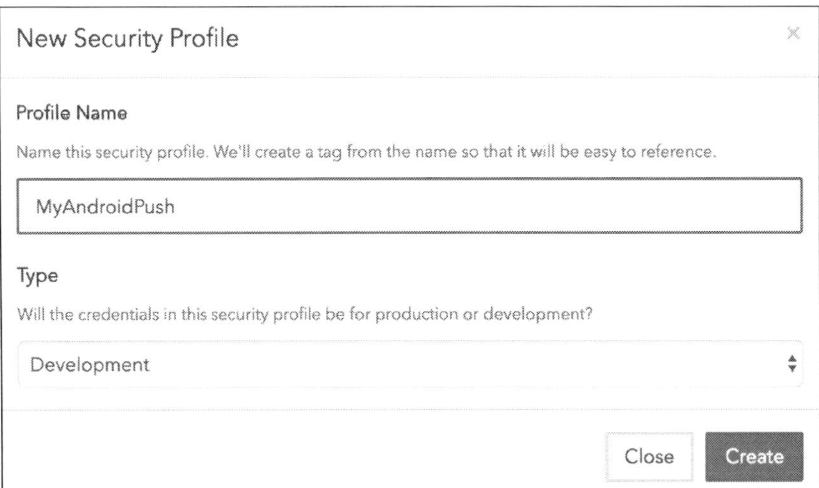

27. Select **EDIT**, as illustrated:

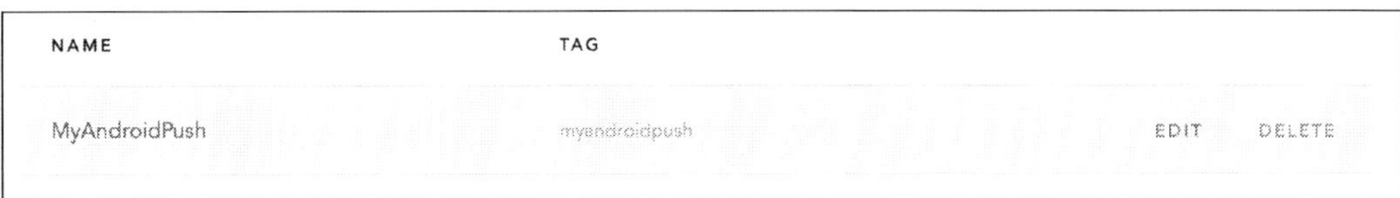

28. Upload your `keystore` file (for example, `MyAndroidPushKey.keystore`,) alias name (for example, `MyAndroidPushKey`), and password from Step 22:

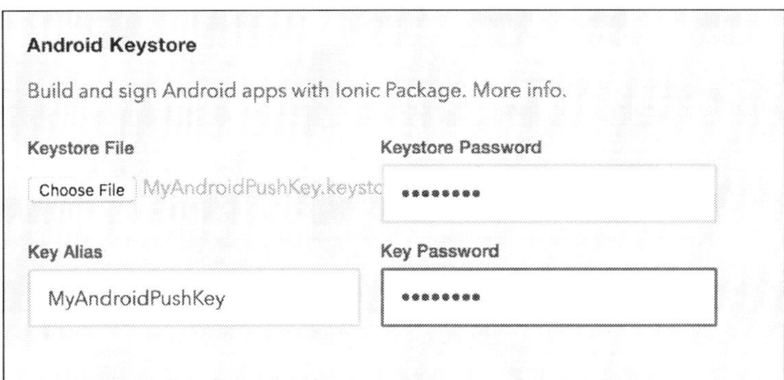

29. Paste **Server key** from Step 13 into the **GCM API Key** input box:

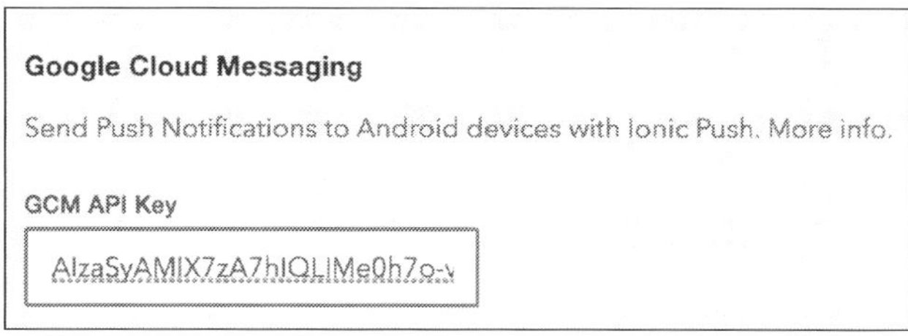

30. Select **Save** to complete creating a security profile.
31. Navigate back to the terminal.
32. Ensure that you are in the app folder and build for the Android platform, as follows:

```
$ ionic emulate android
```

The process to verify push notification for Android is very similar to iOS. Here are the instructions:

1. Navigate to **Ionic Cloud** > your app (**MyAndroidPush**) > **Push**:

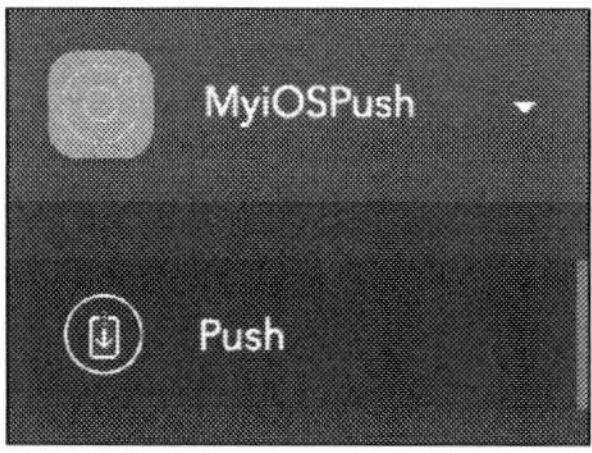

2. Click on the **CREATE YOUR FIRST PUSH** button:

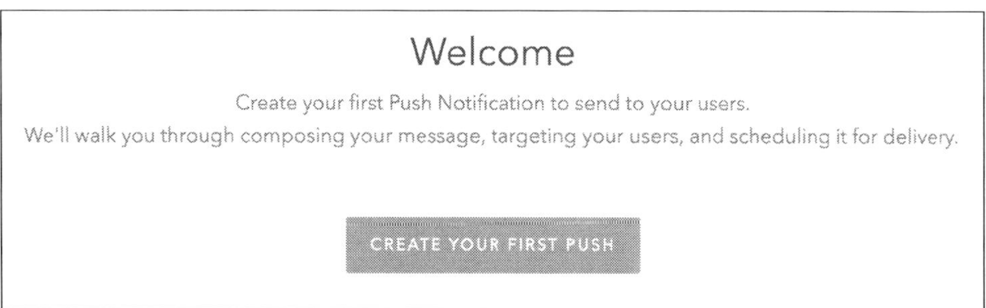

3. Fill in the push notification form from the create your first push message:

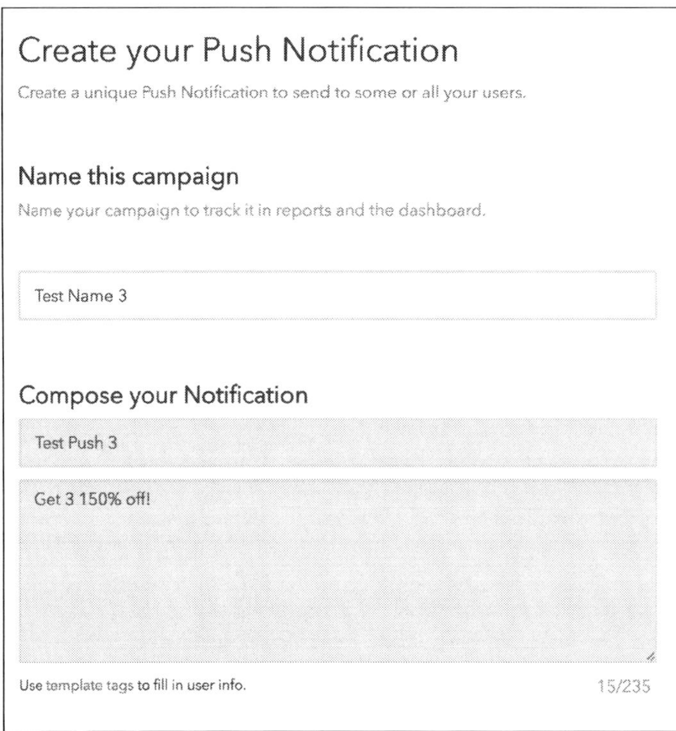

4. Leave the segment as **All users** so that anyone can get the push:

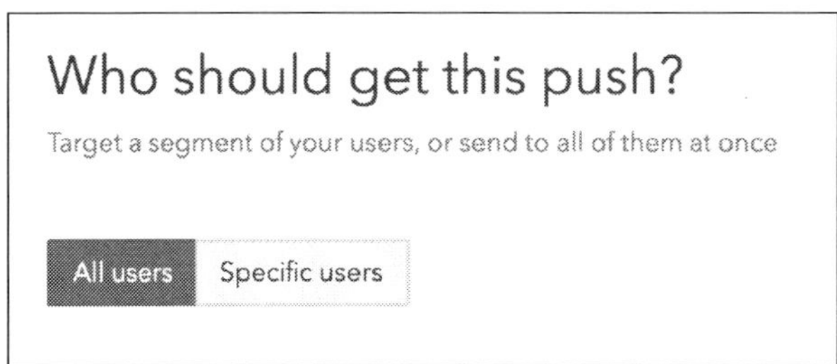

5. Select your security profile (that is, `MyAndroidPush`) that you created earlier. Then, click on the **Send this Push** button. Observe the following screenshot:

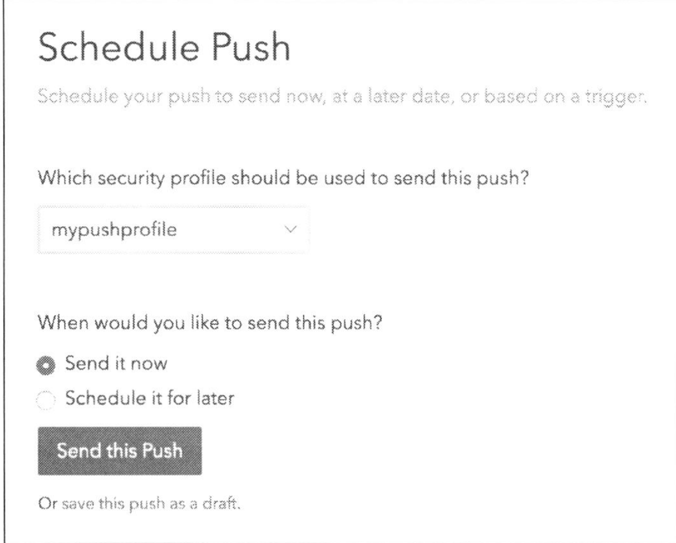

6. Verify that the push notification has been sent successfully from Ionic Cloud. It should have the **Sent** status, as illustrated:

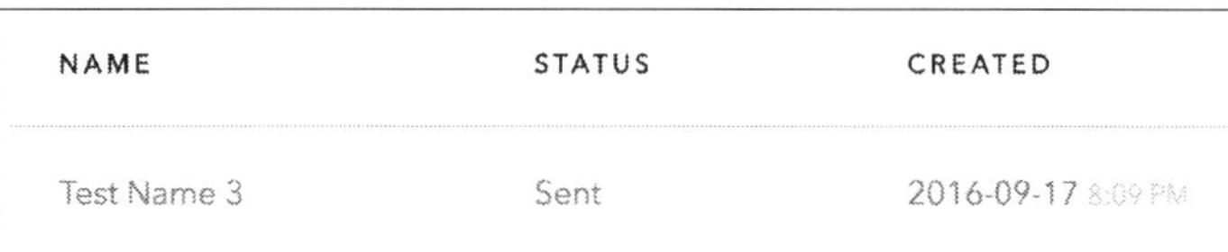

7. In the app on your simulator device, verify that the push message has appeared, as shown:

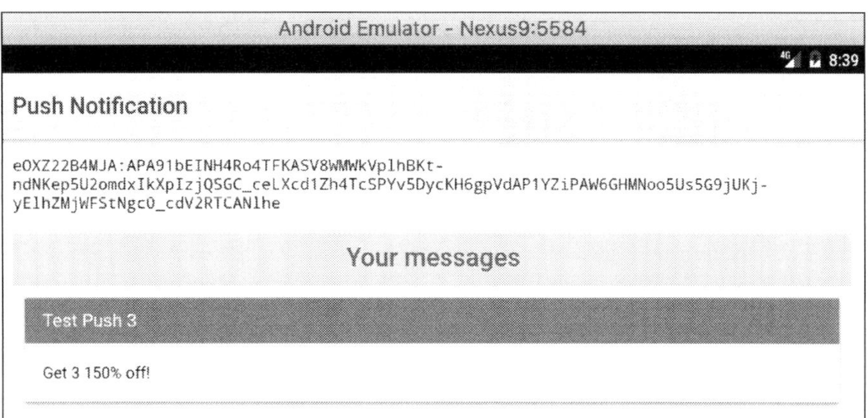

You have successfully completed the verification steps.

How it works...

At a high level, this is the communication process behind the scene:

- Your device sends a registration request for push notification to Google's Firebase server. Your device's app must have the following:
    - Firebase **Project ID**
    - Firebase **Sender ID**
- Google will reply with the registration ID (which is the same as the push token from the Ionic `push` object).
- Your app will send the registration ID to Ionic Cloud (or any push provider server). This process is behind the scene because Ionic Cloud Angular calls Ionic Cloud APIs to execute. However, your Ionic Cloud must have a security profile with four pieces of information, as listed in the following section:
    - Firebase's Server key
    - Keystore
    - Keystore Alias
    - Keystore password
- Ionic Cloud will save this registration ID to request Google to send push notification later. You can trigger notifications via the Ionic Cloud UI.

This is very similar to how Ionic Cloud works with Apple. Everything is simplified into your interactions with the `push` object from the Ionic Cloud Angular module.

To receive the console output, you can navigate to Google's URL at `chrome://inspect/#devices`. This will provide a list of the available simulators to debug. Click on the **inspect** link to open the Google Developer Tool:

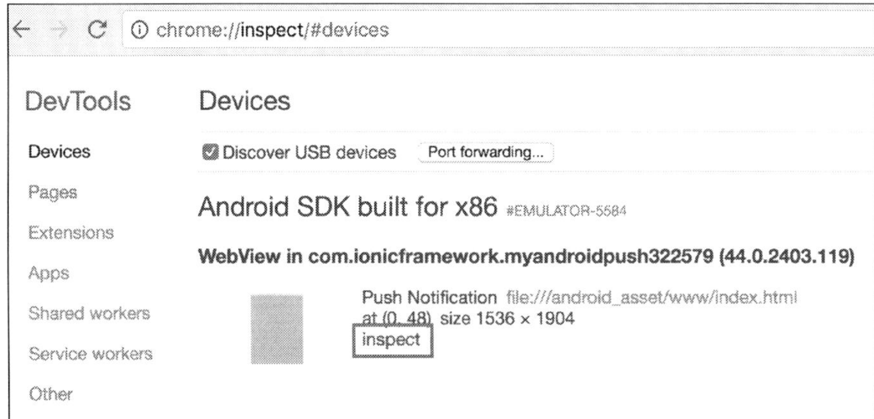

You should be able to see the same screen as follows:

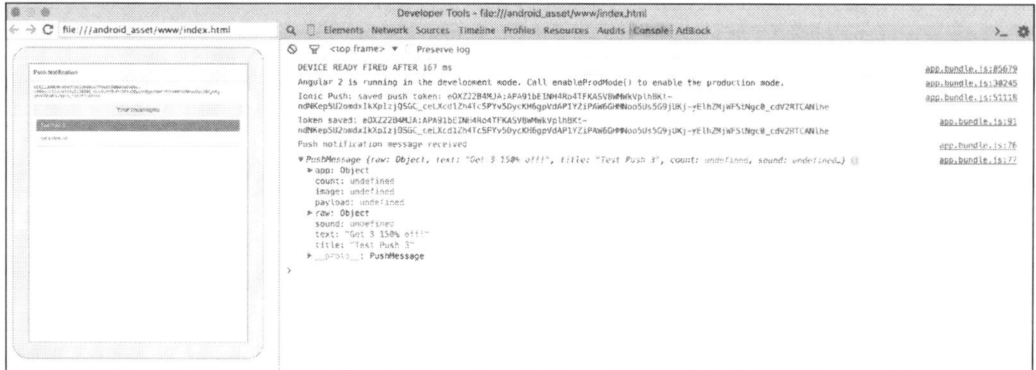

The app outputs a token (that is, a Registration ID) and each push notification will be a `PushMessage` object. You can open and inspect the properties.

In summary, Android push notification works nicely because of the out-of-the-box integration between Ionic Cloud, Ionic Angular module, and Firebase Cloud Messaging.

There's more...

Ionic has its own Android setup instructions pages, as follows:

- `http://docs.ionic.io/setup.html`
- `http://docs.ionic.io/services/profiles/#android-app-keystore`
- `http://docs.ionic.io/services/push/`

For more information about the Firebase Notification service, you can visit the official documentation at `https://firebase.google.com/docs/cloud-messaging/`.

7

Supporting Device Functionalities Using Ionic Native

In this chapter, we will cover the following tasks related to native device feature support:

- Taking a photo using the camera plugin
- Sharing content using the social sharing plugin
- Displaying a term of service using InAppBrowser
- Creating a Taxi app using the Google Maps plugin and geocode support

Introduction

In this chapter, you will learn how to access some common features of a device, such as the camera, contact list, e-mail, and maps. Some of these features can be written in a JavaScript-only environment, but the performance is not on a par with native support.

Cordova has a very well supported community with many plugins. You may want to check out `http://plugins.cordova.io/` to understand what is out there. Luckily, you don't need to deal with these plugins directly. You will use the Ionic Native (`http://ionicframework.com/docs/v2/native/`) service on top of Cordova and Angular 2. Keep in mind that you have to use Ionic Native instead of ngCordova for Ionic 2 because of compatibility issues. You can only use ngCordova for Ionic 1.x.

Taking a photo using the camera plugin

For this section, you will make an app to take a picture using the device camera or load an existing picture from the device album. The picture could be either in the Base64 format or saved in a local filesystem relating to your app. The following is a screenshot of the app:

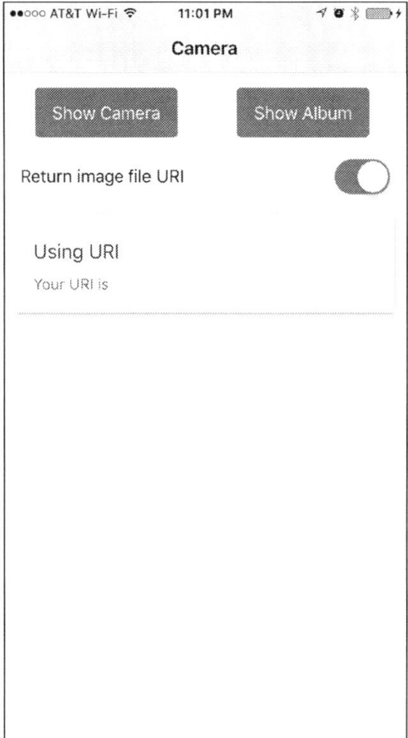

Here is the high-level process:

- Access the Cordova camera plugin to trigger camera capture and get the image back in the Base64 or URI format
- Parse the Base64 data or URI on an `<img>` DOM object
- Display the URI if it's in the URI format
- Capture an event of a toggle component
- Display long data (for example, URI) using horizontal scroll

Getting ready

You should have a physical device ready in order to test the camera capability. It's possible to just run the code via an emulator, but the filesystem support might look different across the various platforms.

How to do it...

The following are the instructions to add camera support:

1. Start a blank project (for example, `MyCamera`) and go to that folder:

   ```
   $ ionic start MyCamera blank --v2
   $ cd MyCamera
   ```

2. Add the Cordova camera plugin using the following code:

   ```
   $ ionic plugin add cordova-plugin-camera
   ```

   > You no longer need to add ngCordova separately. Also, you should not use the `cordova add` command line directly; instead but use `ionic plugin add`

   You should be able to see a new folder `org.apache.cordova.camera` being added in the `/plugins` folder.

3. Replace `./src/pages/home/home.html` with the following code:

   ```
   <ion-header>
     <ion-navbar>
       <ion-title>
         Camera
       </ion-title>
     </ion-navbar>
   </ion-header>

   <ion-content padding>
     <ion-row class="center">
       <ion-col width-50>
         <button ion-button (click)="getPicture(1)">Show Camera</
         button>
       </ion-col>
       <ion-col width-50>
         <button ion-button (click)="getPicture(0)">Show Album</
         button>
       </ion-col>
   ```

```
    </ion-row>

    <ion-item class="no-border">
      <ion-label>Return image file URI</ion-label>
      <ion-toggle energized [(ngModel)]="useURI">
      </ion-toggle>
    </ion-item>

    <ion-card>
      <img [src]="imageData" *ngIf="imageData" />
      <ion-card-content>
        <ion-card-title>
          <div *ngIf="useURI">
            Using URI
          </div>
          <div *ngIf="!useURI">
            Using Base64
          </div>
        </ion-card-title>
        <p *ngIf="useURI">
          Your URI is {{ imageData }}
        </p>
        <p *ngIf="!useURI">
          Your Base64 image has {{ (imageData + '').length }}
          bytes
        </p>
      </ion-card-content>
    </ion-card>
  </ion-content>
```

Since you have only one page, this template will show two buttons and an area to display the image.

4. Replace `./src/pages/home/home.ts` with the following code:

```
import { Component, Input } from '@angular/core';
import { NavController } from 'ionic-angular';
import { Camera } from 'ionic-native';

@Component({
  selector: 'page-home',
  templateUrl: 'home.html'
})
export class HomePage {
  public imageData: string;
```

```
  @Input('useURI') useURI: Boolean = true;

  constructor(public navCtrl: NavController) {
  }

  getPicture(sourceType){
    Camera.getPicture({
        quality: 50,
        allowEdit: true,
        encodingType: Camera.EncodingType.JPEG,
        saveToPhotoAlbum: false,
        destinationType: this.useURI ? Camera.DestinationType.
        FILE_URI : Camera.DestinationType.DATA_URL,
        targetWidth: 800,
        targetHeight: 800,
        sourceType: sourceType
    }).then((imageData) => {
        if (this.useURI) {
          this.imageData = imageData;
        } else {
          this.imageData = "data:image/jpeg;base64,
          " + imageData;
        }
    }, (err) => {
        console.log(err);
    });
  }
}
```

There is only one method: `getPicture()`. This method will return the photo data so that the template can render.

5. Replace `/app/pages/home/home.scss` with the following code:

```
.center {
  text-align: center;
}

.no-border .item-inner {
  border-bottom: 0;
}
```

There are only a few minor changes in the styling so that you can keep them simple.

6. Connect your device to your computer.

7. Go to the Terminal and execute the following command line for iOS:

```
$ ionic run ios
```

> If you are not able to push the app to your physical device using the preceding command line, you can use `ionic run ios --device` to specify the CLI to use the physical device instead of a simulator.

If you want to run the app in your Android device, use the following code:

```
$ ionic run android
```

8. When you run the app and take a picture, you should see the app as shown in the following screenshot:

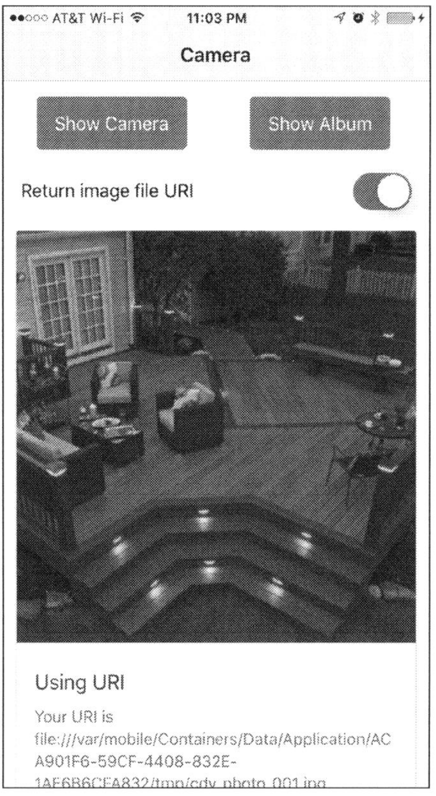

How it works...

`Camera.getPicture()` is just an abstraction of `navigator.camera.getPicture()` from the Cordova camera plugin. If you are already familiar with Cordova or ngCordova from Ionic 1, this should be very familiar. Let's start from the template. You have the following two buttons, which trigger the same, `getPicture()`, method:

- `<button ion-button (click)="getPicture(1)">Show Camera</button>`
- `<button ion-button (click)="getPicture(0)">Show Album</button>`

These are just different ways to access photos: either from the camera itself or from the existing photos in the phone's album. For the photo to render, you need to pass the photo data into the `src` attribute, as follows:

```
<img [src]="imageData" *ngIf="imageData" />
```

Note that you only want to show this `<img>` tag when `imageData` exists with some data. The `imageData` variable could be Base64 or an internal URL of the photo. To specify this option, there is a toggle button, as shown:

```
<ion-toggle energized [(ngModel)]="useURI"></ion-toggle>
```

You will use the `useURI` variable inside the class, as illustrated, to determine which format to return the photo data in.

```
@Input('useURI') useURI: Boolean = true;
```

Both `useURI` and `sourceType` will be used in the `getPicture()` function, as follows:

```
Camera.getPicture({
    quality: 50,
    allowEdit: true,
    encodingType: Camera.EncodingType.JPEG,
    saveToPhotoAlbum: false,
    destinationType: this.useURI ? Camera.DestinationType.FILE_URI
    : Camera.DestinationType.DATA_URL,
    targetWidth: 800,
    targetHeight: 800,
    sourceType: sourceType
}).then((imageData) => {
    if (this.useURI) {
      this.imageData = imageData;
    } else {
      this.imageData = "data:image/jpeg;base64," + imageData;
    }
```

```
    }, (err) => {
        console.log(err);
    });
```

It's important to adjust the quality, `targetWidth` and `targetHeight` to low so that the photo is not too big, which could crash the device, especially when it doesn't have enough memory. When you return the Base64 data, it must be prefixed with the string `data:image/jpeg;base64`.

One item that isn't discussed here is the ability to post image data to the server. The common scenario is to upload the file from the filesystem. It's not a good idea to send data as Base64 because of the data size, which is double the original binary size.

There's more...

It is possible to create Instagram-like filter effects using just JavaScript. You can leverage an existing library, such as Filterous (`https://github.com/girliemac/Filterous`), to modify the image canvas directly.

There is an Instagram plugin (`https://github.com/vstirbu/InstagramPlugin`) for Cordova on GitHub. You could write some extra code to pass the image to Instagram. The user must have Instagram installed on the phone first, though. This idea is nice when you plan to do some cool image processing (for example, adding funny text) before letting Instagram perform the photo filter operation.

You could even add the Cordova's social network plugin and post the resulting images to Twitter or Facebook.

Sharing content using the social sharing plugin

If you develop an app with shareable content, you might want to utilize the native device feature to share via the device's authorized social media accounts. There are several benefits from using this approach. First, users don't need to open a separate browser to log in to their social media account each time they want to share. Second, all the information can be filled out programmatically, such as title, body, link, or image. Finally, since this is a native feature of the device, the menu selection allows users to see multiple accounts, which they are already familiar with, to choose from. The social sharing plugin can greatly enhance the user experience.

This is the app that you will build:

When the user clicks on the **Share** button, the app will show the following native button menu for social media account selection:

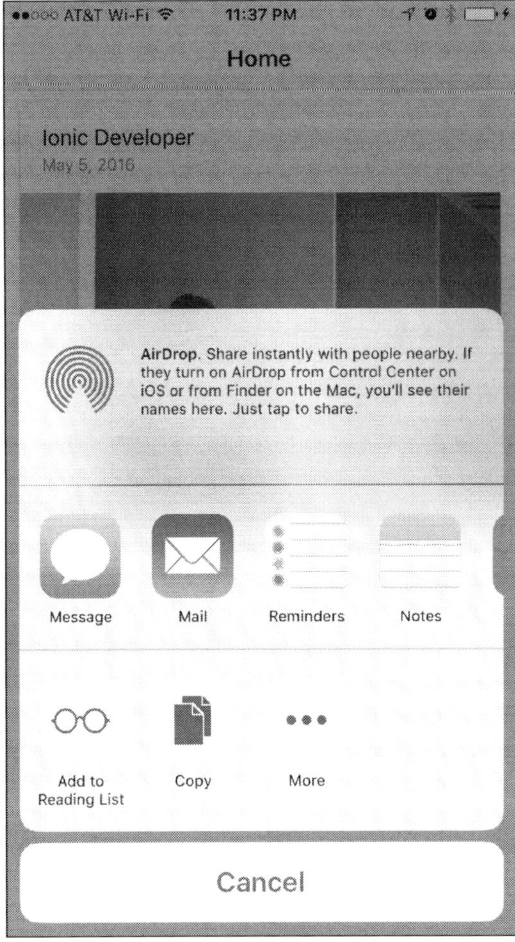

If the user selects Twitter, a popup will show up with all the information prefilled, as illustrated:

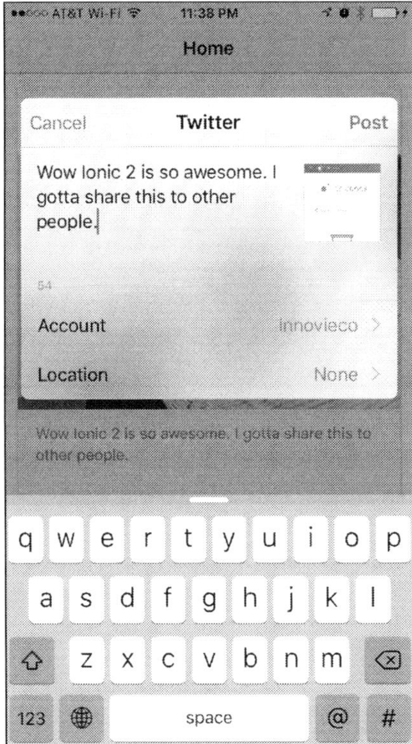

After posting on Twitter, the user goes right back to the app without ever leaving it.

Getting ready

You should have a physical device or simulator ready in order to test the social sharing capability.

How to do it...

The following are the instructions:

1. Start a blank project (for example, `LinkSocialShare`), as follows, and go to that folder:

   ```
   $ ionic start LinkSocialShare blank --v2
   $ cd LinkSocialShare
   ```

2. Add the Cordova camera plugin with the following command line:

   ```
   $ ionic plugin add cordova-plugin-x-socialsharing
   ```

3. Open `./src/pages/home/index.html` and replace its contents with the following code:

```
<ion-header>
  <ion-navbar>
    <ion-title>
      Home
    </ion-title>
  </ion-navbar>
</ion-header>

<ion-content>
  <ion-card>

    <ion-item>
      <h2 #messageSubject>Ionic Developer</h2>
      <p>May 5, 2016</p>
    </ion-item>

    <img src="https:
    //source.unsplash.com/category/technology/600x390">

    <ion-card-content>
      <p #messageBody>Wow Ionic 2 is so awesome.
      I gotta share this to other people.</p>
    </ion-card-content>

    <ion-row>
      <ion-col>
        <button ion-button color="primary"
        clear small icon-left>
          <ion-icon name="thumbs-up"></ion-icon>
          <div>12 Likes</div>
        </button>
      </ion-col>
      <ion-col>
        <button ion-button color="primary"
        clear small icon-left
          (click)="sendShare(messageBody.
          innerText, messageSubject.innerText,
          'http://ionicframework.com/docs/v2/')">
          <ion-icon name="ios-share"></ion-icon>
          <div>Share</div>
        </button>
      </ion-col>
      <ion-col center text-center>
        <ion-note>
```

```
            11h ago
          </ion-note>
        </ion-col>
      </ion-row>

    </ion-card>
  </ion-content>
```

This is a very simple page with the card element. The **Like** button is there just for cosmetic reasons without code implementation. However, all the JavaScript logic will focus on the **Share** button:

1. Open `./src/pages/home/home.ts`, as shown:

   ```
   import { Component } from '@angular/core';
   import { NavController } from 'ionic-angular';
   import { SocialSharing } from 'ionic-native';

   @Component({
     selector: 'page-home',
     templateUrl: 'home.html'
   })
   export class HomePage {

     constructor(public navCtrl: NavController) {
     }

     sendShare(message, subject, url) {
       SocialSharing.share(message, subject, null, url);
     }
   }
   ```

2. Go to the Terminal and execute either of the following command lines:

   ```
   $ ionic run ios
   $ ionic run android
   ```

How it works...

You can start looking at the template because that is where the social media content is extracted from. The subject value is from the `#messageSubject` local variable, as illustrated:

```
<ion-item>
  <h2 #messageSubject>Ionic Developer</h2>
  <p>May 5, 2016</p>
</ion-item>
```

In the preceding case, the subject is `Ionic Developer` because you will access `messageSubject.innerText` later on. `messageSubject` is just referencing your H2 DOM node.

Similarly, the body is from `#messageBody`, as shown:

```
<ion-card-content>
  <p #messageBody>Wow Ionic 2 is so awesome. I gotta share this to
  other people.</p>
</ion-card-content>
```

When the user clicks on the **Share** button, it will trigger the `sendShare()` method, as follows:

```
<button ion-button color="primary" clear small icon-left
          (click)="sendShare(messageBody.innerText,
          messageSubject.innerText,
          'http://ionicframework.com/docs/v2/')">
```

Let's take a look at your `home.ts` to understand how `sendShare()` works.

First, you need to import the `SocialSharing` module from Ionic Native, as illustrated:

```
import { SocialSharing } from 'ionic-native';
```

Ionic 2 makes it very convenient because you don't need to install ngCordova separately. Ionic Native is actually a default option that comes with the project during its creation.

To share your content and trigger the social media menu, the logic, as shown, is very simple:

```
sendShare(message, subject, url) {
  SocialSharing.share(message, subject, null, url);
}
```

If you want to share a file, you can replace the third parameter (where it is `null`) with the URL to the user's local filesystem. This is useful when you want people to send a PDF or JPG via e-mail or post it on Facebook.

There's more...

- To see the latest update of the Social Share plugin, you can visit the documentation page at `http://ionicframework.com/docs/v2/native/social-sharing/`

Displaying a term of service using InAppBrowser

In many apps, you sometimes require users to accept a term of service before they can move on to the next page. The typical approach is to create a popup modal or a new page showing the term of service. Once users finish reading, they can click on the **Done** or **Back** button. However, if the content of your term of service changes, you may need to ask users to update the app. In many cases, users don't update apps often. So, the terms of service that they accepted could be older than your current version. Therefore, there is a need to maintain term of service content separately from the app itself. The InAppBrowser plugin is the best solution for this because you can point users to the same Term of Service page that is already on your website.

The app will just have a simple checkbox and button to demonstrate how InAppBrowser works:

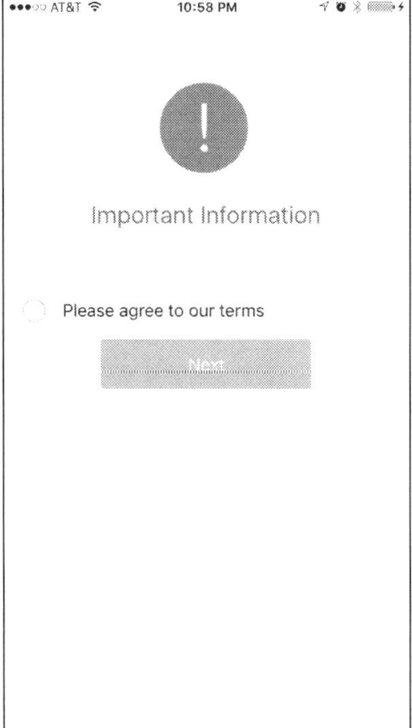

Once the user clicks on the **Please agree to our terms** checkbox, they will go to the InAppBrowser page:

After going through the term of service content, they can click on **Done** and go back to the previous page with the **Next** button enabled:

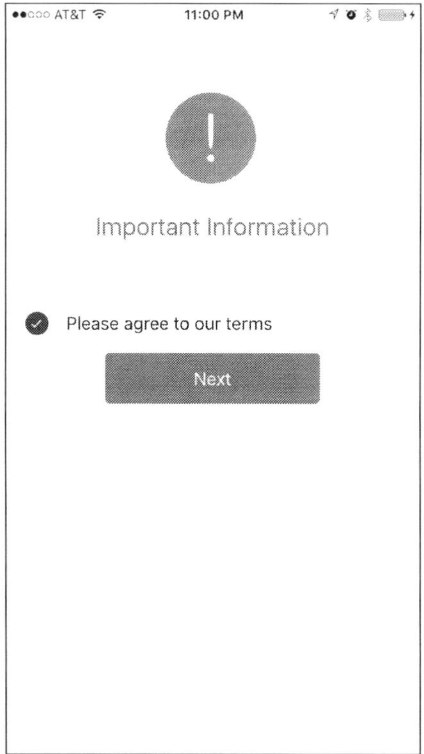

Getting ready

You should have a physical device ready in order to test InAppBrowser, as this won't work in the browser as an iframe.

How to do it...

Here are the instructions:

1. Create a blank Ionic app (for example, `OnlineTOS`) and `cd` to that folder, as shown:

   ```
   $ ionic start OnlineTOS blank --v2
   $ cd OnlineTOS
   ```

2. Install the InAppBrowser plugin using the following command:

   ```
   $ ionic plugin add cordova-plugin-inappbrowser
   ```

3. Open `/config.xml` in the project folder and insert the following two lines under `<access origin="*"/>`, as shown:

   ```
   <allow-navigation href="http://*/*" />
   <allow-navigation href="https://*/*" />
   ```

   This will tell Cordova that it's okay to allow navigation to any website. Otherwise, the device security will block InAppBrowser. You can read more about this on the Cordova documentation page at `https://cordova.apache.org/docs/en/latest/reference/cordova-plugin-whitelist/`.

4. Open `./src/pages/home/index.html` and replace with the following code:

   ```
   <ion-content class="home">
     <div class="top-header center">
       <ion-icon name="alert"></ion-icon>
       <br/>
       <h3>
         Important Information
       </h3>
     </div>
     <ion-item>
       <ion-label>Please agree to our terms</ion-label>
       <ion-checkbox dark (click)="openTOS()"></ion-checkbox>
     </ion-item>
     <div class="center">
       <button ion-button class="long" [(disabled)]="!readTOS">Next</
       button>
     </div>
   </ion-content>
   ```

5. Open `./src/pages/home/home.ts` and replace with the following code:

   ```
   import { Component } from '@angular/core';
   import { Platform } from 'ionic-angular';
   import { InAppBrowser } from 'ionic-native';

   @Component({
     selector: 'page-home',
     templateUrl: 'home.html'
   })
   export class HomePage {
     private platform: any;
     public readTOS: Boolean = false;

     constructor(platform: Platform) {
   ```

```
    this.platform = platform;
  }

  openTOS() {
    this.readTOS = !this.readTOS;
    this.platform.ready().then(() => {
      let ref = new InAppBrowser('https://ionic.io/tos',
      '_blank');
      ref.on('exit').subscribe(() => {
        console.log('Exit In-App Browser');
      });
    });
  }
}
```

6. Open ./src/pages/home/home.scss and replace with the following code:

```
.home {
  .item-inner {
    border-bottom: 0;
  }
}

.top-header {
  margin-top: 50px;
  margin-bottom: 50px;

  ion-icon {
    color: #EB6B56;
    font-size: 100px;
  }

  h3 {
    color: #75706B;
  }
}

.center {
  text-align: center;
}

.long {
  padding: 0 5em;
}
```

This is just to provide minor styling to the page.

7. Run the app in the Terminal using the following command line:

```
$ ionic run ios
$ ionic run android
```

How it works...

First, let's take a look at the `template home.html`:

```
<ion-item>
  <ion-label>Please agree to our terms</ion-label>
  <ion-checkbox dark (click)="openTOS()"></ion-checkbox>
</ion-item>
<div class="center">
  <button ion-button class="long" [(disabled)]="!readTOS">Next</
  button>
</div>
```

There are two areas that you should make a note on. When the `<ion-checkbox>` component is clicked on, it will trigger the `openTOS()` method, which will open the URL via InAppBrowser. The **Next** button is disabled by default (via the `readTOS` variable). So, when the user checks the checkbox, this `readTOS` will be `True` and the button will be enabled.

In your `home.ts`, you must import the `InAppBrowser` module first, as shown:

```
import { InAppBrowser } from 'ionic-native';
```

This will make the `InAppBrowser` object available for use in your class.

Here is the `openTOS()` method:

```
openTOS() {
  this.readTOS = !this.readTOS;
  this.platform.ready().then(() => {
    let ref = new InAppBrowser('https://ionic.io/tos'
    , '_blank');
    ref.on('exit').subscribe(() => {
      console.log('Exit In-App Browser');
    });
  });
}
```

You have to wrap everything inside `platform.ready()` because sometimes Cordova plugin loads more slowly than the app itself and it will cause an error if the user clicks on the button too fast to trigger it InAppBrowser.

To trigger InAppBrowser, you just need to call `InAppBrowser.open` and pass the following three parameters:

1. The URL to load.
2. The target to open the URL. There are four options only—`_self`, `_blank`, and `_system`. `_self` will overwrite your current Ionic app; thus, you should never need to use this option. `_blank` is typically what you want because it leaves you a way to come back to your app. Finally, `_system` opens a separate browser outside the app.
3. Options is the last parameter where you have to pass a string. You can visit the official document for more information (`https://github.com/apache/cordova-plugin-inappbrowser#cordovainappbrowseropen`). In general, you just need to set `location=true` so that the user can see the current URL.

Android and iOS have different options; so, you should check the GitHub page to compare the different platforms.

InAppBrowser also has an `exit` event, where you can listen via `ref.on()`. This is useful when you want to pop up a Thank You dialog or record an event (via the REST API to your server).

There's more...

- To stay up to date with the latest changes in InAppBrowser, you can visit `https://github.com/apache/cordova-plugin-inappbrowser`
- Official support for Ionic Native's InAppBrowser is located at `http://ionicframework.com/docs/v2/native/inappbrowser/`

Creating a Taxi app using the Google Maps plugin and geocode support

Today, many mobile apps utilize different mapping features, such as showing the current location, creating routes, and providing suggestive business searches. This section will show you how to use Ionic Native's Google Maps plugin to provide mapping support.

You will create a Taxi app that can do the following things:

- Display Google Maps in fullscreen
- Add a button overlay on top of the map
- Detect the current device location
- Add a marker with any text

This is the screenshot of the Taxi app:

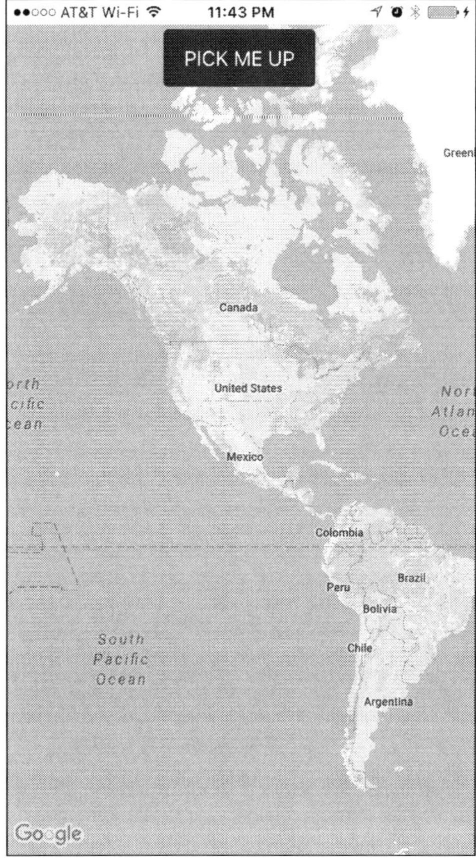

When users click on the **PICK ME UP** button, it will go to the current device location and show longitude and latitude information:

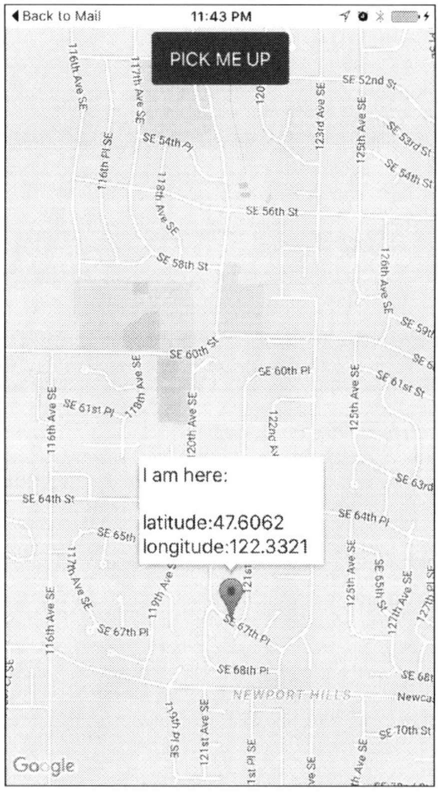

It is possible to use the HTML5 and JavaScript version of geolocation and maps instead of the Cordova plugin's. However, you will see a negative impact on performance. It's very obvious that if you use the SDK, map rendering and optimization tends to be faster. In addition, HTML5 geolocation sometimes has some strange bugs that require the user to accept permission twice—once for the app and once for the inside browser object.

Getting ready

The Google Maps plugin requires a Google Maps API key for your project. You need a Google account and login to get started.

1. Navigate to the Google APIs Console at `https://code.google.com/apis/console/`.

2. Create a project if you don't have one yet. Just fill in the required fields:

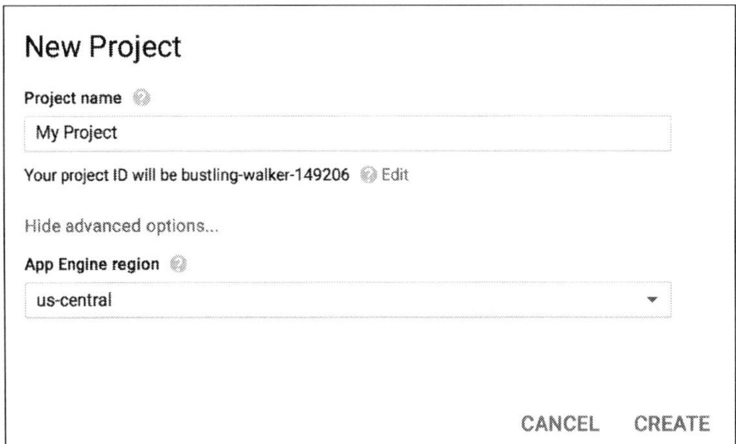

3. You need to enable the **Google Maps SDK for iOS**, the **Google Maps Android API**, or both. It depends on how many platforms you plan to support. Let's select **Google Maps SDK for iOS** for this example:

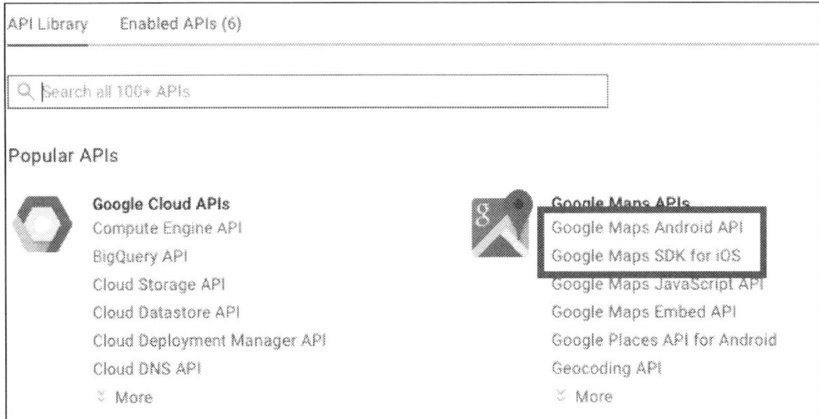

4. Click on the **Enable API** button:

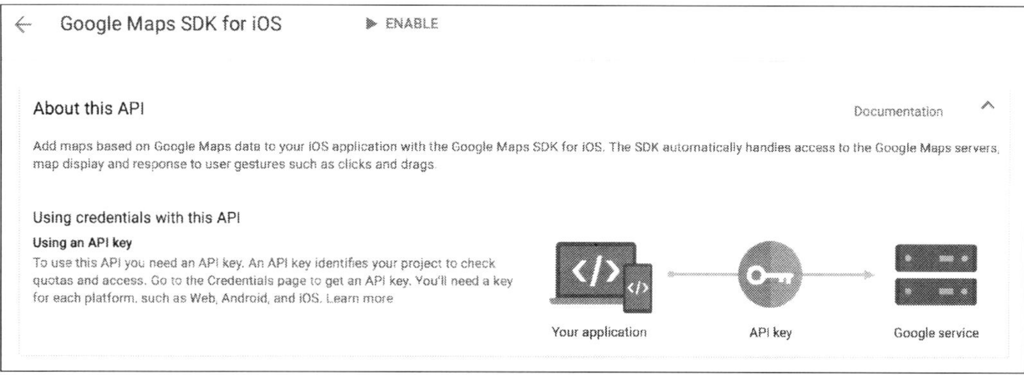

5. Go to **Credentials** to create your own key:

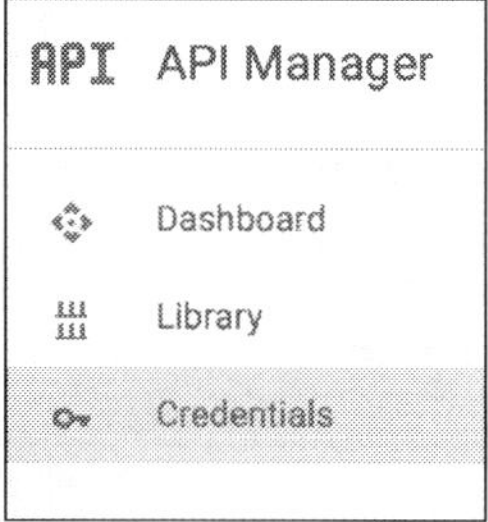

6. Click on the **Create credential** | **API key** option:

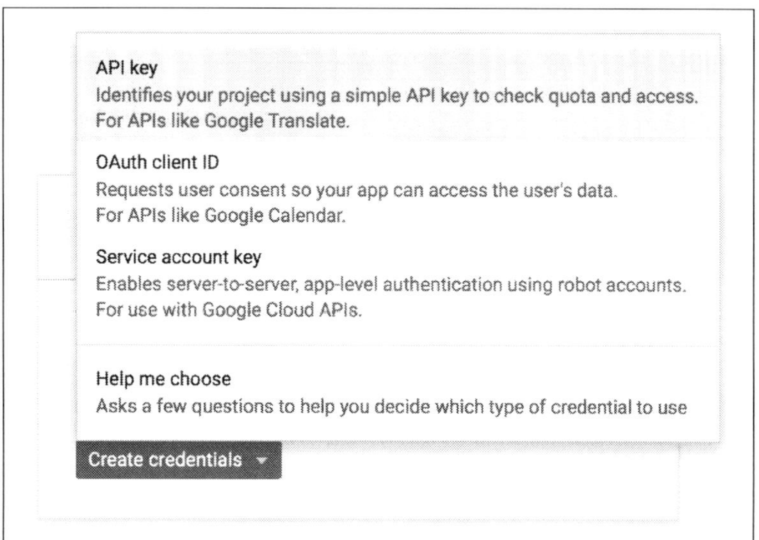

7. Select the restriction option. In the following example, you will select the **iOS apps** radio button:

Key restriction

Key restriction lets you specify which web sites, IP addresses, or apps can use this key. Learn more

- None
- HTTP referrers (web sites)
- IP addresses (web servers, cron jobs, etc.)
- Android apps
- iOS apps

8. Fill in your app's Bundle ID. You might not know exactly what it is yet because Ionic will create a random ID. So just put in `com.ionicframework.starter` and change that later.

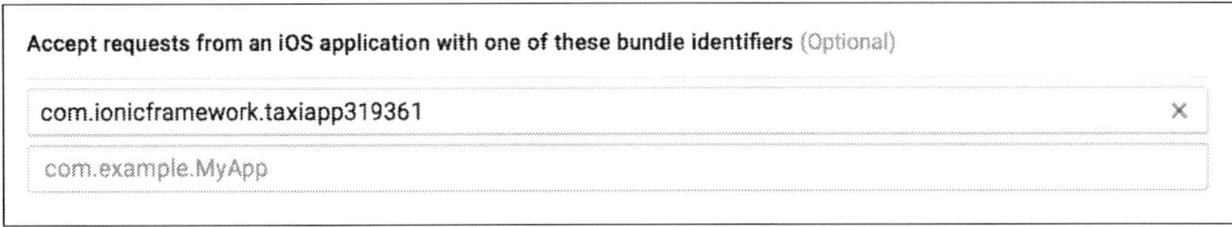

9. Click on the **Save** button.
10. Now you should see the key for the iOS applications section as follows:

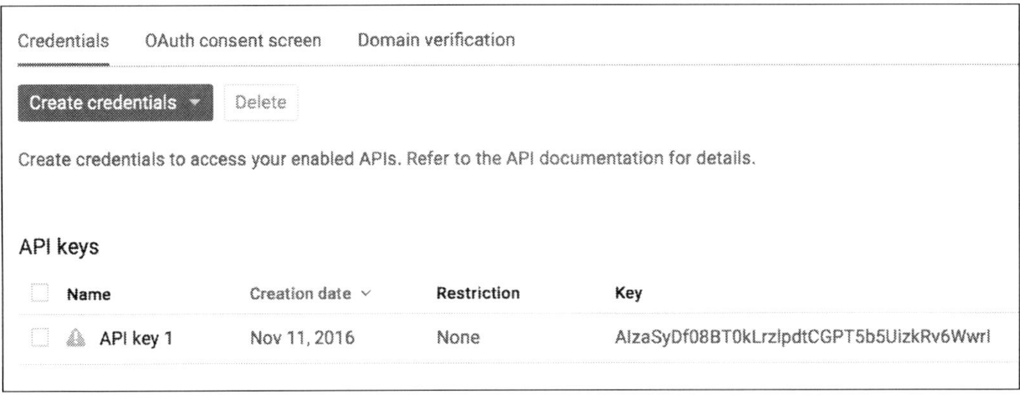

11. Copy the API key so that you can use it to add the Cordova Google Maps plugin.

How to do it...

Let's start an Ionic project from scratch and add Google Maps features, as follows:

1. Create a blank Ionic project, as shown, and go to that folder:

```
$ ionic start TaxiApp blank --v2
$ cd TaxiApp
```

2. Replace the iOS platform with version 3.9.0 with the following command lines:

```
$ ionic platform remove ios
$ ionic platform add ios@3.9.0
$ ionic platform add android
```

You have to pick `ios@3.9.0` specifically because the current version of the Cordova Google Maps plugin only works with this version. Otherwise, your build will fail. You should experiment with the newest version if possible.

3. Install the Google Maps plugin with your copied key replacing `` `YOUR_IOS_API_KEY_IS_HERE ``, as follows:

```
$ cordova plugin add cordova-plugin-googlemaps --variable
API_KEY_FOR_IOS="YOUR_IOS_API_KEY_IS_HERE"`
```

If you do this for both iOS and Android, use the following command line:

```
$ cordova plugin add cordova-plugin-googlemaps --variable
API_KEY_FOR_ANDROID="key" --variable API_KEY_FOR_IOS="key"
```

You have to use the Cordova CLI here because using the Ionic CLI to add Google Maps with the API Key will not work.

4. Open `./src/pages/home/home.html` to modify your template, as shown:

```
<ion-content [ngClass]="{'no-scroll': mapRendered}">
  <div id="map">
    <button ion-button color="dark" (click)="getMyLocation()">PICK
    ME UP</button>
  </div>
</ion-content>
```

The main element here is your `div` with `map` ID because that is where you have to inject the Google Maps object.

5. Edit your `./src/pages/home/home.ts` in the same folder:

```
import { Component } from '@angular/core';
import { NavController, Platform } from 'ionic-angular';
import { GoogleMap, GoogleMapsEvent, GoogleMapsLatLng,
GoogleMapsMarkerOptions, GoogleMapsMarker, CameraPosition }
from 'ionic-native';

@Component({
  selector: 'home-page',
  templateUrl: 'home.html'
})
export class HomePage {
  public map: GoogleMap;
  public mapRendered: Boolean = false;

  constructor(public navCtrl: NavController, public
  platform: Platform) {
    this.platform.ready().then(() => {
      this.showMap();
    });
  }

  showMap(){
    let location = new GoogleMapsLatLng(47.6062,
    -122.3321);
    this.map = new GoogleMap('map', {
      'camera': {
        'latLng': location,
        'tilt': 30,
        'zoom': 15,
        'bearing': 50
      }
    });

    this.map.on(GoogleMapsEvent.MAP_READY).subscribe(()
    => {
      console.log('Map is ready!');
      this.mapRendered = true;
    });
  }

  getMyLocation() {
    this.map.getMyLocation().then((location) => {
      var msg = ["I am here:\n",
```

```
          "latitude:" + location.latLng.lat,
          "longitude:" + location.latLng.lng].join("\n");

        let position: CameraPosition = {
          target: location.latLng,
          zoom: 15
        };
        this.map.moveCamera(position);

        let markerOptions: GoogleMapsMarkerOptions = {
          'position': location.latLng,
          'title': msg
        };
        this.map.addMarker(markerOptions).then((marker:
        GoogleMapsMarker) => {
          marker.showInfoWindow();
        });

      });

    }
  }
```

6. Finally, make some minor adjustments to the stylesheet so that the map can take over the fullscreen. Edit `./src/pages/home/home.scss`, as illustrated:

```
ion-app._gmaps_cdv_ .nav-decor{
  background-color: transparent !important;
}

home-page {
  text-align: center;
  #map {
    height: 100%;
    z-index: 9999;
  }
}

.no-scroll {
  .scroll-content {
    overflow-y: hidden;
  }
}
```

7. Run the app in the Terminal with the following command line:

```
$ ionic run ios --device
$ ionic run android
```

You can use either one of the preceding command lines, depending on the platform.

How it works...

The core of this app is mainly in the JavaScript code—`home.ts`. In order to use the plugin object, you should declare it on top, as shown:

```
import { GoogleMap, GoogleMapsEvent, GoogleMapsLatLng,
GoogleMapsMarkerOptions, GoogleMapsMarker, CameraPosition }
from 'ionic-native';
```

While it might seem that there are a lot of moving parts, the basic flow is very simple, as listed:

1. Whenever Ionic and Cordova are ready, trigger `platform.ready().then` to initialize the map by calling `showMap()` in the constructor of the `HomePage`.
2. When a user clicks on the button, the app will call `getMyLocation` to get the location data.
3. The data will be used to create the marker and move the map's camera to center on that location.

It's important to know that `plugin.google.maps.Map.getMap` does take some time to process, and it will trigger a *ready* event once it has successfully created the map. That's why you need to add an event listener for `plugin.google.maps.event.MAP_READY`. This example does not do anything right after the map is ready, but later, you could add more processing functions, such as jumping to the current location automatically or adding more markers on top of the map.

When the user clicks on the `PICK ME UP` button, it will trigger the `getMyLocation()` method. The location object returned will contain the latitude (`location.latLng.lat`) and longitude (`location.latLng.lng`). To move the camera anywhere, just call `map.moveCamera` by passing the location coordinate (`location.latLng`). To add a marker, call `map.addMarker` with the position and title as HTML.

There's more...

The Cordova Google Maps plugin has many more features, such as the following ones:

- Showing an InfoWindow
- Adding a marker with multiple lines

- Modifying icon
- Text styling
- Base64-encoded icons
- Clicking on a marker
- Clicking on an InfoWindow
- Creating a draggable marker
- Dragging events
- Creating a flat marker

Since you cannot pop up a `div` on top of native Google Maps, the marker features are very handy. Some additional scenarios are as listed:

- **Touch a marker and go to a page**: You just need to listen to the `plugin.google.maps.event.MARKER_CLICK` event and do whatever is needed in the callback function.
- **Show an avatar/profile image as a marker**: The `addMarker` does take the Base64 image string. Thus, you can pass something like this in the argument title—`canvas.toDataURL()`.

Note that Google has a quota on free API usage. For example, you cannot exceed one request per second per use, and you can only have a couple of thousand requests per day. This quota changes all the time, but it's important to know about it. In any case, if you have problems with your key, you have to go back to the **Credentials** page and regenerate the key. In order to change the key manually in your app, you have to edit `` `/plugins/ios.json` ``. Look for the following two places:

```
"*-Info.plist": {
  "parents": {
    "Google Maps API Key": [
      {
        "xml": "<string>YOUR_IOS_API_KEY_IS_HERE</string>",
        "count": 1
      }
    ]
  }
}
```

Along with the following code:

```
"plugin.google.maps": {
  "API_KEY_FOR_IOS": "YOUR_IOS_API_KEY_IS_HERE",
  "PACKAGE_NAME": "com.ionicframework.starter"
}
```

You just need to edit the `YOUR_IOS_API_KEY_IS_HERE` line and replace it with your new key.

There are a lot of ways to work with Google Maps. You can visit the GitHub page of the Google Maps plugin to learn more, at `https://github.com/mapsplugin/cordova-plugin-googlemaps`.

8
Theming the App

In this chapter, we will cover the following tasks related to app theme customization:

- Viewing and debugging themes for a specific platform
- Customizing themes based on the platform

Introduction

Although Ionic has its own out-of-the-box default themes, you might want to even customize your app's look and feel further. There are several methods, as follows:

- Change style sheet within Sass file
- Detecting platform-specific type (iOS, Android, Windows) in JavaScript and applying custom classes or AngularJS conditions

Either of the above two methods should work, but it's highly recommended to apply customization in a Sass file before the app is built in order to achieve maximum rendering performance.

Viewing and debugging themes for a specific platform

One of the biggest challenges in developing an app is to ensure that it has the desired look and feel for each platform. Specifically, you want to write the code and theme once and have it just work. Another challenge is figuring out the workflow on a daily basis, from writing code and previewing it in the browser to deploying to a device for testing purposes. You want to minimize a lot of unnecessary steps. It's certainly difficult if you have to rebuild the app and test it independently for each mobile platform.

Ionic 2 CLI provides seamless integration to improve your workflow to ensure that you can *catch* all the issues for each platform ahead of time. You can quickly view the app on various platforms in the same browser window. This feature is powerful because now one can make a side-by-side comparison for each screen with specific interaction. If you want to debug JavaScript code, you employ the same web developer tool that you have been using in the browser. This capability will save you a lot of time instead of waiting to push the app to a physical device, which could take minutes if your app is getting larger.

In this example, you will learn how to modify a theme quickly using Sass variables. Then, you will run the app and inspect different platforms for UI consistency.

Getting ready

There is no need to test the theme on a physical device because Ionic can render iOS, Android, and Windows Phone in the browser.

How to do it...

Here are the instructions:

1. Create a new app using the `tutorial` template, as shown, and go to the folder:

   ```
   $ ionic start ThemeApp tutorial --v2
   $ cd ThemeApp
   ```

> In Ionic 1, you need to set up Sass dependencies because Ionic uses a number of external libraries for this. However, Ionic 2 has no such requirements because all the dependencies are added when you create the project.

2. Open the `/app/theme/app.variable.scss` file and replace the `$colors` variable with the following commands:

   ```
   $colors: (
     primary:    #2C3E50, // #387ef5,
     clear:      white,
     secondary:  #446CB3, // #32db64,
     danger:     #96281B, // #f53d3d,
     light:      #BDC3C7, // #f4f4f4,
     dark:       #6C7A89, // #222,
     favorite:   #16A085 // #69BB7B
   );
   ```

The default color codes can be commented out as shown in the preceding code.

3. Open `app.html` and add the `clear` attribute to the following code block:

```
<ion-toolbar clear>
  <ion-title>Pages</ion-title>
</ion-toolbar>
```

4. Open the `./src/pages/hello-ionic/hello-ionic.html` file and replace the contents with the given code:

```
<ion-header>
  <ion-navbar primary>
    <button ion-button menuToggle>
      <ion-icon name="menu"></ion-icon>
    </button>
    <ion-title>Hello Ionic</ion-title>
  </ion-navbar>
</ion-header>


<ion-content padding class="getting-started">

  <h3>Welcome to your first Ionic app!</h3>

  <p>
    This starter project is our way of helping you get a
    functional app running in record time.
  </p>
  <p>
    Follow along on the tutorial section of the Ionic docs!
  </p>
  <p>
    <button ion-button color="secondary" menuToggle>Toggle Menu</
     button>
  </p>

</ion-content>
```

5. Test-run the app in the browser and you should be able to see a screen as follows:

```
$ ionic serve -l
```

The `-l` (lima) command means render the app for all three platforms.

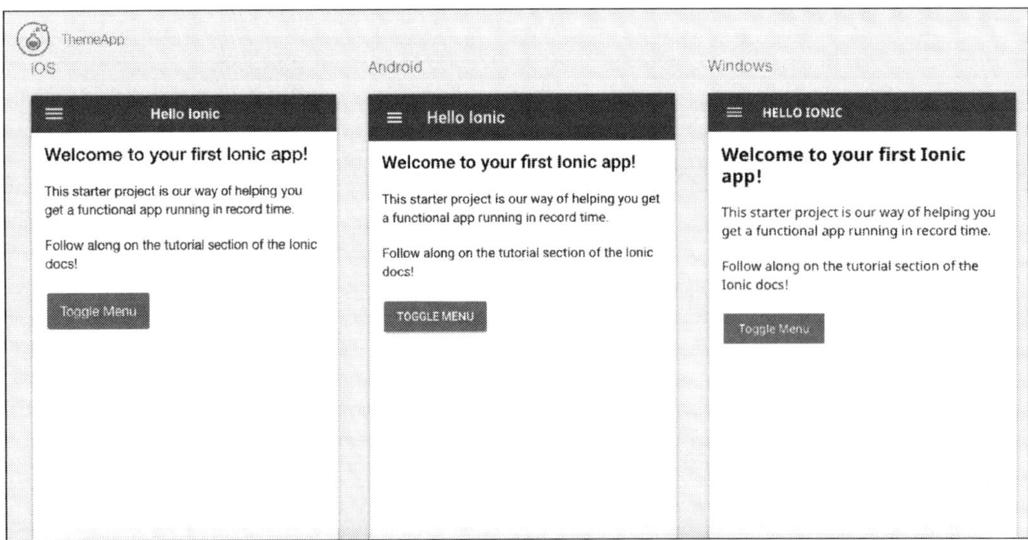

How it works...

Ionic 2 has made it very easy to develop and test themes for different platforms. Your typical flow is to modify the theme variable in `app.variables.scss` first. You should not modify any `.css` files directly. Also, Ionic 2 project now makes it safe so that you can't accidently edit the wrong core theme files because those core files are no longer in the app folder location.

To update the default color, you just have to modify the color code in `app.variables.scss`. You can even add more color names, such as `clear: white`, and Ionic 2 will automatically take care of the rest. That means the `clear` keyword is available as an attribute to any Ionic element that takes a color name. A few examples are as follows:

```
<ion-navbar primary>
<button ion-button color="secondary" menuToggle>
<ion-toolbar clear>
```

The Ionic CLI is a very useful tool for debugging your theme in different platforms. To get help on how to use the Ionic CLI, you can type the following command line in the console:

```
$ ionic -h
```

This will list all the options available for you to choose from. Under the `serve` option, you should familiarize yourself with some of the important features, which are as follows:

Parameters	Description
`--consolelogs|-c`	Print app console logs to Ionic CLI
`--serverlogs|-s`	Print dev server logs to Ionic CLI
`--browser|-w`	Specifies the browser to use (Safari, Firefox, and Chrome)
`--browseroption|-o`	Specifies a path to open to (`/#/tab/dash`)
`--lab|-l`	Tests your apps on multiple screen sizes and platform types

There's more...

You can get more color palettes by visiting Matheus Cruz Rocha's cloned repository at `https://github.com/innovieco/ionic-flat-colors`.

Customizing themes based on the platform

Each mobile platform vendor has its own design guideline. This section will go over an example of a typical workflow to develop, view, debug, and address the app theme differently for iOS, Android, and Windows Phone. In traditional development (of using either the native language or other hybrid app solutions), you have to keep separate repositories for each platform in order to customize the theme. This could be very inefficient in the long-run.

Ionic 2 has many built-in features to support theme changes based on the detected platform. It makes it very convenient by separating Sass variables for each platform. This will eliminate a lot of unnecessary customizations. As a developer, you'd rather focus on the app experience than spend time managing the platform.

The example in this section covers two possible of customizations using Sass and JavaScript. The following screenshot shows an iOS, Android, and Windows app with a different title bar color and text:

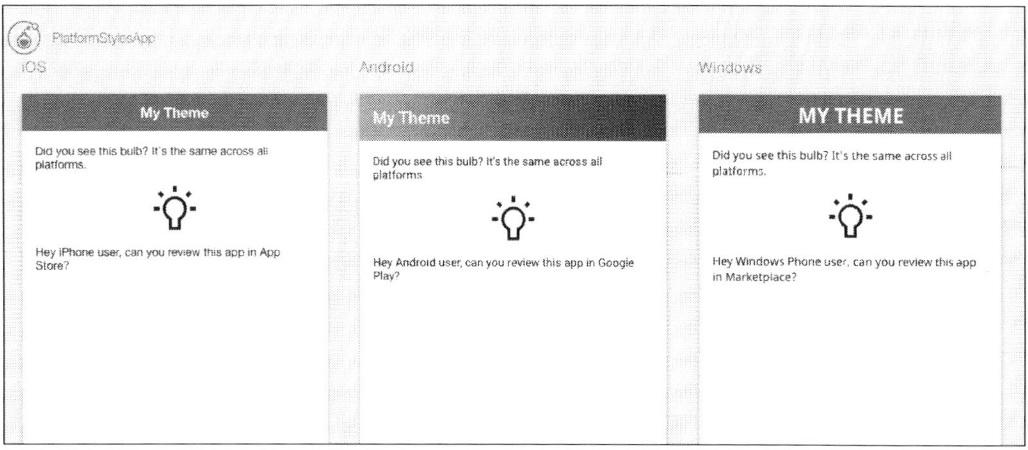

Getting ready

There is no need to test themes on a physical device because Ionic can render all three platforms in the browser.

How to do it...

Here are the instructions:

1. Create a new app using the `blank` template and go into the project folder:

   ```
   $ ionic start PlatformStylesApp blank --v2
   $ cd PlatformStylesApp
   ```

2. Open the `./src/app/app.module.ts` file and replace the entire body with the following:

   ```
   import { NgModule } from '@angular/core';
   import { IonicApp, IonicModule } from 'ionic-angular';
   import { MyApp } from './app.component';
   import { HomePage } from '../pages/home/home';

   @NgModule({
     declarations: [
       MyApp,
       HomePage
     ],
     imports: [
       IonicModule.forRoot(MyApp, {
         backButtonText: 'Go Back',
         iconMode: 'md',
         modalEnter: 'modal-slide-in',
         modalLeave: 'modal-slide-out',
         tabbarPlacement: 'bottom',
         pageTransition: 'ios',
       })
     ],
     bootstrap: [IonicApp],
     entryComponents: [
       MyApp,
       HomePage
     ],
     providers: []
   })
   export class AppModule {}
   ```

   This example expands the use of Ionic Bootstrap, which will be discussed now.

3. Open `./src/pages/home/home.ts` and replace the code with the following:

```
import { Component } from '@angular/core';
import { Platform } from 'ionic-angular';
import { NavController } from 'ionic-angular';

@Component({
  selector: 'page-home',
  templateUrl: 'home.html'
})
export class HomePage {
  platform: any;
  isIOS: Boolean;
  isAndroid: Boolean;
  isWP: Boolean;

  constructor(private navController: NavController, platform:
Platform) {
    this.platform = platform;
    this.isIOS = this.platform.is('ios');
    this.isAndroid = this.platform.is('android');
    this.isWP = this.platform.is('windows');
    console.log(this.platform);
  }
}
```

4. Open the `./src/pages/home/home.html` file and change the template to:

```
<ion-header>
  <ion-navbar primary [ngClass]="{'large-center-title': isWP}">
    <ion-title>
      My Theme
    </ion-title>
  </ion-navbar>
</ion-header>

<ion-content padding>
  Did you see this bulb? It's the same across all platforms.
  <p class="center">
    <ion-icon class="large-icon" name="bulb"></ion-icon>
  </p>

  <p *ngIf="isIOS">
    Hey iPhone user, can you review this app in App Store?
  </p>
```

```
  <p *ngIf="isAndroid">
    Hey Android user, can you review this app in Google Play?
  </p>
  <p *ngIf="isWP">
    Hey Windows Phone user, can you review this app in
    Marketplace?
  </p>
</ion-content>
```

This is the only template for the app, but its UI will look different depending on the detected platform.

5. Replace `./src/pages/home/home.scss` with the following stylesheet:

```
.large-icon {
  font-size: 60px;
}

.center {
  text-align: center;
}

.md .toolbar[primary] .toolbar-background {
  background: #1A2980;
  background: -webkit-linear-gradient(right, #1A2980, #26D0CE);
  background: -o-linear-gradient(right, #1A2980, #26D0CE);
  background: linear-gradient(to left, #1A2980, #26D0CE);
}

.large-center-title {
  text-align: center;
  .toolbar-title {
    font-size: 25px;
  }
}
```

There is no need to change the global variables. Thus, you only modify the styles for one page. The purpose is to demonstrate the ability to customize for each platform.

6. Test-run the app in the browser using the following command:

```
$ ionic serve -l
```

How it works...

Ionic automatically created platform-specific parent classes and put them at the `<body>` tag. The iOS app will include the `.ios` class. The Android app will have `.md class`. So, for stylesheet customization, you can leverage those existing classes to change the look and feel of your app.

Ionic 2 documentation has a list of all platform modes and configuration properties at `http://ionicframework.com/docs/v2/theming/platform-specific-styles/`.

Platform	**Mode**	**Details**
iPhone/iPad/iPad	`ios`	The iOS style is used across all Apple products
Android	`md`	*md* means **Material Design** as this is the default design for Android devices
Windows Phone	`wp`	Viewing on any windows device inside Cordova or Electron uses the Windows styles
Core	`md`	Material Design is the default for all others

First, let's take a look at the Ionic Bootstrap class from Ionic Angular. You declared this in `app.ts` file:

```
IonicModule.forRoot(MyApp, {
    backButtonText: 'Go Back',
    iconMode: 'md',
    modalEnter: 'modal-slide-in',
    modalLeave: 'modal-slide-out',
    tabbarPlacement: 'bottom',
    pageTransition: 'ios',
})
```

This statement basically instructs the app to bootstrap with the `MyApp` object. The third parameter is where you can inject your customized configuration properties. There is a list of all `Config` properties at `http://ionicframework.com/docs/v2/api/config/Config/`.

One main thing to point out here is `iconMode`. Icons are very different for each platform in Ionic 2. The entire Ionicons set is now separated by the platform name. There are three platforms according to Ionic 2's documentation page, at `http://ionicframework.com/docs/v2/ionicons/`.

You can even search for the icon name using the **Search Ionicons**, buttons as follows:

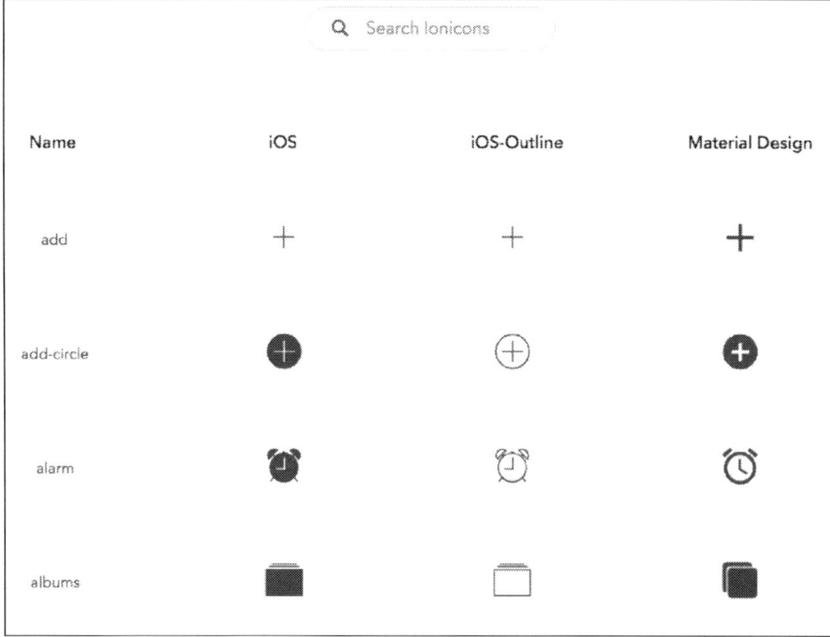

Note that you don't need to worry about which icon to pick for which platform. Even though, in this example, the code forces you to choose iOS icon for all three platforms, you could just use the icon name and let Ionic 2 decide which icon to use:

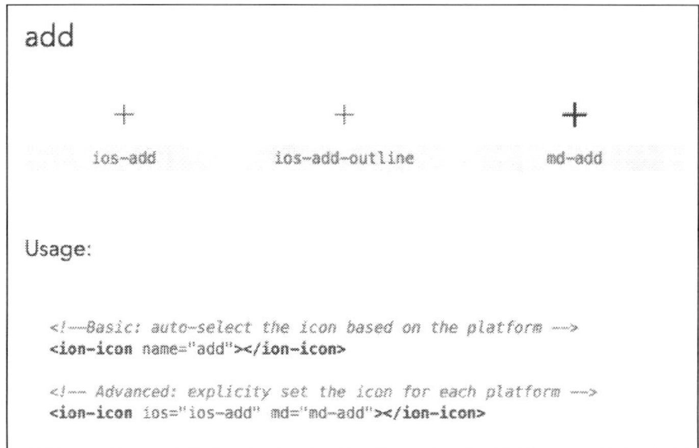

For example, when you state the icon name as `"add"`, Ionic 2 will use `"md-add"` if the user is using Android, as follows:

```
<ion-icon name="add">
</ion-icon>
```

There are several ways to theme your app based on the platform. First, you could add variables to detect the current platform as in the `HomePage` class, as illustrated:

```
export class HomePage {
  platform: any;
  isIOS: Boolean;
  isAndroid: Boolean;
  isWP: Boolean;

  constructor(private navController: NavController, platform:
Platform) {
    this.platform = platform;
    this.isIOS = this.platform.is('ios');
    this.isAndroid = this.platform.is('android');
    this.isWP = this.platform.is('windows');
    console.log(this.platform);
  }
}
```

`this.platform = platform` is what Ionic 2 provides. If you open up the browser console while running the app, you can inspect the `platform` object:

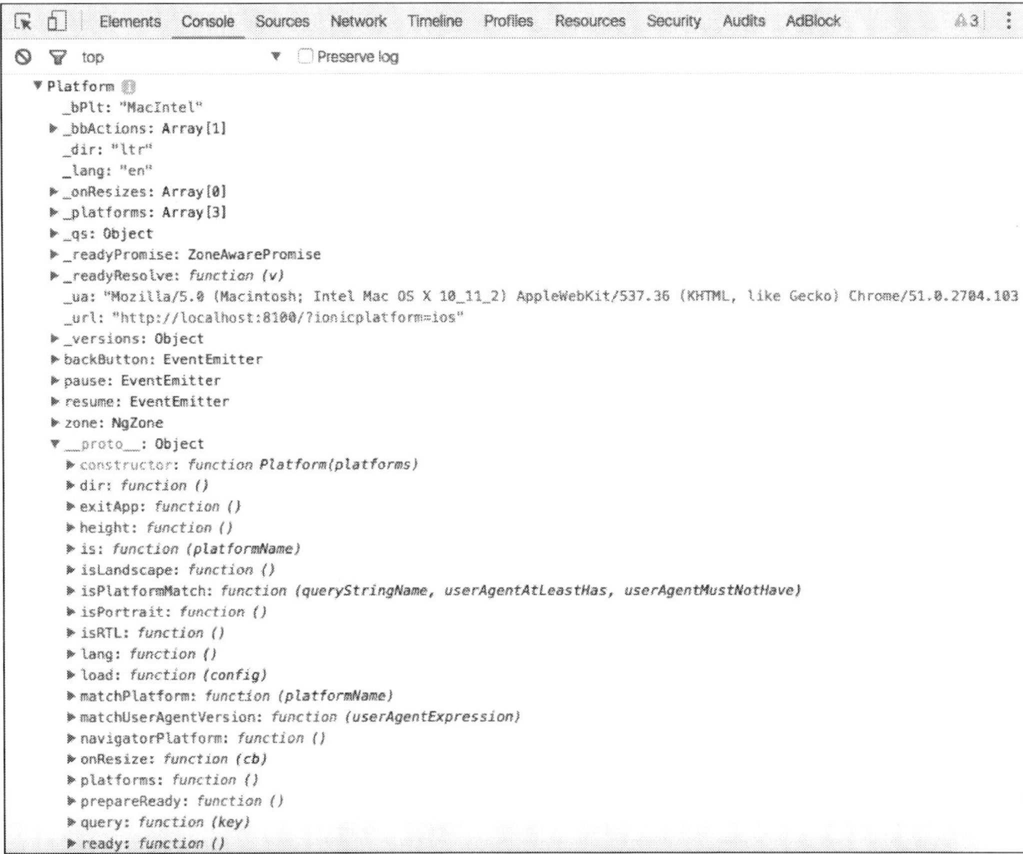

This `platform` object has a rich amount of information. This is similar to `ionic.platform` in Ionic 1. However, it has been restructured significantly.

By making the platform variables available to the view, you can use it to hide or show a specific DOM using `ngIf`. It's recommended to use `ngIf` instead of `ngShow` because `ngShow` may show and hide the element right away, creating a *flickering* effect. The following is the code in the template relating to using those platform variables:

```
<p *ngIf="isIOS">
  Hey iPhone user, can you review this app in App Store?
</p>
<p *ngIf="isAndroid">
  Hey Android user, can you review this app in Google Play?
</p>
```

```
<p *ngIf="isWP">
  Hey Windows Phone user, can you review this app in Marketplace?
</p>
```

Finally, you could change the theme using platform classes directly. Consider the following example:

```
.md .toolbar[primary] .toolbar-background {
  background: #1A2980;
  background: -webkit-linear-gradient(right, #1A2980, #26D0CE);
  background: -o-linear-gradient(right, #1A2980, #26D0CE);
  background: linear-gradient(to left, #1A2980, #26D0CE);
}
```

This means that, whenever it's a Material Design mode (`.md` class), you will override the classes with your own styles. The preceding example shows an interesting CSS gradient, which works very nicely in mobile devices.

There's more...

Further, device information is available from the `Platform` class. You can even detect iPad devices at `http://ionicframework.com/docs/v2/api/platform/Platform/`.

9
Publishing the App for Different Platforms

In this chapter, we will cover the following tasks related to publishing and future-proofing an app:

- Adding versioning to future proof the app
- Building and publishing an app for iOS
- Building and publishing an app for Android

Introduction

In the past, it was very cumbersome to build and successfully publish an app. However, there is much documentation and many unofficial instructions on the internet today that can pretty much address any problem that you may run into. In addition, Ionic also comes with its own CLI to assist in this process. This chapter will guide you through the app building and publishing steps at a high level. You will learn how to do the following things:

- Add versioning to future proof the app
- Publish your app to App Store or Google Play

The purpose of this chapter is to provide ideas on what to look for and some *gotchas*. Apple and Google are constantly updating their platforms and processes; so, the steps may not look exactly the same over time.

Adding versioning to future proof the app

It's typical that you don't think about keeping track of the app version for a particular user. However, as the app grows in the number of users as well as releases, you will soon face the problem of update issues and incompatibilities. For example, a user may run an old version of your app but all your backend APIs are now expecting new parameters from a newer app version. Therefore, you may want to think about a strategy to detect the app version locally in order to notify the users for an update requirement. This is also helpful if your backend processes differently for a specific app version.

The app you are going to build is very simple. It will detect the current version and store the information in a service. This is the screenshot of the app:

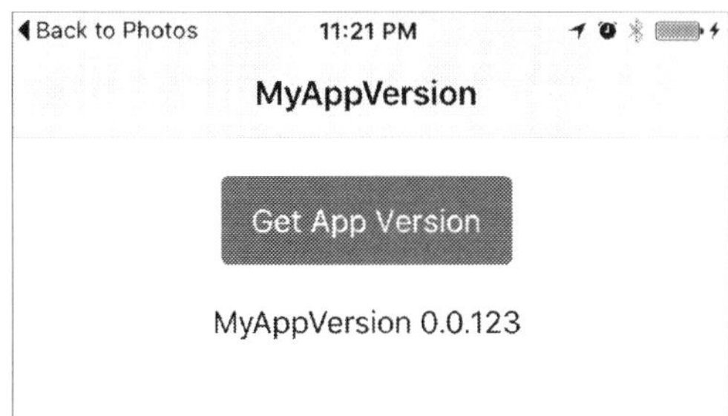

Getting ready

This app example must run on a physical device or a simulator.

How to do it...

Observe the following instructions:

1. Create a new `MyAppVersion` app using the `blank` template, as follows, and go to the `MyAppVersion` folder:

   ```
   $ ionic start MyAppVersion blank --v2
   $ cd MyAppVersion
   ```

2. Install the `app-version` plugin:

   ```
   $ ionic plugin add cordova-plugin-app-version
   ```

3. Edit `./config.xml` by changing the version number, as follows:

   ```
   <widget id="com.ionicframework.myappversion637242"
   version="0.0.123" xmlns="http://www.w3.org/ns/widgets"
   xmlns:cdv="http://cordova.apache.org/ns/1.0">
   ```

Note that your `widget id` might be different from the one mentioned here. You only need to change the version number. In this case, it is the `0.0.123` version.

1. Create the `services` folder inside the app folder, as shown:

   ```
   $ mkdir ./src/services
   ```

2. Create `myenv.ts` in the `services` folder with the following code:

   ```
   import {Injectable} from '@angular/core';
   import {AppVersion} from 'ionic-native';

   @Injectable()
   export class MyEnv {
     public appVersion: any;

     constructor() {
       this.appVersion = AppVersion;
     }

     getAppVersion() {
       return this.appVersion.getVersionCode();
     }
   }
   ```

   This is your only service for this app. In the real-world project, you will need multiple services because some of them will have to communicate directly with your backend.

3. Open and edit your `./src/app/app.module.ts`, as follows:

   ```
   import { NgModule } from '@angular/core';
   import { IonicApp, IonicModule } from 'ionic-angular';
   import { MyApp } from './app.component';
   import { HomePage } from '../pages/home/home';
   import { MyEnv } from '../services/myenv';

   @NgModule({
     declarations: [
       MyApp,
       HomePage
     ],
     imports: [
       IonicModule.forRoot(MyApp)
     ],
     bootstrap: [IonicApp],
     entryComponents: [
       MyApp,
       HomePage
   ```

```
  ],
  providers: [MyEnv]
})
export class AppModule {}
```

The main modification in this file is to inject the `MyEnv` provider for the entire app.

4. Open and replace `./src/pages/home/home.html` with this code:

```
<ion-header>
  <ion-navbar>
    <ion-title>
      MyAppVersion
    </ion-title>
  </ion-navbar>
</ion-header>

<ion-content padding class="center home">
  <button ion-button (click)="getVersion()" >Get App Version</
button>
  <p class="large" *ngIf="ver">
    MyAppVersion {{ ver }}
  </p>
</ion-content>
```

5. Open and replace `./src/pages/home/home.ts` with the following code:

```
import { Component } from '@angular/core';
import { NavController } from 'ionic-angular';
import { MyEnv } from '../../services/myenv';

@Component({
  selector: 'page-home',
  templateUrl: 'home.html'
})
export class HomePage {
  public ver: string;

  constructor(private navCtrl: NavController, public myEnv: MyEnv)
{
    this.myEnv = myEnv;
  }

  getVersion() {
    console.log(this.myEnv.getAppVersion());
    this.myEnv.getAppVersion().then((data) => this.ver = data);
  }
```

```
}
```

6. Open and edit `home.scss` in the same folder:

```
.home {
  p.large {
    font-size: 16px;
  }
}

ion-content {
  &.center {
    text-align: center;
  }
}
```

7. Go to your terminal and run the app. If you want to run the app on your physical device, type the given command:

```
$ ionic run ios
```

For Android, type the following command:

```
$ ionic run android
```

How it works...

In a nutshell, the `AppVersion` plugin does all the *heavy lifting*. It's not possible for an Ionic app to find out the current version in its code using Javascript. You may think that using local storage or cookie is an alternative, but the users could also delete that storage manually. In order to have a permanent solution, the `AppVersion` plugin should be used because it can read your `config.xml` file and get the version for you.

It's the best practice to create a separate service for all environment variables. That's why you should have a service, called `MyEnv`. Also, you should inject `MyEnv` as a provider at the *app level* because you want to instantiate it only once, instead of doing it every time a new component is created. Observe the following code:

```
providers: [MyEnv]
```

Since all the `AppVersion` methods are based on `promise`, you should return the entire object as a promise. Let's take a look at the `getAppVersion()` method in your `myenv.ts` file:

```
getAppVersion() {
  return this.appVersion.getVersionCode();
}
```

Then, in your page files, such as `home.ts`, you should call the `getAppVersion` method, as shown, and use the `.then()` method to get the result:

```
getVersion() {
  console.log(this.myEnv.getAppVersion());
  this.myEnv.getAppVersion().then((data) => this.ver = data);
}
```

If you open the console to inspect the `promise` object, you will see that it has your app version value and the `.then()` method. Observe the following screenshot:

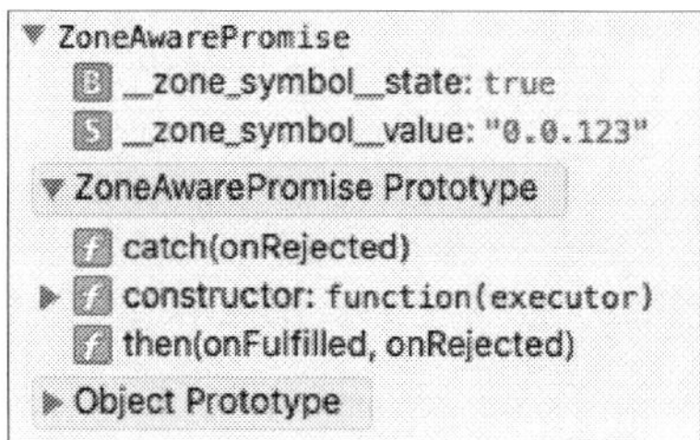

For more information about the `AppVersion` plugin, you may want to refer to the official AppVersion documentation at `https://github.com/whiteoctober/cordova-plugin-app-version`.

Building and publishing an app for iOS

Publishing on App Store could be a frustrating process if you are not well prepared upfront. In this section, you will walk through the steps to properly configure everything in Apple Developer Center, iTunes Connect and local Xcode project.

Getting ready

You must register for Apple Developer Program in order to access `https://developer.apple.com/macos/touch-bar/` and `https://itunesconnect.apple.com`, because those websites will require an approved account.

In addition, the following instructions a the specific version of these components:

- Mac OS X El Capitan 10.11.2
- Xcode 7.2
- Ionic CLI 2.0
- Cordova 5.4.1

How to do it...

Here are the instructions:

1. Ensure that you are in the app folder and build for the iOS platform:

   ```
   $ ionic build ios
   ```

   Go to the `/platforms/ios` folder to open the `.xcodeproj` file in Xcode. Observe the following screenshot:

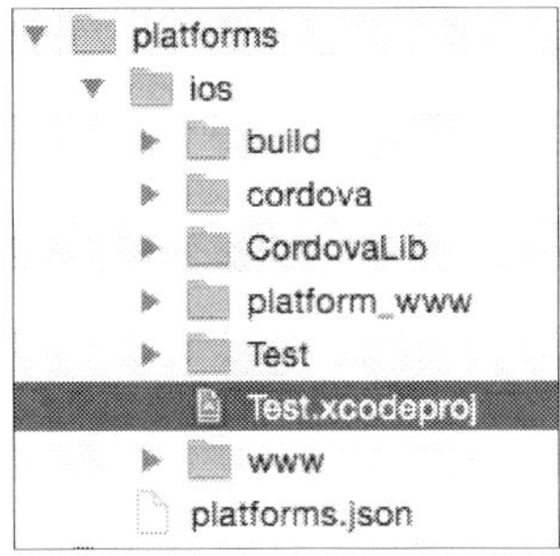

2. Go through the **General** tab, as illustrated in the following screenshot, to make sure that you have the correct information for everything, especially **Bundle Identifier** and **Version**. Change and save as needed:

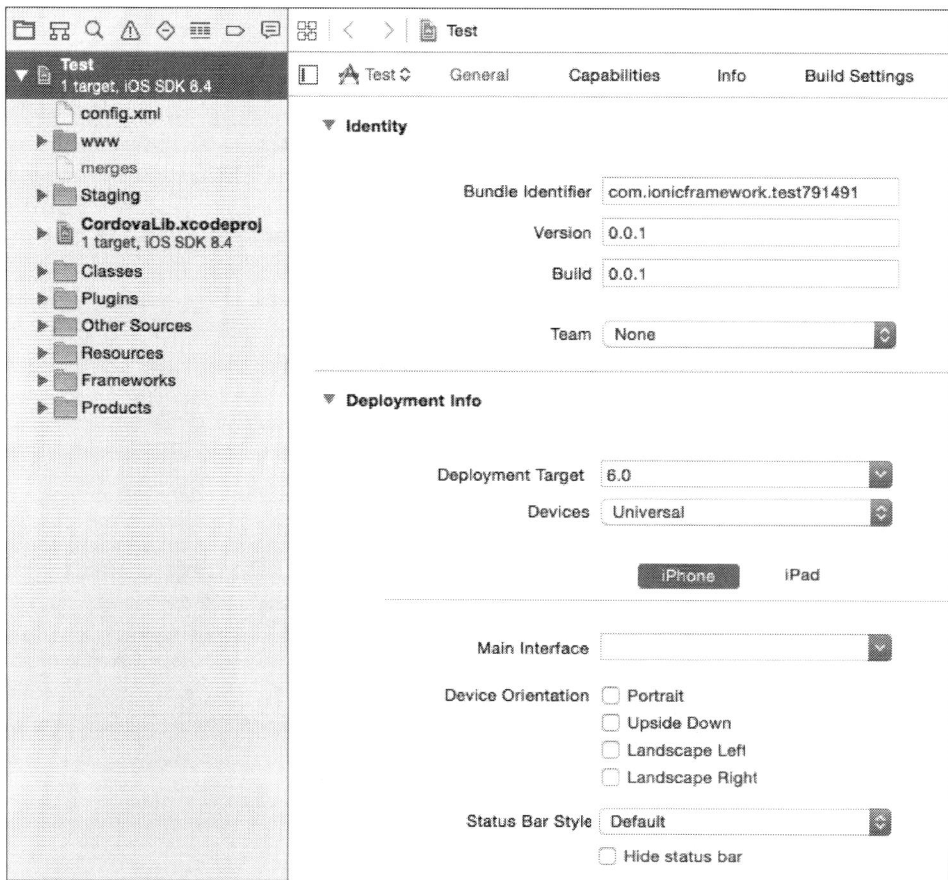

3. Visit the Apple Developer website and click on **Certificates, Identifiers & Profiles**, as illustrated:

4. Select the correct device platform you are targeting. In this case, it will be **iOS, tvOS, watchOS** as shown:

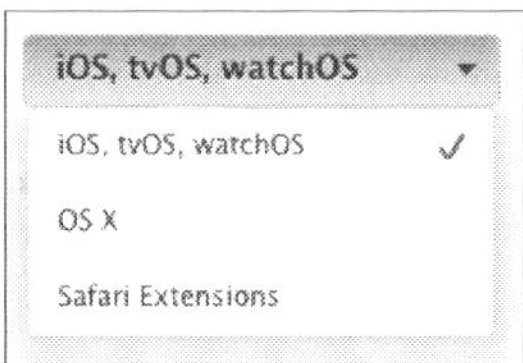

5. For the iOS app, you need the certificate, app ID, test device, and provisioning profile.

   To start with the certificate, navigate to **Certificates** | **All**, as follows:

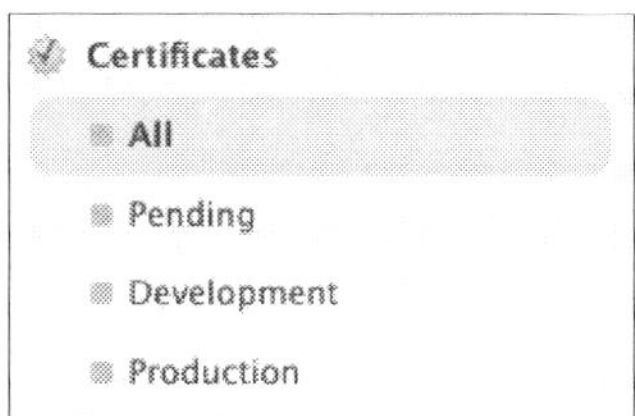

6. Click on the (**+**) plus button, as shown in the following screenshot:

7. You just have to go through the steps in the website to fill out the necessary information, as depicted in the following screenshot:

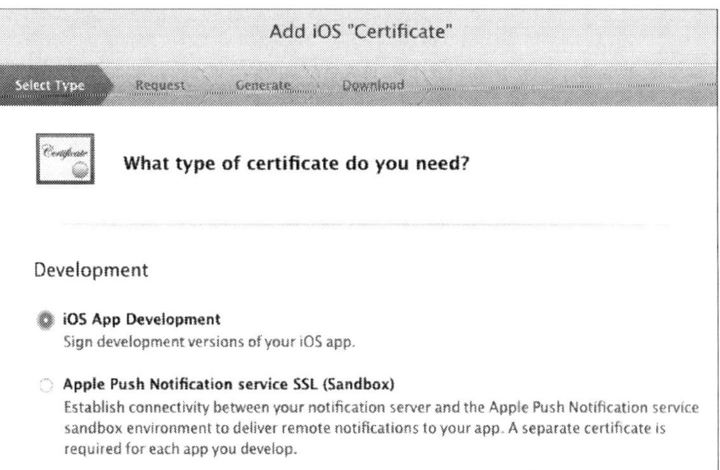

8. Once you've completed the form, you can save the CSR file and import it to your Mac's **Keychain Access**.
9. Navigate to **Identifiers** | **App IDs**, as follows, to create an app ID:

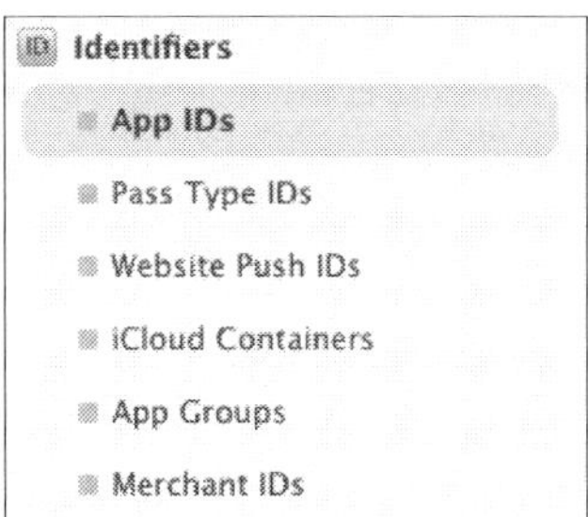

10. Click on the plus (**+**) button at the top right of the screen, as follows:

11. Fill in the form to register your **App ID**, as shown:

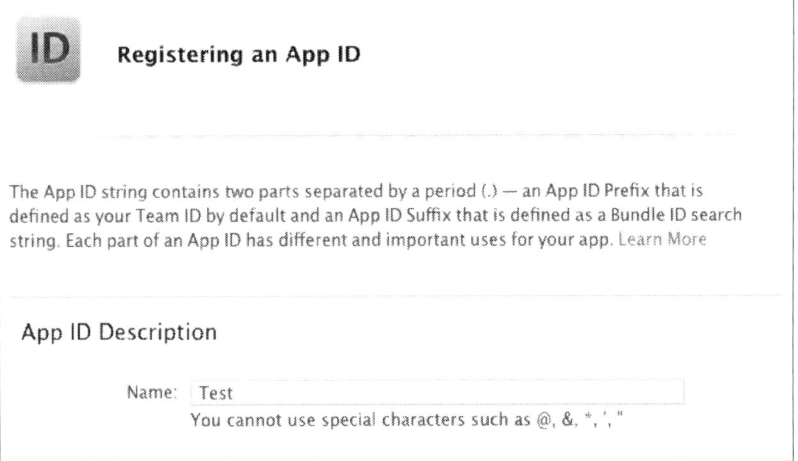
ID
Registering an App ID
The App ID string contains two parts separated by a period (.) — an App ID Prefix that is defined as your Team ID by default and an App ID Suffix that is defined as a Bundle ID search string. Each part of an App ID has different and important uses for your app. Learn More
App ID Description
Name: Test
You cannot use special characters such as @, &, *, ', "

12. The important part here that you need to do correctly is the **Bundle ID**, as shown in the following screenshot, because it must match your **Bundle Identifier** in Xcode:

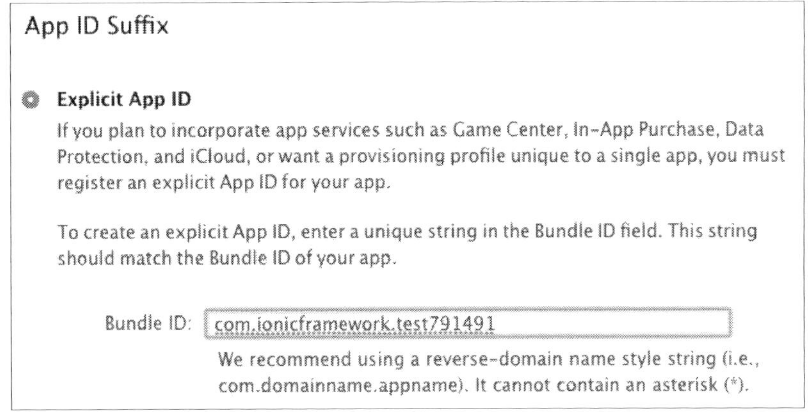
App ID Suffix
Explicit App ID
If you plan to incorporate app services such as Game Center, In-App Purchase, Data Protection, and iCloud, or want a provisioning profile unique to a single app, you must register an explicit App ID for your app.
To create an explicit App ID, enter a unique string in the Bundle ID field. This string should match the Bundle ID of your app.
Bundle ID: com.ionicframework.test791491
We recommend using a reverse-domain name style string (i.e., com.domainname.appname). It cannot contain an asterisk (*).

13. If your app needs **Push Notifications** or other **App Services**, you need to check those services on the page:

App Services

Select the services you would like to enable in your app. You can edit your choices after this App ID has been registered.

Enable Services:
- [ ] App Groups
- [ ] Apple Pay
- [ ] Associated Domains
- [ ] Data Protection
  - Complete Protection
  - Protected Unless Open
  - Protected Until First User Authentication
- [x] Game Center
- [ ] HealthKit
- [ ] HomeKit
- [ ] iCloud
  - Compatible with Xcode 5
  - Include CloudKit support (requires Xcode 6)
- [x] In-App Purchase
- [ ] Inter-App Audio
- [ ] Personal VPN
- [x] Push Notifications
- [ ] SiriKit
- [ ] Wallet
- [ ] Wireless Accessory Configuration

14. If you need to push the app to a specific device, you must register the device. Navigate to **Devices** | **All**, as illustrated:

15. Click on the plus (**+**) button, as shown:

16. Provide the device **UDID**, as follows, and save it in order to register the device:

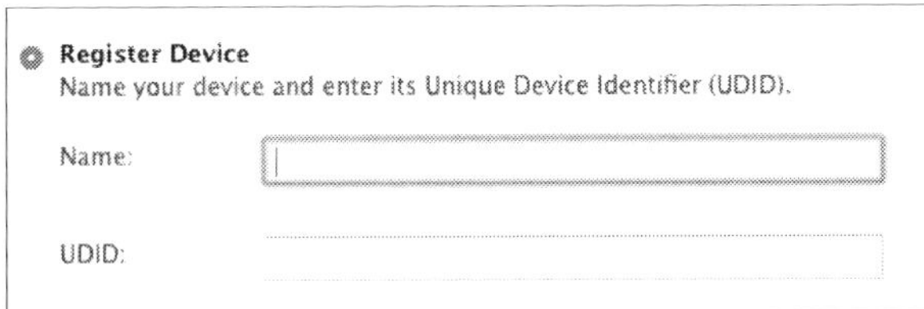

17. Finally, you need a provisioning profile if one doesn't exist yet. Usually, Xcode will create one automatically. However, you could create your own by navigating to **Provisioning Profiles** | **All**, as shown:

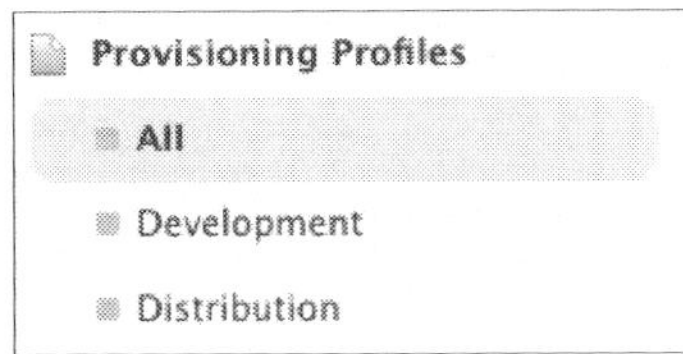

18. Click on the plus (**+**) button, as follows:

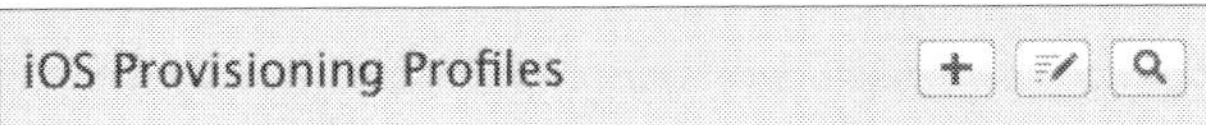

19. Select App Store as your provisioning profile, as illustrated:

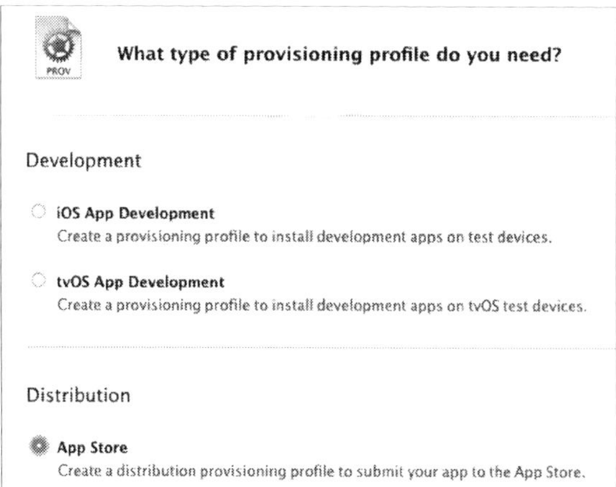

20. Select the correct **App ID** in the drop-down menu and save to finalize your provisioning profile creation, as follows:

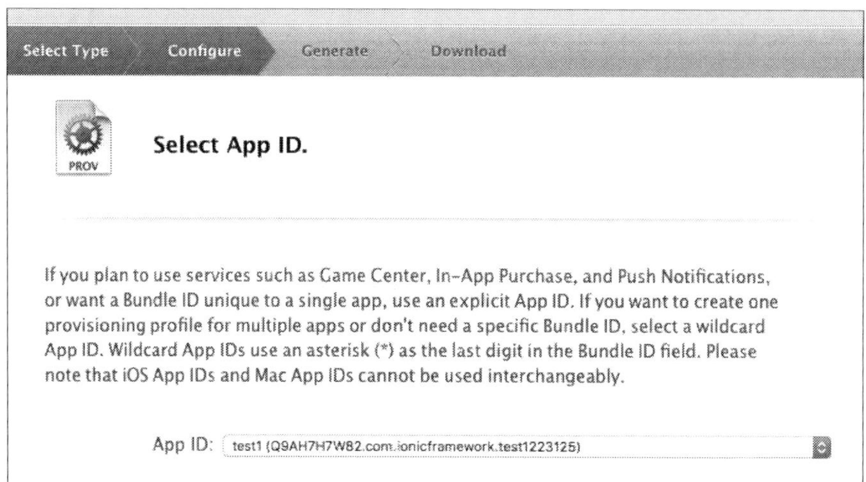

21. Visit iTunes Connect at `https://itunesconnect.apple.com` and click on the **My Apps** button, shown as follows:

22. Select the plus (**+**) icon to select **New App**, as shown:

23. Fill out the form and ensure that you select the right **Bundle Identifier** of your app:

There are several additional steps to provide information about the app, such as screenshot, icon, and address. If you just want to test the app, you could provide some place holder information initially and come back to edit later.

That's it to prepare your Developer and iTunes Connect account.

24. Now, open **Xcode** and select **iOS Device** as the archive target. Otherwise, the **Archive** feature will not turn on. You will need to archive your app before you can submit to the App Store:

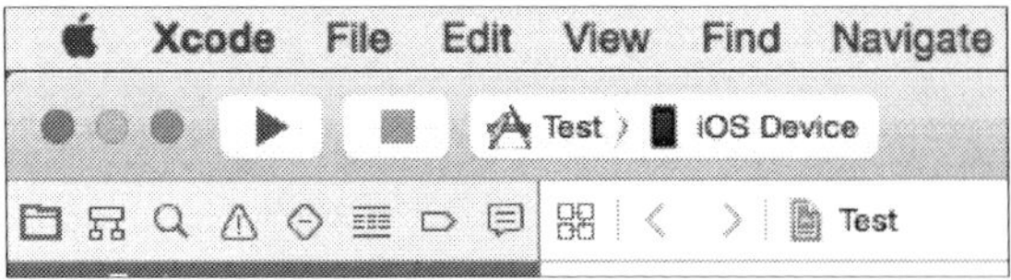

25. Navigate to **Product** | **Archive** in the top menu, as illustrated:

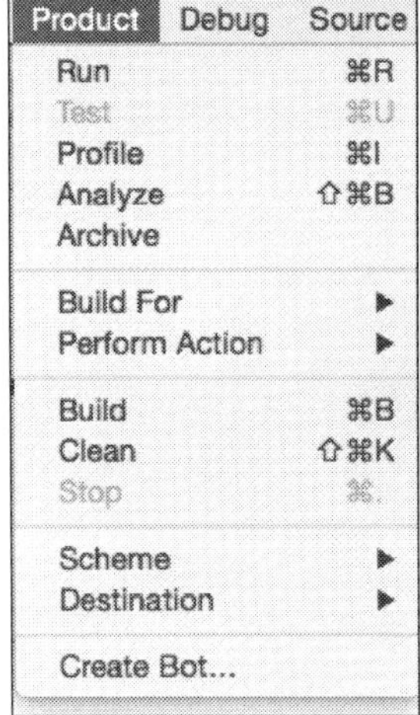

26. After the archive process is completed, select **Submit to App Store** to finish the publishing process.
27. To publish, select **Submit for Beta App Review**. You may want to go through other tabs, such as **Pricing** and **In-App Purchases**, to configure your own requirements.

How it works...

Obviously, this section does not cover every bit of detail in the publishing process. In general, you just need to ensure that your app is tested thoroughly, locally, on a physical device (either via USB or *TestFlight*) before submitting it to the App Store.

If for some reason the **Archive** feature doesn't build, you could manually go to your local Xcode folder to delete that specific temporary archived app to clear cache, as shown:

```
~/Library/Developer/Xcode/Archives
```

There's more...

TestFlight is a separate subject by itself. The benefit of *TestFlight* is that you don't need your app to be approved by Apple in order to install the app on a physical device for testing and development. You can find out more information about *TestFlight* at `https://developer.apple.com/library/content/documentation/LanguagesUtilities/Conceptual/iTunesConnect_Guide/Chapters/BetaTestingTheApp.html`.

Building and publishing an app for Android

Building and publishing an Android app is a little more straightforward than iOS because you just interface with the command line to build the .apk file and upload it to Google Play's Developer Console.

The Ionic Framework documentation also has a great instruction page for this, which is `http://ionicframework.com/docs/guide/publishing.html`.

Getting ready

The requirement is to have your Google Developer account ready and to log in to `https://play.google.com/apps/publish`.

Your local environment should also have the right SDK as well as `keytool`, `jarsigner`, and `zipalign` command line for that specific version.

How to do it...

Here are the instructions:

1. Go to your app folder and build for Android with the following command:

```
$ ionic package build --release android
```

2. You will see the `android-release-unsigned.apk` in the `/platforms/android/build/outputs/apk` folder. Go to that folder in the terminal:

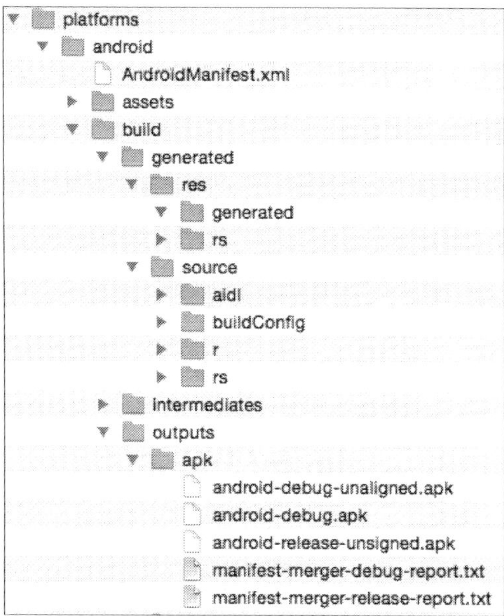

3. If this is the first time you created this app, you must have a `keystore` file. This file is used to identify your app for publishing. If you lose it, you cannot update your app later on. To create a `keystore`, type the following command line and ensure that it's the same `keytool` version of the SDK:

```
$ keytool -genkey -v -keystore my-release-key.keystore -alias
alias_name -keyalg RSA -keysize 2048 -validity 10000
```

4. Once you fill out the information in the command line, make a copy of this file somewhere safe because you will need it later.

5. The next step is to use that file to *sign* your app so that it will create a new `.apk` that Google Play allows users to install:

```
$ jarsigner -verbose -sigalg SHA1withRSA -digestalg SHA1 -keystore
my-release-key.keystore HelloWorld-release-unsigned.apk alias_name
```

6. To prepare for the final .apk before upload, you must package it using zipalign, as follows:

```
$ zipalign -v 4 HelloWorld-release-unsigned.apk HelloWorld.apk
```

You need to ensure that zipalign is in PATH or you have to specify the absolute path. The app name could be anything you like or you can use the same name as created in this chapter:

1. Log in to Google Developer Console and click on **Add new application**, as shown:

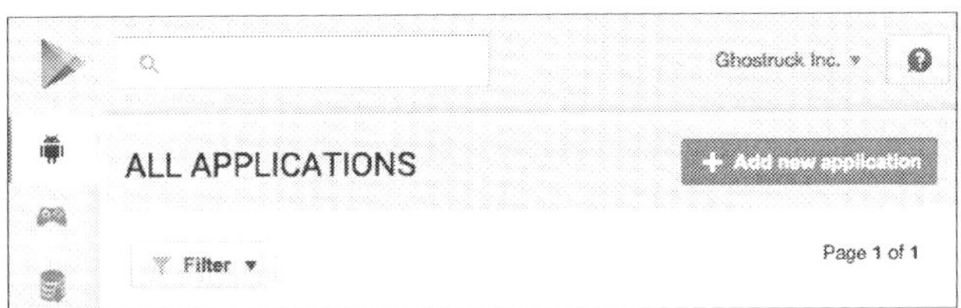

2. Fill out content rating and other information as possible for your app using the left menu:

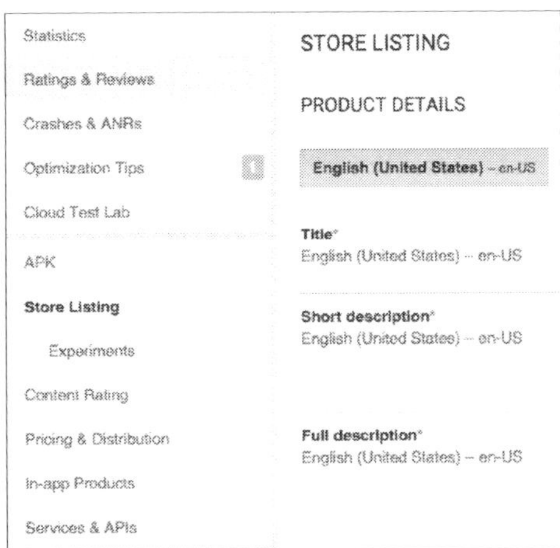

3. Now you are ready to upload your `.apk` file. First is to do a Beta:

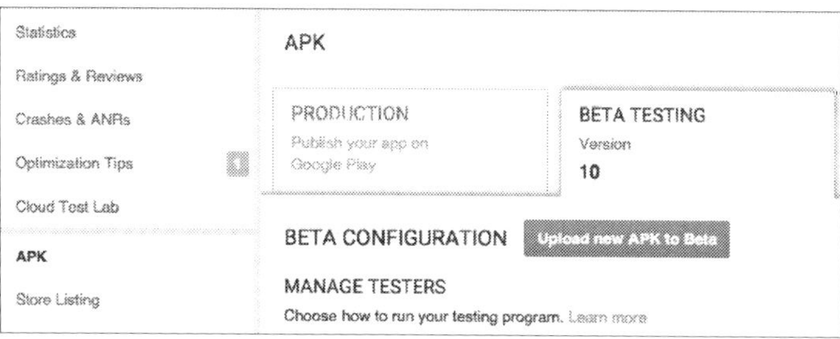

4. Once you are done with Beta testing, you can follow Developer Console instructions to push the app to production.

If you run into any problem while publishing the app, it's helpful to look at the "Why can't I publish?" link in the dashboard's top right corner. Google will guide you on specific steps that must be completed or fixed.

How it works...

This section does not cover other Android marketplaces, such as Amazon app store, because each of them has different processes. However, the common idea is that you need to completely build the unsigned version of the `.apk`, sign it using an existing or new `keystore` file, and, finally, `zipalign` to prepare it for upload.

Index

I

J

L

M

N

O

P

R

S

T

U

V

W

X

Printed in Great Britain
by Amazon